# Frequently Asked Antitrust Questions

## Second Edition

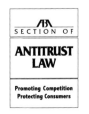

SECTION OF

**ANTITRUST LAW**

Promoting Competition
Protecting Consumers

AMERICAN BAR ASSOCIATION
Defending Liberty
Pursuing Justice

This volume should be officially cited as:

ABA SECTION OF ANTITRUST LAW,
FREQUENTLY ASKED ANTITRUST QUESTIONS, SECOND EDITION (2013)

Cover design by ABA Publishing.

ISBN: 978-1-61438-926-2
Library of Congress Catalog Number: 2013935336

Discounts are available for books ordered in bulk. Special consideration is given to state bars, CLE programs, and other bar-related organizations. Inquire at Book Publishing, ABA Publishing, American Bar Association, 321 N. Clark Street, Chicago, Illinois 60654-7598.

17 16 15      5 4 3 2

www.ShopABA.org

# CONTENTS

## Chapter IV
## Pricing ..............................................................................................103

**Chapter VIII**

# FOREWORD

The Section of Antitrust Law of the American Bar Association is pleased to publish the second edition of *Frequently Asked Antitrust Questions*. In addition to updating the law since the 2004 edition, this revision of *Frequently Asked Antitrust Questions* provides more in-depth discussion than its predecessor. The second edition continues the tradition of providing an easy to read, quick introduction to a wide variety of competition issues that lawyers, particularly in-house corporate counsel, face frequently.

The first edition of *Frequently Asked Antitrust Questions* was very well received. Given the substantial changes to the law since 2004, such as *Twombly* and *Leegin*, it became clear that a revision was required. Although this is not one of the Section's larger publications, it still required substantial time and effort to complete. This edition of *Frequently Asked Antitrust Questions* was shepherded to completion by the current leadership of the Section's Corporate Counseling Committee. Particular thanks go to Eric J. Stock and Jerome A. Swindell for their time and diligence in overseeing the team of volunteers that did the actual drafting. The Section appreciates the experience, expertise and effort that are required to bring superior publications to our membership and we believe this publication will become a valuable resource for your practice.

February 2013

Theodore Voorhees, Jr.
*Chair*, Section of Antitrust Law
American Bar Association
2012-13

# PREFACE

The Antitrust Section's Corporate Counseling Committee is pleased to provide this *Second Edition* of the Committee's publication *Frequently Asked Antitrust Questions*. This book was conceived of by our Committee as a basic guide to provide antitrust counselors, especially in-house corporate counsel, with clear and concise answers to basic antitrust questions that arise in the day-to-day business of corporate clients. This publication also seeks to assist counselors in identifying those situations where additional, more detailed, research may be needed, and to provide guidance on where the more detailed answers to these questions may be found.

The editors and contributors to this *Second Edition* are heavily indebted to those who originally conceived of this book, including and especially former Committee Chair Brian Henry and current Committee Co-Chair Steven J. Cernak, who led the drafting process for the *First Edition*. For this *Second Edition*, the drafting process was led by Committee Vice-Chair Jerome A. Swindell, as well as Co-Chair Eric J. Stock. We greatly appreciate the hard work and expertise provided by the lead Chapter Editors John W. Treece, Thomas Ensign, Joel M. Cohen, Claudia R. Higgins, Paula W. Render, David K. Park, and Peggy Ward. The effort to finalize the drafting process was led by Jerome A. Swindell and Eric J. Stock, as well as Committee Co-Chair Steven J. Cernak, and Books and Treatises Committee Vice-Chair Patrick Bock and Co-Chair Kimberly Ketalas. Other contributors to the final volume include: Jack R. Bierig, Keith D. Edelman, Neeraj K. Gupta, Jodi A. Lucena-Pichardo, Elizabeth L. Maxeiner, Kate McMillan, Craig Minerva, Adam N. Murad, Daniel J. O'Brien, Dennis M. Quinio, William H. Rawson, Rebecca Tracy Rotem, Heather M. Schneider, Daniel E. Shulak, Jesse Solomon, Courtney E. Silver, and Molly M. Wilkens.

We are very grateful for the hard work provided by all of the contributors to this volume, and hope that this publication continues to serve as a useful guide for antitrust practitioners who seek clear and simple answers to frequently asked antitrust questions.

February 2013

Steven J. Cernak
Eric J. Stock
*Co-Chairs*, Corporate Counseling Committee
Section of Antitrust Law
American Bar Association
2012-13

# INTRODUCTION

*Frequently Asked Antitrust Questions* is a different kind of ABA publication. It is not meant to provide exhaustive answers to complex antitrust questions. It will not provide much help to an antitrust litigator writing an appellate brief.

What *Frequently Asked Antitrust Questions* aims to provide is a quick, jargon-free framework to help answer common antitrust questions that lawyers face every day. For the antitrust lawyer, the publication provides a brief reminder of some antitrust basics plus a list of additional reading materials to help get started and to help ensure that the antitrust lawyer asks the right questions of the client. For the lawyer who does not need to answer antitrust questions every day, this publication provides quick guidance to help meet client needs.

If you are looking for crisp, clear answers to common antitrust questions, this book will be a valuable resource.

CHAPTER I

# DEALING WITH COMPETITORS

## A. What Are the Basic Rules That Govern My Company's Interactions with Competitors?

The principal concern raised by "dealing with competitors"—the subject of this chapter—is a concern under Section 1 of the Sherman Act, which makes it illegal to enter an agreement that unreasonably restrains trade.[1] An agreement or conspiracy between or among *competitors* with the sole or principal effect of limiting competition among them along any parameter—on price, terms, output, or product quality, either generally or with respect to a specific customer—will likely violate this statute, exposing both the individual and his employer to enormous criminal sanctions and civil liability. Because these consequences are so severe, this chapter focuses not only on what specific conduct might violate Section 1, but also on how to advise clients to conduct themselves in a manner that minimizes the risk of being accused unfairly of violating the statute, i.e., the "best practices" for avoiding even the appearance of an antitrust violation.

Although antitrust laws sometimes seem complex, a Section 1 violation can be established by proving just two elements: (1) an agreement that (2) unreasonably restrains trade. Below, we briefly explore the meaning of thoese two elements.

---

1. Section 1 of the Sherman Act provides that "[e]very contract, combination in the form of trust or otherwise, or conspiracy, in restraint of trade or commerce among the several States, or with foreign nations, is declared to be illegal." 15 U.S.C. § 1. The case law has the terms "contract, combination . . . or conspiracy" interchangeably with the term "agreement." 1 PHILLIP E. AREEDA & HERBERT HOVENKAMP, ANTITRUST LAW: AN ANALYSIS OF ANTITRUST PRINCIPLES AND THEIR APPLICATION ¶ 1403 (3d ed. 2006).

## 1.  Agreement

A firm or individual cannot violate Section 1 by acting unilaterally; rather, Section 1 requires an "agreement" between or among at least two persons or entities with separate economic interests.[2] Thus, an agreement that violates Section 1 of the Sherman Act can be between a company and its competitor, its upstream supply channel, its downstream distribution channel, its ultimate customers, its joint venturers, or even a joint venture in which it is one of the joint venturers.

It is important to understand that for Section 1 purposes, an "agreement" can be, but does not have to be, reflected in a written document, a firm handshake, or a verbal acknowledgement. An agreement exists for Section 1 purposes if the parties merely share a "conscious commitment to a common scheme designed to achieve an unlawful objective."[3]

Such a "conscious commitment" can be proven by direct evidence. That evidence may take the form of a written contract which contains a provision that is alleged to restrain competition unreasonably, such as an exclusivity provision, a resale price maintenance provision, a territorial restriction on commercial activities, or the like. Or, it may take the form of an eye witness to an agreement to fix prices, or an admission by a party that it has participated in such a conspiracy. Or, a verbalized suggestion, followed by a responsive "knowing wink," may be enough evidence to show the requisite "conscious commitment to a common scheme."[4]

---

2.      The Supreme Court has held that an agreement between a parent company and its wholly owned subsidiary is not an agreement for Section 1 purposes because those two entities do not have independent economic incentives. Copperweld Corp. v. Independence Tube Corp., 467 U.S. 752 (1984). This rationale has been extended to find that agreements between parent companies and their majority-owned subsidiaries do not fall within the ambit of Section 1. *See* Freeman v. San Diego Ass'n of Realtors, 322 F.3d 1133, 1148 (9th Cir. 2003) ("Where there is substantial common ownership . . . individual firms function as an economic unit and are generally treated as a single entity."); *see also* Novatel Commc'ns v. Cellular Tel. Supply, 1986 WL 798475 (N.D. Ga. 1986).

3.      Monsanto Co. v. Spray-Rite Serv. Corp., 465 U.S. 752, 764 (1984).

4.      The American Bar Association's Model Jury Instructions provide that, "[t]o establish the existence of a conspiracy, the evidence does not need to show that its members entered into any formal or written agreement . . . . The agreement may itself have been entirely unspoken." *See* ABA SECTION OF ANTITRUST LAW, MODEL JURY INSTRUCTIONS IN CIVIL

Alternatively, an agreement can be proven by circumstantial evidence from which the trier-of-fact may infer an agreement or conspiracy. Importantly, a court or jury may infer a "conscious commitment to a common scheme" based largely on the *conduct* of the alleged conspirators. Specifically, an agreement for Section 1 purposes can be inferred from an opportunity to conspire (such as that provided by meeting with competitors) followed by similar and reasonably contemporaneous business conduct (such as price increases, output restrictions, or reductions in quality) that arguably would not be in any single competitor's economic self-interest if it were acting alone.[5]

Many cases brought under Section 1 involve such "parallel conduct" by competitors. (The antitrust cases use the term "parallel conduct" to refer to circumstances in which competitors engage in substantially similar business conduct at about the same time.) Often, the parallel conduct in question involves price increases, and the question is whether competitors' substantially similar and reasonably contemporaneous price increases "stem[] from independent decision or from an agreement, tacit or express."[6] This is often a very difficult question to answer because, as the courts have long recognized, there are often innocent explanations for parallel conduct, including parallel price increases.

---

ANTITRUST CASES B-2 (2005). *See also* Esco Corp. v. United States, 340 F.2d 1000, 1007 (9th Cir. 1965) ("A knowing wink can mean more than words."); Weit v. Cont'l Ill. Nat'l Bank & Trust Co. of Chi., 641 F.2d 457, 475 (7th Cir. 1981) ("This exchange of information regarding the 'regular' interest rate and the interest rate being charged by Pullman is analogous to '(a) knowing wink (which) can mean more than words' in determining whether defendants agreed to fix prices."). But note that in *In re High Fructose Corn Syrup Antitrust Litigation*, 295 F.3d 651, 654 (7th Cir. 2002), the Seventh Circuit Court of Appeals said that the:

> language [of the Sherman Act] is broad enough ... to encompass a purely tacit agreement to fix prices, that is, an agreement made without any actual communication among the parties to the agreement .... Nevertheless, it is generally believed ... an agreement involving actual, verbalized communication, must be proved in order for a price-fixing conspiracy to be actionable under the Sherman Act.

*Id.* at 654. Thus, a verbalized suggestion, followed by a "knowing wink," is enough to infer an agreement for Section 1 purposes.

5.　*See High Fructose Corn Syrup*, 295 F.3d at 654-55; City of Tuscaloosa v. Harcros Chems., 158 F.3d 548, 570-71 (11th Cir. 1998).

6.　Theatre Enters. v. Paramount Film Distrib. Corp., 346 U.S. 537, 540 (1954).

- In many industries, competitors will often make parallel responses to changes in market forces which affect them similarly.[7] For example, if the cost of a significant input to the products made by all or most competitors were to increase rapidly, one would expect all or most of them to respond by increasing their prices; while competitors' prices would rise "in parallel," one need not hypothesize a conspiracy to explain that parallel behavior. Similarly, if in a developing consumer market, consumers responded well to the option, offered by one competitor, to purchase "bundles" of products rather than individual products, one would expect the other firms in the industry to quickly follow suit with parallel bundled offers.[8]
- In concentrated industries, competitors' pricing decisions are often interdependent—meaning that each competitor will consider the other competitors' likely competitive responses before implementing a pricing decision. In such industries, "follow the leader" pricing is often expected and may not suggest a price-fixing agreement.[9]

Because parallel business behavior is often a common feature of competitive markets, "antitrust law limits the range of permissible inferences from ambiguous evidence," so that a plaintiff attempting to prove an agreement based on parallelism "must present evidence 'that

---

7.   *See* Donald F. Turner, *The Definition of Agreement Under the Sherman Act: Conscious Parallelism and Refusals to Deal*, 75 HARV. L. REV. 655, 663 (1962) (noting that parallelism often "involves simply the independent responses of a group of competitors to the same set of economic facts").

8.   *See* FED. TRADE COMM'N, AN FTC GUIDE TO THE ANTITRUST LAWS (July 6, 2010), *available at* http://www.ftc.gov/bc/antitrust/factsheets/antitrustlawsguide.pdf.

9.   Clamp-All Corp. v. Cast Iron Soil Pipe Inst., 851 F.2d 478 (1st Cir. 1988) ("A firm in a concentrated industry typically has reason to decide (individually) to copy an industry leader."); *In re* Citric Acid Litig., 191 F.3d 1090, 1102 (9th Cir. 1999) ("A section 1 violation cannot, however, be inferred from parallel pricing alone, nor from an industry's follow-the-leader pricing strategy.") (internal citations omitted); Reserve Supply Corp. v. Owens-Corning Fiberglas Corp., 971 F.2d 37, 55 (7th Cir. 1992) ("Because of the interdependence of the fiberglass insulation industry, consciously parallel pricing alone does not indicate a conspiracy.").

tends to exclude the possibility' that the alleged conspirators acted independently."[10] Put another way, a plaintiff attempting to prove an illegal agreement on the basis of parallel conduct must show that the defendant "acted in a way that, but for a hypothesis of joint action, would not be in its own interest."[11] Conversely, "[a] defendant is entitled to summary judgment when it 'provides a plausible and justifiable alternative interpretation of its conduct that rebuts the alleged conspiracy.'"[12] Moreover, the courts have concluded that if the explanation for parallel conduct could "just as well be independent action" as it could be illegal conspiracy, then no inference of an illegal agreement will be permitted.[13] That is, when an innocent explanation for parallel conduct is equally likely as the hypothesis of conspiracy, the courts are to find no violation of Section 1.

Plaintiffs can often find arguments as to why a defendant's parallel conduct would not have been in its economic self-interest if it had been acting alone. As a result, the determination of whether allegedly parallel conduct can support an inference of an illegal agreement is often complex and difficult, particularly for the typical jury for whom such issues are entirely foreign. An important point, however, is that before the court or jury has to wrestle with that question, the plaintiff must first show that the defendants had the opportunity to conspire and as a practical matter, suggest that the conduct at issue was the subject of communication among defendants. Accordingly, as discussed below, limiting so-called opportunities to conspire and the subject matter of

---

10. Matsushita Elec. Indus. v. Zenith Radio Corp., 475 U.S. 574, 588 (1968) (quoting Monsanto Co. v. Spray-Rite Serv. Corp., 465 U.S. 752, 764 (1984)).

11. Illinois Corporate Travel v. Am. Airlines, 806 F.2d 722, 726 (7th Cir. 1986).

12. Market Force v. Wauwatosa Realty Co., 906 F.2d 1167, 1174 (7th Cir. 1990) (quoting City of Long Beach v. Standard Oil Co., 872 F.2d 1401, 1406 (9th Cir.1989)); *see also* AD/SAT, Div. of Skylight, Inc. v. Associated Press, 181 F.3d 216 (2d Cir. 1999); Reserve Supply Corp. v. Owens-Corning Fiberglas Corp., 799 F. Supp. 840, 844 (N.D. Ill. 1990), *aff'd*, 971 F.2d 37 (7th Cir. 1992).

13. Bell Atl. Corp. v. Twombly, 550 U.S. 544, 557 (2007); *see also* Starr v. Sony BMG Music Entm't, 592 F.3d 314, 327 (2d Cir. 2010) ("Under *Twombly*, allegations of parallel conduct that could 'just as well be independent action' are not sufficient to state a claim. However, in this case plaintiffs have alleged behavior that would plausibly contravene each defendant's self-interest 'in the absence of similar behavior by rivals.'" (internal citation omitted)).

communications with competitors are important ways to avoid or minimize antitrust exposure.

## 2. *Restraint of Trade*

As to the second required element for a Section 1 violation—that the agreement unreasonably restrains competition—the law has created a largely unrebuttable presumption that certain types of agreements among competitors unreasonably restrain trade. These kinds of agreements are said to be per se illegal and are sometimes called "hard core" offenses because experience has taught that they almost never have any redeeming, procompetitive benefits.[14] Per se illegal agreements are almost always agreements reached between or among competitors to limit competition between them, such as agreements to fix or maintain prices (including classic bid-rigging or cartel behavior), to restrict output or limit quality, to allocate markets or customers among competing suppliers, to limit innovation, or otherwise to deprive customers of the benefits of vigorous competition.[15]

It is important to remember, however, that agreements that are not per se illegal may still be found to restrain trade unreasonably in violation of Section 1 of the Sherman Act if, after a thorough analysis of their probable effects on competition, called a "rule of reason" analysis, their anticompetitive effects outweigh their procompetitive benefits. Such a rule of reason analysis typically considers a host of factors—such as the structure of a relevant market, market concentration, the possibility of new entry, the nature of relationships between sellers and buyers, the speed and significance of innovation, and the like—in order to understand the competitive effects of agreements that are not per se illegal but are nonetheless challenged under Section 1 as unreasonably restraining competition.

As this brief discussion shows, it is not illegal to deal with competitors. In fact, competitors deal with each other all the time—at civic events, during lobbying efforts, at trade association or industry meetings, or in the context of joint ventures—without running afoul of the antitrust laws. It is only illegal under Section 1 of the Sherman Act to enter into agreements with competitors that unreasonably restrain competition. Nonetheless, because the criminal sanctions and civil

---

14.    *See* Catalano, Inc. v. Target Sales, 446 U.S. 643, 647-48 (1980); United States v. Socony-Vacuum Oil Co., 310 U.S. 150, 223 (1940).

15.    1 AREEDA & HOVENKAMP, *supra* note 1, ¶ 1910.

liability exposure associated with a violation of Section 1 are so severe, antitrust lawyers frequently advise clients to conduct themselves in a manner that minimizes the risk that an antitrust enforcement agency or trier-of-fact will draw the erroneous inference that the client entered an illegal agreement. This chapter will therefore focus on these "best practices" for minimizing antitrust risks when dealing with competitors.

## B. Our Employees Occasionally Participate with Their Counterparts from Our Competitors in Civic Events and Industry Trade Associations. How Should We Prepare for Such Events?

The antitrust laws are not intended to discourage your client's employees from participating in charitable events, civic events, or trade associations—even if competitors' employees will be there too! There is nothing illegal about simply talking to, socializing with, or participating in charitable or civic events with a competitor's employees. Similarly, employees who participate in industry gatherings can interact with competitors' employees without violating the antitrust laws. As discussed in Part A, what Section 1 prohibits is reaching an agreement with a competitor that unreasonably restrains competition. One can socialize, pursue civic objectives, and attend industry conferences without entering anticompetitive agreements.

Nonetheless, informal communications between or among competitors in these settings can raise antitrust risks that should not be ignored, in part because of the possibility that a larger set of facts may unfold over which the socializing employees have no knowledge or control. For example, assume that shortly after two competitors' senior executives spend a day together working on a charitable or civic endeavor, both companies, simultaneously or within a short period, were to raise their prices substantially. A plaintiff seeking to establish a Section 1 violation would question whether the executives had used the opportunity of the event to reach an agreement to raise prices. If the question were investigated years later—and discovery in antitrust cases often occurs many years after the relevant events—the executives may have no recollections that would allow them to deny forcefully that they had any discussions about general market conditions, their companies' actual or expected responses to those conditions, the behavior of their mutual competitors, what their companies or other companies should charge, or other competitively sensitive subjects. Worse, what if they actually *had* commiserated generally about the poor market conditions their companies were facing and discussed in general terms the desperate need some companies had to get prices up—but without any intent to agree on a price increase or any expectation that the conversation would result in any action by either company? And worse yet, what if one of the participants had recounted the exchange in an e-mail to a friend or colleague, explaining that the conversation had convinced him that his competitor "agreed" that everyone in the industry was suffering and was eager to find solutions? Each of these scenarios provides evidence from which a plaintiff's attorney could argue to a jury that the price increases resulted from an agreement between the two competitors—an agreement that is per se illegal.

Your client's employees may also communicate with competitors' employees at trade shows or industry conferences. The antitrust risks associated with these events are even greater than those associated with civic or charitable events because (1) by definition competitors will attend the same industry event; (2) conversations about certain competitively sensitive topics, discussed below, may occur as your client's employees and competitors' employees discuss products, prices, and perhaps other competitively sensitive topics with their sometimes-mutual customers; and (3) the attendees at such industry events are likely to have responsibilities for competitively sensitive functions like pricing, sales, marketing, or product development.

The solution to these risks is to alert your client's employees to the risks and to provide them with training and some simple "best practices" rules about how they should conduct themselves when in the company of competitors' employees.

First, employees should be taught not to discuss *any* competitively sensitive information with competitors. This general admonition, which goes beyond antitrust concerns, will go a long way in avoiding them. However, not sharing competitively sensitive information is insufficient to protect against inappropriate casual comments or industry chit-chat that could provide the basis to infer an illegal agreement, because employees may not appreciate that chit-chat about even publicly available information can lead to serious antitrust risks.

Second, all employees should be trained that they are simply forbidden from discussing certain topics with competitors. These prohibited topics include the following:

- *Past, Present, or Future Prices.* Simply put, your client's employees should never discuss with competitors, in any setting, whether formal or informal, the prices that their company or any competitor has charged, does charge, should charge, could charge, or will charge for its products—to the market generally or to any specific customer. This prohibition includes not only discussions about specific prices but also discussions about pricing policies or structures, such as package or bundled pricing, rebate programs, discounts, discount levels, surcharges, fees and the like. It also includes discussions about whether to bid at all for certain business or to certain customers.

In fact, discussion of any price-related subject should be off limits. This includes terms and conditions of sale, such as credit terms, returned goods policies, minimum purchase commitments or requirements, or performance requirements that customers must satisfy to qualify for preferential prices.

All of these price-related topics should be off-limits during conversations with competitors. There is almost never a legitimate reason for these types of discussions with competitors—certainly, a jury is unlikely to see a legitimate purpose.[16]

- *Output, Capacity Utilization, or Outages.*[17] An agreement among competitors to restrict output, which has the almost inevitable effect of raising prices, is a per se violation of Section 1 just as much as a collusive agreement to raise prices. Your client's employees should never discuss their employer's output decisions or plans with a competitor. This includes discussions about plant expansions, production curtailments, or outages.

- *Marketing or Sales Plans, Future Business Plans and Strategies.*[18] Your client's employees should never discuss their company's marketing or sales plans or its business plans or strategies with competitors. If this information is shared with competitors, they may reduce their competitive vigor with respect to certain markets or customers, denying those customers of the benefits of such competition.

- *Product Development.*[19] Particularly in "high tech" industries, companies sometimes compete primarily not on the basis of

---

16. *See* United States v. U.S. Gypsum Co., 438 U.S. 422 (1978).

17. *See* NCAA v. Bd. of Regents of Univ. of Okla., 468 U.S. 85, 109-10 (1984).

18. U.S. DEP'T OF JUSTICE & FED. TRADE COMM'N, ANTITRUST GUIDELINES FOR COLLABORATIONS AMONG COMPETITORS § 3.31(b) (2000), *available at* http://www.ftc.gov/os/2000/04/ftcdojguidelines.pdf.

19. *See* 1 AREEDA & HOVENKAMP, *supra* note 1, ¶ 2115(b)-(c).

price, but on the basis of their ability to develop and introduce new products. Agreements to limit this competition—i.e., agreements not to enter certain technologies or not to develop or introduce certain innovative products—may also violate the antitrust laws. Consequently, your client's employees should not discuss product development plans with competitors, including decisions *not* to engage in certain research and development or *not* to pursue certain development projects.

- *Supply and/or Demand Conditions in the Industry.*[20] Although it seems entirely natural for competitors to commiserate about supply or demand conditions that are largely outside of their control and have driven prices or profitability down—i.e., over-supply or slack demand—those discussions must be avoided. It is a short distance from "agreeing" that industry conditions are terrible to an "agreement" about what to do about it—for example, set prices or limit output.

- *Specific Customers or Classes of Customers.*[21] It may also seem natural to commiserate with a competitor about a particularly difficult or querulous customer, but it is a per se violation of Section 1 for competitors to agree not to deal with a particular customer (or how or on what terms to deal with it). Accordingly, discussions about specific customers should be treated as off-limits.

- *Specific Suppliers or Classes of Suppliers.*[22] Similarly, it can be per se illegal for competitors to agree whether or under what terms and conditions to deal with a supplier or class of suppliers. Discussions of this topic are also forbidden.

Why is it so important to train employees that certain topics of discussion are simply forbidden when talking to competitors' employees? If an antitrust challenge is made to a company's decision to increase prices, restrict output, adopt a certain pricing structure, etc., that challenge may come years after the fact. Employees may not have a distinct memory of what was discussed at the charity, civic, or industry

---

20.  *See* Standard Iron Works v. ArcelorMittal, 639 F. Supp. 2d 877 (N.D. Ill. 2009); *In re* OSB Antitrust Litig., 2007 WL 2253419 (E.D. Pa. 2007).

21.  *See* FTC v. Superior Court Trial Lawyers Ass'n, 439 U.S. 411 (1990); FTC v. Ind. Fed'n of Dentists, 476 U.S. 447 (1986).

22.  *See* Eastern States Retail Lumber Ass'n v. United States, 234 U.S. 600 (1914); Seagood Trading Corp. v. Jerrico, Inc., 924 F.2d 1555 (11th Cir. 1991).

event, but if they have been adequately trained and are clear about the rules of engagement with competitors' employees, they will nonetheless be in a position to deny forcefully and unequivocally, any suggestion that a problematic discussion occurred. For this reason, employees should be trained to properly document interactions with competitors.

Third, your client's employees should be advised to "control the setting" in which they interact with competitors. Part of this control should be attending only meetings for which there is a preapproved agenda and where minutes will be taken and distributed. Simply put, they should avoid settings which appear clandestine, even if the conversation is not. If possible, their interactions with competitors' employees should be open and public, rather than private and one-on-one. The point is that the setting should dispel the inference of collusion. Thus, collusion seems unlikely during meetings or events attended by customers or public officials; meetings with competitors in hotel rooms, bars, or hospitality suites create a very different impression.

The admonition to "control the setting" becomes even more important in the context of trade shows or other industry gatherings. On the one hand, the floor of a large industry trade show, with customers swarming suppliers' booths, seems like a highly unlikely environment in which to reach an illegal agreement that deprives those customers of the benefits of competition. To the contrary, the environment is an inherently competitive one, as each firm tries to grab the customers' attention away from its competitor. On the other hand, trade shows and conferences typically offer many activities that occur away from the scheduled events. Your client's employees should be trained to be aware of their surroundings and to avoid being alone with competitors' employees in hospitality suites, bars, or hotel rooms. Indeed, in some concentrated, antitrust-sensitive industries, firms prohibit their employees from visiting competitors' hospitality suites—and bar competitors from their own.

There is another sense in which employees should be trained to "control the setting." A significant difference between attending a civic or charitable event with a competitor and attending a trade show is the presence of customers and/or suppliers who may be there in large part to discuss with your client's employees some of the "forbidden topics" outlined above that are off-limits in discussions with competitors. That is, customers have a keen and legitimate interest in discussing future prices, products, and marketing plans, industry dynamics or trends, or new products in the pipeline. The antitrust laws do not discourage these conversations between suppliers and their customers and to the contrary, recognize that the free flow of information between a supplier and its customers makes markets more efficient. These conversations are therefore to be encouraged.

But holding these conversations in the mixed company of suppliers, customers, *and competitors* carries a heightened risk that either the conversation itself or subsequent documentation of it—i.e., the competitor's e-mails about what they learned at the trade show they attended—could be perceived as improper. To minimize these risks, your client's employees should be reminded to tailor conversations appropriately to their audiences. Topics that may be discussed with customers or suppliers who have legitimate reasons to inquire may not be appropriate to discuss openly in the presence of competitors. (A hospitality suite open only to customers, and not competitors, is a good venue for such discussions.) Even a discussion of competitively sensitive views or information in a public setting, such as on an analyst call, can create antitrust exposure, especially in a concentrated industry, because plaintiffs or government enforcement agencies have sometimes argued that, particularly in such an industry, such seemingly public statements were in fact intended to signal competitors that a price increase, output restriction, or other reduction of competitive pressures would be welcomed.

Fourth, employees should be sensitized about how they document their contacts with competitors and/or competitive intelligence that they learn as a result.

- Most important, any documentation about meeting with, talking to, or receiving information from a competitor should, on its face, dispel any erroneous suggestion that your client's employees received competitively sensitive information directly from a competitor in circumstances that were not open and public. It is not good enough for an e-mail to say, "while at the meeting, I learned that . . ." because that statement does not rule out the possibility that the competitive information was received in a one-on-one, private conversation with a competitor that raises suspicions. Instead, such documentation should include the source of competitively sensitive information and the legitimate circumstances in which it was received or learned.
- If any document that originated with a competitor is obtained, the individual who received it should mark it in a way that makes clear and unambiguous the circumstances under which, and from whom, the information was legitimately received. More often than not, announcements (including price increase

announcements) or other materials that originated with competitors come from public sources or customers; that fact should be noted on the face of the document so that years later, there can be no suggestion that the materials came directly from the competitor. Simply, the recipient of these materials should write, on the face of the document, "Received from J. Smith of Our Customer, Inc. on 7-7-2012."

- If a competitor's employee's name appears on any trip or expense report, the legitimate purpose of the expense should also be stated clearly.
- Avoid the use of the ambiguous word "agree." An e-mail that recounts that the attendees at a conference "agreed" that the market has deteriorated and prices need to be higher to sustain the industry may have been meant as a simple statement of economic fact, but it could be read to suggest an illegal conspiracy.
- Do not state rumors as facts. Competitive intelligence about future events is inherently uncertain, and any description of such competitive intelligence should reflect that uncertainty. Rather than stating that "Company X will launch a new product in September," the description should acknowledge the source and the uncertainty: "I heard a rumor from three different customers (A, B, and C) that Company X will launch in September."

Finally, your client's employees should be trained that if an employee from a competitor approaches them and begins to discuss any of the prohibited topics, they must immediately make it *very clear* that they will not participate in such a discussion.[23] They should simply and clearly state, "I can't talk about that. My company's policy doesn't allow it." If this occurs at a meeting, the employee should insist that his departure is reflected in the minutes. Employees must be trained to take these extra steps because the law is unforgiving to a competitor who stands by idly, listening to others conspire or invite participation in an illicit agreement, even if he himself does not evidence assent. It is instead incumbent on the "bystander" to make it very clear that he will not participate and to walk away.

---

23. *See* United States v. Therm-All, Inc., 373 F.3d 625 (5th Cir. 2004) (finding that phone records may be used as circumstantial evidence of participation in a price-fixing conspiracy).

Employees should also be taught that if they are approached by a competitor in a manner that raises antitrust concerns, they should immediately report such conduct to the company's legal department and, with their help, document their refusal to participate in such discussions or take other action necessary to dispel any inference of an agreement.

An especially difficult situation arises when a competitor's employee discloses competitively sensitive information to your client's employee, without suggesting or soliciting any actual agreement. What should the employee do? The competitive intelligence may be useful to the company—and the antitrust laws do encourage aggressive competition, after all—but can it be passed on ethically and without undue antitrust risk? Employees should be trained that if they receive unsolicited competitive intelligence from a competitor, they should consult the legal department. Sometimes, the circumstances will allow the employee to document the source of the competitive intelligence in a way that would dispel any reasonable inference that the information was obtained illicitly or in the context of an anticompetitive agreement. If so, the company may choose to use the information to its competitive advantage. In other cases, however, the competitive intelligence should not be passed on or used because the circumstances, including other contemporaneous events, may make it difficult to prove unequivocally that the information was obtained innocently.

In sum, even social interactions among your client's employees and competitors' employees present antitrust risks. Those risks are heightened when the interaction occurs at industry events. Your client's employees should therefore be trained to follow "best practices" that reduce these risks and minimize the chance that they or the company are unfairly accused of violating the antitrust laws.

## C. A Competitor Contacted Us to Complain That Our Company Is Offering Illegal Discounts, or Imposing "Anticompetitive" Conditions on the Availability of Discounts, but They've Got Their Facts All Wrong. Can We Advise the Competitor of Its Factual Errors and the True Facts?

Any discussion with a competitor about prices, including discounts and other price-related terms and conditions of sale, raises serious antitrust risks that a per se illegal agreement might be inferred from the discussion. The question presented—one competitor complaining about another's pricing—provides a good example of why this is so.

If a competitor's *lawyer* complains that your client is "offering illegal discounts or imposing 'anticompetitive' conditions on the availability of discounts," you should of course take those complaints very seriously and investigate any allegation of illegality, especially if the client has significant market or monopoly power and could be subject to a Sherman Act Section 2 claim for monopolization or attempted monopolization. But if after such an investigation, you are satisfied that your client's pricing would not run afoul of the Sherman Act, then a simple letter responding that the company takes compliance with the antitrust laws seriously, that you have investigated the matter, and that you are satisfied that the company's pricing complies with all applicable laws should be a sufficient response. If such a response is not sufficient to quell the threat of a lawsuit by the competitor, of course, the matter may have to be discussed counsel-to-counsel.

But if the complaint came to one of your client's executives from an executive at a competitor, it would be a very bad idea to allow a business-to-business response. Accordingly, your executives should be trained to bring *any* request for a meeting among competitors to counsel's attention, and in this instance, you should respond to the competitor that such a meeting is inappropriate.

Fundamentally, a competitor's complaint about allegedly illegal discounts (or "anticompetitive" conditions on the availability of discounts) can be read to be a complaint that your client's prices are too low—firms rarely complain that competitors have set their prices too high—and the competitor might be viewed as rattling the saber of purported illegality to convince your client to raise its prices. For example, the competitor may be claiming that after discounts, your client's prices are "predatory" because they appear to be too low relative to costs. Or, it may be claiming that discounts offered to customers who agree to purchase a bundle of your client's products are illegal because the competitor has a narrower product line and cannot afford to match the discounts on your client's bundle. Or, it may be claiming that your client's discounts create price differences that are illegal under the Robinson-Patman Act. In all of these cases, there are risks associated with trying to "set the record straight."

First, any "explanation" carries a high likelihood of becoming a discussion that goes beyond the question presented—the legality of your client's pricing—to become a discussion about pricing more generally. Indeed, even if the discussion were limited to disclosing the facts that are strictly necessary to respond to the allegation of illegality, the other side may not record or remember it that way.

Second, there is virtually no good way to characterize such a discussion from an antitrust perspective. Why would your client even agree to meet with its competitor to "set the record straight?" Why is it in its interest to do so? If the competitor mistakenly believes your client's prices are *higher* than they actually are, then your client should have no interest in disabusing the competitor of its mistake since the competitor will presumably continue to bid higher than it needs to take the business away from your company. Conversely, if the competitor believes that your company's prices are *lower* than they are—if it has been under a misapprehension about the extent of your company's discounts or the ease with which customers can avail themselves of those discounts— then "setting the record straight" means that the competitor will perceive less competitive pressure and may stop trying to compete with the non-existent discounts that it mistakenly perceives. In short, the competitor may raise its prices. While that may be good for your client, the "record" from an antitrust perspective would be that (1) the two companies met and discussed prices, and (2) the competitor raised its prices. This is an outline for a per se offense.

In short, any complaint by a competitor purportedly about the legality of your client's pricing should be referred to counsel, and a response, if any, should be made counsel-to-counsel. However, even counsel-to-counsel discussions of this nature carry risks, and so you should think through carefully whether it could later be claimed that the response itself—"setting the record straight"—chilled competition by eliminating or reducing uncertainty for your client or its competitor.

## D. My Sales Team Has Been Told by a Customer That It Has Received a Lower Priced Offer from a Competitor. May We Ask the Competitor to Verify the Truth of the Customer's Assertion?

As discussed in Part A, any horizontal agreement on price—whether that price applies to all customers or to a single customer—is per se illegal. While a theoretical argument exists that one could "verify" prices with a competitor without entering a price-fixing or price-stabilizing agreement, the antitrust risks of "price verification" activities are so significant that your client should follow an ironclad rule: Do not verify competitive prices with or for competitors. This is true both because the exchange of information with the competitor could be used as direct evidence of an agreement itself, and because the exchange of information along with parallel conduct could be used to infer an agreement.

As discussed in Part A of this chapter, a Sherman Act Section 1 violation requires just two elements: (1) an agreement that (2) unreasonably restrains competition.

A pattern of verifying prices between competitors can satisfy the agreement element of Section 1. For example, in *United States v. Container Corp. of America*,[24] competitors contacted each other regularly to verify customers' claims of lower prices. When one of Company A's customers demanded that it lower its price to meet Company B's allegedly lower price, Company A would call Company B to verify the price. If the lower price was verified, Company A would then match it.[25] The Supreme Court found that this conduct established an agreement under Section 1 of the Sherman Act, reasoning that "[e]ach defendant on receiving that request usually furnished the data with the expectation that it would be furnished reciprocal information when it wanted it."[26]

Even in the absence of a regular pattern of price verifications by competitors, an agreement can be easily inferred from instances of price verification followed by parallel price movements because, as the Supreme Court's language suggests, it is very difficult to explain why a firm would verify its prices to a competitor in the absence of an understanding to receive "reciprocal information." If your client asks its competitor to verify a price and the competitor admits to the lower price, your client would know that the customer is not bluffing and will presumably have the opportunity to match the lower price in order to get the customer's business, effectively defeating any advantage that the competitor had by giving a discount. Thus, verifying a lowered price would not normally be seen as in the self-interest of the verifying company, absent an agreement by the requesting company to furnish reciprocal information in the future.

In sum, even though the two price-verifying competitors have not "fixed" a price in the sense that they have not agreed on a specific price to charge the market or a specific customer, they are at substantial risk of being found to have entered an agreement that is a per se violation of Section 1 of the Sherman Act.

---

24.   United States v. Container Corp. of Am., 393 U.S. 333 (1969).
25.   *Id*. at 339-40.
26.   *Id*. at 335.

### E. Our Competitor Just Implemented a New Pricing Scheme That We Would Like to Adopt as Well. Are There Any Antitrust Problems We Should Consider?

It is not illegal to make an independent decision to adopt a competitor's pricing scheme or structure any more than it is illegal to match its price increase. However, adopting a competitor's pricing scheme may invite antitrust scrutiny, and so it is important to understand the risks and then follow "best practices" in order to minimize them.

The risk presented by the proposal to adopt a "pricing scheme" that has been recently adopted by a competitor is the risk of an accusation that the two companies agreed or coordinated on adoption of the new prices. This risk will be greater if the change from the old to the new prices would prejudice certain customers or classes of customers, particularly if certain customers could argue that, by making pricing structures uniform, one company has abandoned a structure which allowed it to compete more effectively for its business. Ultimately, then, the question will be whether your client's adoption of the scheme can be characterized as "parallel conduct" that could support an inference of collusion because (1) your client and its competitor had the opportunity to conspire, and (2) an argument exists that your client's adoption of the pricing scheme would not be in its independent economic self-interest if it were acting alone, i.e., absent the hypothesis of collusion.

With that background, the risks of adopting a competitor's pricing scheme or structure are largely dependent on the following factors:

- How recently did the competitor adopt its pricing scheme? If a significant period of time has passed since the competitor implemented its pricing structure, and it is reasonably clear that your client has simply observed customers' favorable reactions to it or its success over time, a decision to match the competitor's scheme should not be found to be "parallel."[27] Similarly, if a competitor has increased its price and your client has observed over some reasonable period of time that the

---

27.    City of Tuscaloosa v. Harcros Chems., 158 F.3d 548, 572 (11th Cir. 1998) ("[P]laintiffs first must produce evidence showing that the defendants engaged in consciously parallel action."); Quality Auto Body, Inc. v. Allstate Ins. Co., 660 F.2d 1195, 1200 (7th Cir. 1981) (finding defendants' conduct not parallel); *In re* Baby Food Antitrust Litig., No. 92-5495, slip op. at 21, 22-23 (D.N.J. July 25, 1997), *aff'd*, 166 F.3d 112 (3d Cir. 1999).

competitor did not lose many sales, then matching that price cannot be fairly characterized as parallel conduct.[28]

- Have your client's executives who are responsible for designing and approving the scheme had occasion to meet or communicate recently with the competitor whose scheme is being adopted? An illegal agreement cannot be inferred in the absence of an "opportunity to conspire," but if such opportunities existed, then (1) the legitimate reasons for the earlier competitor contacts should be assessed and documented, and (2) more care should be taken to document internally the independent reasons for adopting the pricing structure.

- How did your client learn about the competitor's pricing scheme? Can it establish that it became aware of it through legitimate means, such as from a customer or from publicly available information?

- Most important, why does your client want to adopt the competitor's pricing scheme? Why is it advantageous as compared to the current pricing structure? If your client has an independent business justification for adopting the scheme—one that makes sense whether or not competitors match it—then there is little room to argue that your client is adopting it as a result of a collusive agreement.[29]

- Can your client document the independent reasons for adopting the new scheme? Particularly if the competitor recently implemented the pricing scheme and if you cannot substantially rule out the possibility of contacts between your client and the competitor, then it would be prudent to document the procompetitive justifications for adopting the competitor's pricing structure as part of the decision-making process.

---

28. *See* Brooke Grp. v. Brown & Williamson Tobacco Corp., 509 U.S. 209, 227 (1993); *In re* Late Fee & Over-Limit Fee Litig., 528 F. Supp. 2d 953, 964 (N.D. Cal. 2007).

29. *See In re* Elevator Antitrust Litig., 502 F.3d 47, 51 (2d Cir. 2007) ("[S]imilar pricing can suggest competition at least as plausibly as it can suggest anticompetitive conspiracy."); City of Moundridge v. Exxon Mobil Corp., 409 F. App'x 362, 363 (D.C. Cir. 2011) ("Appellants' burden was to present evidence that tends to exclude the possibility that the alleged conspirators acted independently." (internal quotation marks omitted)).

In sum, there is no reason why your client cannot adopt a pricing scheme that it believes to be in its independent best interests, even if it is the same as or similar to one adopted by a competitor. However, to protect against the allegation that it followed its competitor's pricing structure as part of a collusive agreement, your client should answer the questions posed above if it is at risk of an adverse inference and, if so, take the defensive steps described to protect against it.

### F. Our Operations Employees Want to Meet with Their Counterparts from Our Competitor to Share Some Best Practices. Is That Okay?

The exchange of operational and other business data for the purpose of evaluating "best practices" in a given industry or across industries is frequently referred to as "benchmarking."[30] The antitrust authorities recognize that the exchange of "benchmarking" or "best practices" information may be procompetitive, potentially leading to increased productivity, product improvements, and reductions in consumer prices.[31] For example, they may benchmark the use of certain types of software, pension benefit structures, or methods of tracking intellectual property rights.

The fact that benchmarking is often procompetitive is evidenced by the fact that oftentimes, the companies involved in a benchmarking exercise may come from entirely different industries. In these situations, there are no evident antitrust concerns, and yet, the participating companies devote time and resources to these exercises for clearly procompetitive reasons.

Nonetheless, when benchmarking exercises include competitors, they raise the same risks associated with many types of information exchanges among competitors. We will therefore discuss the risks of benchmarking and information exchanges together.

---

30.  Jeffrey S. Ross, *Benchmarking and the Antitrust Laws*, ANDREWS ANTITRUST LITIG. REP., Nov. 1997, at 3.

31.  *See* Foss Mar. Co., Business Review Letter (B.R.L.) 01-557, 2001 WL 1564270 (DOJ Oct. 25, 2001) (outlining the Dep't of Justice's response to a business review letter written by maritime services companies, proposing to conduct industry survey); *see also In re* Citric Acid Litig., 191 F.3d 1090, 1098 (9th Cir. 1999) (holding that the collection and annual dissemination of aggregated sales and production statistics served the legitimate purpose of "informing members of worldwide [industry] conditions").

First, the mere interactions among competitors associated with an exchange of benchmarking data or competitively sensitive information may later be viewed as having provided the participating firms with an opportunity to reach an anticompetitive agreement that is per se illegal or as having served as a mechanism by which the participants were able to monitor each other's compliance with such an agreement.[32] Accordingly, your client's employees who are involved in benchmarking activities or information exchanges with competitors should be trained in the "best practices" for dealing with competitors discussed in Part B above.

Second, information exchanges and benchmarking activities can potentially violate Section 1 even in the absence of a per se violation. Specifically, because benchmarking and exchanges of information are generally procompetitive, they are not themselves condemned as per se illegal.[33] Nonetheless, the courts recognize that in certain limited circumstances, the exchange of information—and particularly, price information—may have the effect of causing competition to be less vigorous than if there were no exchange, thereby perhaps making the exchange illegal under a "rule of reason" analysis.

The dilemma therefore is that, on the one hand, an exchange of information among competitors can clearly be procompetitive; on the other hand, it might either mask or facilitate an explicit cartel or tacit collusion. Between those two extremes, the exchange of information may or may not make competition less vigorous.

---

32. *See In re* New Motor Vehicles Canadian Exp. Antitrust Litig., 522 F.3d 6 (1st Cir. 2008) (finding that dissemination of best practices presented, in conjunction with other competitor communications, as evidence of an alleged conspiracy to unreasonably restrain trade); Todd v. Exxon Corp., 275 F.3d 191, 207-11 (2d Cir. 2001) (reversing dismissal of claim that competitors within the oil and petrochemical industry had violated § 1 of the Sherman Act by regularly exchanging detailed salary and wage information); Reed v. Advocate Health Care, 268 F.R.D. 573 (N.D. Ill. 2009) (involving allegations that an exchange of information regarding RN wages violated § 1 of the Sherman Act).

33. *See* United States v. U.S. Gypsum Co., 438 U.S. 422, 441 n.16 (1978) ("The exchange of price data and other information among competitors does not invariably have anticompetitive effects; indeed such practices can in certain circumstances increase economic efficiency and render markets more, rather than less, competitive. For this reason, we have held that such exchanges of information do not constitute a per se violation of the Sherman Act."); ABA SECTION ON ANTITRUST LAW, MODEL JURY INSTRUCTIONS IN CIVIL ANTITRUST CASES B-32-33 (2005).

The resolution of this dilemma can be largely discerned from four Supreme Court cases. In *American Column & Lumber Co. v. United States*,[34] a majority of the lumber companies in the southeastern United States participated in a so-called "Open Competition Plan," in which they provided to a secretary detailed product information, past and present customer-specific price information, and details about their future plans. The secretary prepared detailed reports for the companies on market conditions and recommended prices and production levels. The Court found that the "Open Competition Plan" was no more than a "gentleman's agreement" to stabilize prices, i.e., a price-fixing agreement, as the plan dictated price and output decisions as a cartel does.

By contrast, in *Maple Flooring Manufacturers' Ass'n v. United States*,[35] the defendants collectively produced 70 percent of the maple flooring in the United States, but the Court noted that they owned only a small proportion of the total stand of maples, so that potential competitors could enter the market easily if prices rose above competitive levels. The companies provided a secretary with detailed sales, price, and inventory information, all of which dealt "exclusively with past and closed transactions."[36] The secretary then aggregated this historical information and sent it to members without revealing specific respondents' or customers' identities. On these facts, the Court found there was no violation, and in fact, the exchange of past information was not anticompetitive; it did not enable the members to predict confidently what other members would quote to specific customers, but provided market information that was useful to the participants.

In *United States v. Container Corp. of America*,[37] the Court took *American Column* one step farther, holding that an information exchange may violate Section 1 even in the absence of the "gentlemen's agreement" found in the earlier case. In *Container Corp.*, the defendants comprised 90 percent of the corrugated box market; the market was dominated by a few sellers; the products were fungible; and demand was inelastic. In short, the structure of the market made it vulnerable to explicit or tacit collusion. The defendants exchanged information regarding current prices being charged to specific, identified customers, "not a statistical report on the average cost to all members."[38] The Court

---

34.    American Column & Lumber Co. v. United States, 257 U.S. 377 (1921).
35.    Maple Flooring Mfrs.' Ass'n v. United States, 268 U.S. 563 (1925).
36.    *Id.* at 573.
37.    United States v. Container Corp. of Am., 393 U.S. 333 (1969).
38.    *Id.* at 334.

found that the agreement to exchange information provided the "agreement" element of a Section 1 violation and that the nature of the industry and the type of information exchanged established that the exchange of current transaction-level price information had a price-stabilizing effect. Accordingly, the exchange was found to be illegal.

Finally, in *United States v. U.S. Gypsum Co.*,[39] the Court reaffirmed that the mere exchange of price information is not per se illegal, but held that a court must apply a "rule of reason" analysis that considers both the structure of the industry and the nature of the information exchanged to determine whether the exchange unreasonably restrains trade.

As these cases suggest, whether an exchange of information will be deemed to have anticompetitive effects depends on the structure of the industry and the nature of the information that is exchanged. Moreover, as described below, the antitrust enforcement agencies have issued guidelines that have been interpreted to define a "safe harbor" for such activities that also reflect these considerations.

## 1. Structure of the Industry

Benchmarking activities are unlikely to raise antitrust concerns if the participants are not competitors, but they may raise concerns when they are. Concerns increase when the participants comprise a substantial portion of the competitors in a market that is structurally susceptible to collusion, i.e., a market (1) that is highly concentrated, (2) that has high barriers to entry, (3) in which the products are fungible, and (4) in which customers are not especially price sensitive.[40]

- *Market Concentration and Exchange Participation Rate.* Collusion is easier when a market is concentrated because less coordination is required. In the context of benchmarking or an information exchange, where the industry is concentrated, only a few sellers need to react to the information that is the subject of the exchange in order for it to have a market impact.

  Conversely, collusion tends not to succeed if any significant number of rivals do not participate because non-participating rivals can steal customers away from colluders who set artificially high prices. Thus, an exchange among companies that represent a small share of the industry suggests only an intent to

---

39. United States v. U.S. Gypsum Co., 438 U.S. 422 (1978).
40. *See* Todd v. Exxon Corp., 275 F.3d 191, 207-11 (2d Cir. 2001).

provide information, not an intent to collude to affect prices. However, an exchange of information among competitors that collectively represent a large portion of the market raises the possibility that the exchange may have an effect on market prices.

- *Barriers to Entry*. Low barriers to entry make collusion a largely futile exercise. Consequently, an information exchange in an industry with low barriers to entry is less likely to have anticompetitive effects. Instead, it most likely represents simply a procompetitive exchange of information the participants find helpful.

- *Fungible Products*. An exchange of price information is more likely to stabilize prices if products are fungible because sellers can more easily police prices for identical products than they can for differentiated products. For example, it's easier for colluders to fix the price of gravel than the price of software.

- *Elasticity of Demand*. Collusion is less likely if consumers will respond to higher prices by simply not buying the products, i.e., if demand is highly elastic. If demand is relatively inelastic, however, consumers will more likely absorb the price increases without switching away. Thus, information exchanges regarding products with inelastic demand are more problematic.

## 2. *Nature of the Information Exchanged*

The antitrust risks of an exchange of price or other competitively sensitive information will also vary depending on whether (1) the information is competitively sensitive, (2) the information is accompanied by recommendations, and (3) historical, present, or future prices are exchanged.[41]

- *Competitive Sensitivity*. Some benchmarking information is simply not competitively sensitive. Sharing information, even among competitors, about the pros and cons of back office software, "best practices" in a variety of human resources department practices, or pension investment returns is unlikely to affect price or output and so, is unlikely to raise any antitrust concern. But sharing information about prices—particularly, customer-specific or customer class-specific prices—suggests

---

41.    *Id*. at 211-13.

that a deeper antitrust analysis of the exchange should be undertaken to determine if the exchange may affect market prices.

- *Recommendations.* The results of any information exchange, including benchmarking, should *never* be accompanied by a price or output recommendation to suppliers. Courts are extremely hostile to such recommendations, which have been viewed as a strong indication that more is happening than the mere exchange of information to enable the participants to make better independent decisions.

- *Timeliness of Information.* The more easily the exchanged information can be used to predict participants' current or future prices, the more likely it can be used to facilitate collusion. As a result, the courts are extremely hostile to the exchange of information about pricing plans, as well as current or future prices—even when the structure of the market is not conducive to collusion. Consequently, information about current or future pricing should almost never be exchanged with a competitor.

## 3. Procedures Used to Exchange the Information

The antitrust risk of an exchange of price or other competitively sensitive information also may vary depending on the procedures used for collecting and disseminating the information

- *Frequency and Regularity of Exchanges/Discussions.* Frequent exchanges of competitive information increases the antitrust risks of these exercises. Perhaps more important, discussions about the information—including e-mail surveys and questionnaires that follow up on the information—raise concerns that the exchange is being used to police an agreement.

- *Aggregated or Customer-Specific Information.* The regular and systematic exchange of information that is customer-specific or disaggregated by customer class is viewed as particularly suspect because it may enable firms to predict with some confidence how competitors will price to specific customers in the future and/or because it is viewed as a tool for policing an earlier agreement. Conversely, the exchange of aggregated data is generally useful for neither purpose and is therefore viewed with much less suspicion.

- *Use of Third-Party Aggregator.* Using a third party to collect and aggregate the data supplied by competitors will not immunize the activity from antitrust scrutiny,[42] but this practice is nonetheless viewed favorably compared to the alternative of direct competitor-to-competitor communications on competitively sensitive subjects.

### 4. Government Guidelines/Safe Harbor

The foregoing analysis is reflected for the most part in guidelines for the exchange of fee, cost, and price information among competitors set out in the Statements of Antitrust Enforcement Policy in Health Care issued jointly by the Department of Justice and the Federal Trade Commission in 1996.[43] Those guidelines were developed specifically for the health care industry, but they are generally viewed as applicable more broadly. The guidelines are believed to create a "safe harbor" for the exchange of fee, cost or price information, but only if the following conditions are satisfied:

- the collection, analysis, and dissemination of data is managed by an independent third party;
- the information exchanged is at least three months old;
- the information is provided by at least five competitors;
- when the information is disseminated in an aggregated form, no individual company's information represents more than 25% of the weighted basis of any statistic; and
- the results disseminated are sufficiently aggregated.[44]

Each of the three factors discussed above—the structure of the market, the nature of the information exchanged, and the exchange procedures—should be evaluated prior to engaging in benchmarking activities or other forms of information exchanges with competitors.

---

42.    *Id.* at 212-13.
43.    U.S. Dep't of Justice & Fed. Trade Comm'n, Statements of Antitrust Enforcement Policy in Health Care (1996) [hereinafter DOJ & FTC Health Care Guidelines], *available at* http://www.justice.gov/atr/public/guidelines/0000.htm; *see also* Foss Mar. Co., B.R.L. 01-557, 2001 WL 1564270 (DOJ Oct. 25, 2001).
44.    DOJ & FTC Health Care Guidelines 63 (Statement 6).

Then, if your client decides to engage in these activities, there are a few additional steps that can be taken to minimize antitrust exposure.[45]

First, the client should develop and document a plan, approved by counsel, that clearly presents the topics that will be addressed and the procompetitive justifications for the exchange.

Second, the ad hoc exchange of information between employees—like all other communications with competitors about competitively sensitive issues—should be avoided. If companies communicate directly, the role and responsibilities of the employees involved in the process may affect the degree of risk involved. Some courts have recognized that, though not immune from antitrust scrutiny, communications between low level employees or "operations" employees not responsible for pricing or other competitive strategies raise less of a concern than communications between employees with such responsibilities.[46]

Finally, all participating employees should receive sufficient training so they are familiar with the antitrust requirements and risks associated with information exchanges.

### G. We Need to Know More about Our Competition. What Information Are We Allowed to Gather and How?

Gathering information about competitors is an important part of many businesses. Moreover, collecting and analyzing competitive intelligence may be procompetitive. This information can spur the recipient to lower its prices, be more efficient, introduce new products, or adopt innovative business models. Accordingly, there is nothing inherently unlawful under the antitrust laws about obtaining information about other companies.

Nonetheless collecting and analyzing competitive intelligence can, in some circumstances, raise concerns under Section 1 of the Sherman Act (as well as under privacy or property rights laws). Specifically, your client should avoid collecting competitive intelligence in a way that might provide the basis for inferring that it conspired with one or more of

---

45. *See* DOJ & FTC HEALTH CARE GUIDELINES. See also Brian R. Henry, *Benchmarking and Antitrust*, 62 ANTITRUST L.J. 483 (Winter 1994).

46. *See, e.g., In re* Coordinated Pretrial Proceedings in Petroleum Prods. Antitrust Litig., 906 F.2d 432, 458 (9th Cir. 1990) (finding that the lack of pricing authority on the part of the employee communicating with competitors regarding prices did not preclude the use of such communications to support an inference of conspiracy).

its competitors not to compete, or to compete less vigorously, on any aspect of competition.

Your client should not obtain competitive intelligence directly from competitors or provide that type of information directly to competitors, except for a limited and properly structured exchange of aggregated information such as that described in Part F of this chapter. The risks associated with such a direct exchange of competitively sensitive information far outweigh the potential benefits. If the information concerns a competitive parameter—such as current or future prices or output, product development plans, or any of the other "forbidden topics" identified in Part B above—then giving or receiving that information directly to or from a competitor can too easily be the basis to infer an agreement not to compete on those parameters. For example, *companies should never exchange information about future or prospective pricing*. This means that employees should never provide a price list (or information from which a price can be derived) to a competitor; nor should employees accept price lists from competitors. This is true even if the price list is already in effect and widely available to customers.

The advice not to receive competitive intelligence or information directly from competitors affects how your client should collect and treat such information received from other sources as well. For example, obtaining competitive information from publicly available sources is generally appropriate. There is no antitrust concern, for instance, if a manufacturer reviews publicly available reports comparing the manufacturing costs and revenues of competitive manufacturers. Trade publications often include extensive information about particular markets, which a company may review and use without running afoul of the antitrust laws. However, after collecting competitive intelligence, employees typically use or report it in some manner. It is important that employees be trained to identify clearly the source of competitive intelligence when reporting or using it. Specifically, the source of the competitive intelligence should be identified with enough detail to dispel any possible inference that it was obtained from a competitor.

Similarly, it is generally lawful to obtain information, including competitive pricing information, from customers or third parties. The antitrust laws recognize that markets are more efficient when suppliers and customers talk to each other about market conditions and each others' capabilities and needs. There is nothing wrong, therefore, if a customer or a third party provides information about a price change that it expects a competitor to announce. Again, however, it is critical that if this competitive intelligence is reported or repeated within the company, or otherwise documented, its source be clearly identified. An unattributed statement that "Competitor A is going to increase its price by \$5" leaves far too much room for the inference that your client and Competitor A had a discussion about the prices A would charge. Thus, employees should be trained not only to document the source of competitive intelligence themselves, but to insist that their reports and colleagues do so as well.

There is a second caveat about obtaining competitive information from customers or third parties. It must be done in a way that does not suggest that the customer or third party has been used as a conduit or "hub" through which competitors communicate competitive information to each other. Thus, it is appropriate to ask a customer whether it has heard of any upcoming price increases in the market—so long as any resulting information is clearly identified as coming from the customer. But, it is not appropriate for your client (1) to ask a customer to find out how competitors would react if your client announced a price increase, or (2) to tell a customer how it would react to competitors' price announcements with the knowledge or expectation that the customer will pass that information on to its competitors.

What should an employee do if a competitor's employee discloses competitively sensitive information? As discussed in Part B of this chapter, there is no antitrust prohibition against using such information—which, in fact, could enable your client to compete more effectively—but once again, the danger is the risk of a perception that it was received as part of an explicit or tacit agreement not to compete. Employees should be trained that, if a competitor discloses competitively sensitive information, they should consult the company's legal. Sometimes, the information can be used after documenting its source clearly. Other times, however, the circumstances may make it difficult to prove unambiguously that the information was obtained innocently, and the decision may be made not to use it.

## H. We Want to Coordinate with Our Competitors to Pursue Legislation That Will Advantage Our Industry. Can We Do That?

Your client is almost certainly able to lobby for competitively helpful legislation, or otherwise engage in the legislative process, without a concern about antitrust liability.

The First Amendment to the U.S. Constitution protects the right of all citizens—both individuals and corporations—"to petition the

Government for a redress of grievances."[47] In a line of cases that created what is known as the *Noerr-Pennington* doctrine,[48] the Supreme Court ruled that this constitutional guarantee protects a private party's right to petition the government to enact legislation or regulations, or to take other actions, that are in the petitioner's economic self-interest. As a result, such requests or "petitioning activities" cannot form the basis for antitrust liability because imposing liability in these circumstances would chill the exercise of First Amendment rights.

The *Noerr-Pennington* doctrine protects not only an individual company's petitioning activities, but also joint petitioning activities. That is, the Court has held that the First Amendment guarantees that companies with common interests be permitted "to advocate their causes and points of view respecting ... their business and economic interests."[49] As the Court stated in *United Mine Workers of America v. Pennington (Pennington)*[50]:

> Joint efforts to influence public officials do not violate the antitrust laws even though intended to eliminate competition. Such conduct is not illegal, either standing alone or as part of a broader scheme itself violative of the Sherman Act.[51]

By way of example, the defendant railroads in *Eastern Railroad Presidents Conference v. Noerr Motor Freight (Noerr)*[52] staged a public relations campaign to persuade the public (and, by extension, the legislature and governor) to oppose legislation that would have permitted the plaintiff truckers to haul heavier loads. The Supreme Court held that even if the railroads' intent was to destroy their competitors, and even if the lobbying campaign was misleading, the campaign was immune from antitrust scrutiny because the railroads had a First Amendment right to lobby. Then, in *Pennington*, the Court extended the immunity given for legislative lobbying found in *Noerr* to immunity for petitioning administrative bodies. In that case, the Court held that the joint efforts of

---

47.    U.S. CONST. amend. I.
48.    Eastern R.R. Presidents Conference v. Noerr Motor Freight, 365 U.S. 127 (1961); United Mine Workers of Am. v. Pennington, 381 U.S. 657 (1965).
49.    California Motor Transp. Co. v. Trucking Unlimited, 404 U.S. 508, 511 (1972).
50.    *Pennington*, 381 U.S. 657 (1965).
51.    *Id.* at 670.
52.    *Noerr*, 365 U.S. 127 (1965).

a union and large coal mine operators to convince the Secretary of Labor to establish a minimum wage were immune from antitrust scrutiny. Following these two cases, the immunity became known as the *Noerr-Pennington* doctrine. In the Court's 1972 decision in *California Motor Transport Co. v. Trucking Unlimited*,[53] the doctrine was extended to attempts to influence adjudicatory processes. Thus, the *Noerr-Pennington* doctrine, though not unlimited for the reasons discussed below, provides protection from antitrust scrutiny for petitioning activity before any branch of government.

Furthermore, the doctrine protects not only joint petitioning activity itself, but also ancillary organizational efforts undertaken to make the joint activity effective, such as meetings, public relations campaigns, public policy research efforts, and communications among firms in an industry in which they discuss, plan, and execute their lobbying and related public relations strategies.[54]

Despite the broad immunity provided by the *Noerr* doctrine, there are still reasons for your client's employees who are engaged in lobbying or other "petitioning" activities to be antitrust-cautious. First, although lobbying and the ancillary organizational activities related to it are *Noerr*-protected, that does not mean that everything that goes on during those activities is immune from the antitrust laws. To use an extreme example, competitors' lobbyists could not fix prices in a meeting during which they also planned their lobbying strategies and then claim that their legitimate lobbying activities immunized their price-fixing agreement from antitrust scrutiny.

As a result, employees who are involved in lobbying efforts that involve competitors should be trained in the "do's" and "don'ts" of dealing with competitors that are described in Part B of this chapter. As a general matter, they should restrict their discussions with competitors' employees to the legitimate subject matter of the lobbying efforts, and steer away from discussion of other competitively sensitive topics. That said, however, the scope of what discussions or exchanges of information are permissible in this context under a "best practices" approach to antitrust compliance is not always clear. For example, competitors are often asked to provide financial or other competitively sensitive information in order to build a persuasive, industry-wide argument to

---

53.    California Motor Transp. Co. v. Trucking Unlimited, 404 U.S. at 508.
54.    *Id.* at 511; Lawline v. Am. Bar Ass'n, 956 F.2d 1378, 1383-84 (7th Cir. 1992); Federal Prescription Serv. v. Am. Pharm. Ass'n, 471 F. Supp. 126 (D.D.C. 1979), *rev'd on other grounds*, 663 F.2d 253 (D.C. Cir. 1981).

legislators or regulators. The exchange of information for this purpose is protected by the *Noerr-Pennington* doctrine, but at the same time, if the same information were then disseminated more broadly than is necessary to accomplish the legitimate lobbying objectives, there is a risk that the participants will be accused of using the lobbying activity to mask anticompetitive behavior. Accordingly, employees engaged in joint petitioning activities should also be trained to bring to the legal department's attention requests to supply competitively sensitive information in order to support lobbying activities.

Second, the *Noerr-Pennington* doctrine does not protect anticompetitive agreements reached even if they are intended to influence governmental decision makers. For example, in *FTC v. Superior Court Trial Lawyers Ass'n*[55], the Supreme Court held that the doctrine did not protect an agreement among lawyers to boycott court appointments to represent criminal defendants until the court-authorized fee for those engagements is increased.[56] Similarly, an agreement among pharmaceutical companies to *limit* their price increases to increases in the Consumer Price Index were not immune from antitrust scrutiny, even if the agreement was reached in order to dissuade Congress from enacting price control legislation.[57] Nor does *Noerr-Pennington* immunity extend to improper attempts to influence the standard-setting process of a private association, even where those standards are routinely adopted by legislatures.[58]

The governing principal in these cases is that, although the defendants cannot be liable under the antitrust laws for collectively petitioning for higher lawyers' fees, against price controls, or for restrictive construction standards, they cannot use an anticompetitive agreement as a vehicle to pressure or persuade government authorities to endorse a particular position. Making such an agreement is not "petitioning" activity. The advice to your client's employees is therefore straightforward: commercial agreements among competitors, even those entered to support lobbying efforts, are not protected by the *Noerr-Pennington* doctrine.

Third, although there is some doubt on the issue, you should assume conservatively that *Noerr-Pennington* immunity does not apply when the government acts in a commercial capacity or as a market participant.

---

55.    FTC v. Superior Court Trial Lawyers Ass'n, 493 U.S. 411 (1990).
56.    *Id.*
57.    *In re* Brand Name Prescription Drugs Antitrust Litig., 186 F.3d 781 (7th Cir. 1999).
58.    Allied Tube & Conduit Corp. v. Indian Head, Inc., 486 U.S. 492 (1988).

Thus, the Supreme Court did not apply *Noerr-Pennington* immunity to efforts to influence a foreign government acting in a commercial capacity.[59] Similarly, the First Circuit has held that *Noerr-Pennington* "does not extend to efforts to sell products to public officials acting under competitive bidding statutes,"[60] while lower courts have split on whether to recognize such an exception.[61]

Finally, the *Noerr-Pennington* doctrine, even when applicable, is not absolute; it is limited by the "sham exception." That is, *Noerr* itself, while emphasizing the importance "[i]n a representative democracy . . . [of] the ability of the people to make their wishes known to their representatives,"[62] contemplated the possibility of antitrust liability when the purported petitioning activity is not "a genuine effort" to influence the government but rather a "mere sham to cover what is actually nothing more than an attempt to interfere directly with the business relationships of a competitor."[63] This is commonly called the "sham exception" to *Noerr-Pennington* immunity.

The scope of the sham exception may depend on the branch of government involved. On the one hand, in the legislative or political context, misrepresentations, deception, and strong-arming are considered part of the "no holds-barred" political process that is beyond the regulation of antitrust. In that context, *Noerr-Pennington* immunity enjoys its broadest sweep—and the sham exception, its narrowest application, if it applies at all.[64] On the other hand, in *California Motor*

---

59. Continental Ore Co. v. Union Carbide & Carbon Corp., 370 U.S. 690 (1962).

60. George R. Whitten, Jr., Inc. v. Paddock Pool Builders, 424 F.2d 25, 33 (1st Cir. 1970) ("We doubt whether the Court, without expressing additional rationale, would have extended the Noerr umbrella to public officials engaged in purely commercial dealings when the case turned on other issues." (citing *Continental Ore*, 370 U.S. 690)).

61. *Compare* Ticor Title Ins. Co. v. FTC, 998 F.2d 1129 (3d Cir. 1993) (recognizing a market participant exception), *and* Federal Prescription Serv. v. Am. Pharm. Ass'n, 663 F.2d 253 (D.C. Cir. 1981) (same), *with* Independent Taxicab Drivers' Emps. v. Greater Houston Transp. Co., 760 F.2d 607 (5th Cir. 1985) (rejecting market participant exception), *and In re* Airport Car Rental Antitrust Litig., 693 F.2d 84 (9th Cir. 1982) (same).

62. Eastern R.R. Presidents Conference v. Noeer Motor Freight, 365 U.S. 127, 137 (1961).

63. *Id*. at 144.

64. Allied Tube & Conduit Corp. v. Indian Head, Inc., 486 U.S. 492, 499-500 (1988) ("A publicity campaign directed at the general public, seeking

*Transport*, the Court grappled with the balance between an antitrust defendant's constitutional right to seek redress from the judicial branch and the risk that it would abuse that right for anticompetitive purposes; it concluded that the "sham exception" to *Noerr-Pennington* immunity applies to a "pattern of baseless, repetitive claims" brought "regardless of the merits."[65] Then, in *Professional Real Estate Investors v. Columbia Pictures Industries*,[66] the Court clarified that for the "sham litigation exception" to apply, the lawsuit must be first be found to be "objectively baseless," meaning that no reasonable litigant could expect to prevail and that its position would be sanctionable under Federal Rule of Civil Procedure 11. If the suit was objectively baseless, then the trier-of-fact must determine if it was subjectively motivated not by a desire for a favorable outcome, but by an intent to use the litigation process itself to interfere directly with a competitor's business relationships.[67]

Lying between these two extremes is the question of how the "sham exception" applies to the petitioning of administrative agencies. Those agencies serve both quasi-legislative functions—i.e., making rules or regulations—and adjudicative functions. It is generally believed that the "sham exception" should have little application to petitioning an agency to act in its quasi-legislative capacity for the same reason the "sham exception" has little application to legislative lobbying. In that context, it is difficult to imagine what "objectively baseless" petitioning would be. One commentator has suggested that a party would have to ask an agency for rules that are "manifestly inconsistent with the authorizing statute" in order for such petitioning activity to be "objectively baseless."[68] The *Professional Real Estate Investors* standard for "sham litigation," however, is likely to apply to petitions requiring an agency to act in its adjudicative capacity. As a result, such petitioning activity can lose its *Noerr-Pennington* protection if the petition is "objectively baseless" or if the petitioner makes intentional, material

---

legislation or executive action, enjoys antitrust immunity even when the campaign employs unethical and deceptive methods.").
65.   California Motor Transp. Co. v. Trucking Unlimited, 404 U.S. 508, 512-14 (1972).
66.   Professional Real Estate Investors v. Columbia Pictures Indus., 508 U.S. 49 (1993).
67.   *Id.* at 60-61.
68.   1 Areeda & Hovenkamp, *supra* note 1, ¶ 204(b).

misrepresentations or omissions that materially affect the outcome of the proceedings or deprive them of their legitimacy.[69]

In sum, asking the legislature for legislation, or regulators for regulations, that are in one's economic self-interest (and contrary to a competitor's interests) is protected by the First Amendment and, under the *Noerr-Pennington* doctrine, immune from antitrust attack. Legitimate petitioning activity also can be conducted jointly with competitors that have similar interest in government decision-making. Although there are requirements of good faith and truthfulness that apply when petitioning courts or administrative agencies in certain circumstances, your client is free to pursue a legislative agenda of its choosing or to pursue that agenda with like-minded corporations, including competitors.

## I. A Company That Competes with Our Company to Repair Our Company's Products Wants to Buy Spare Parts from Us. Can We Refuse to Do Business with Our Competitor?

It has long been held that, as a general matter, a firm has no duty to help, and may refuse to deal with, its competitor.[70] A limited exception to this general rule was provided by the Supreme Court in *Aspen Skiing Co. v. Aspen Highland Skiing Corp.*[71] In that case, the Court found a violation of Section 2 of the Sherman Act, which prohibits monopolization and attempts to monopolize, when the owner of three large ski areas cancelled a joint ticket program it had previously offered to consumers in cooperation with a smaller ski slope operator and further

---

69.   *See* Mercatus Grp. v. Lake Forest Hosp., 641 F.3d 834 (7th Cir. 2011); Kottle v. Nw. Kidney Ctrs., 146 F.3d 1056 (9th Cir. 1998); Bath Petroleum Storage v. Mkt. Hub Partners, 129 F. Supp. 2d 578 (W.D.N.Y. 2000), *aff'd*, 229 F.3d 1135 (2d Cir. 2000).

70.   Pacific Bell Tel. Co. v. Linkline Commc'ns, 555 U.S. 438, 448 (2009) (citing United States v. Colgate & Co., 250 U.S. 300, 307 (1919)); Verizon Commc'ns v. Law Offices of Curtis V. Trinko, LLP, 540 U.S. 398 (2004); *see also* Four Corners Nephrology Assocs. v. Mercy Med. Ctr. of Durango, 582 F.3d 1216, 1221 (10th Cir. 2009) ("The Supreme Court has recently emphasized the general rule that a business, even a putative monopolist, has no antitrust duty to deal with its rivals at all."(internal quotation marks omitted)); *In re* Elevator Antitrust Litig., 502 F.3d 47, 52 (2d Cir. 2007) ("[A] refusal to deal with competitors does not typically violate § 2."); American Cent. E. Tex. Gas Co. v. Union Pac. Res. Grp., 93 F. App'x 1, 9 (5th Cir. 2004) ("Courts admittedly must be cautious in finding exception to the right to refuse to deal.").

71.   Aspen Skiing Co. v. Aspen Highland Skiing Corp., 472 U.S. 585 (1985).

refused to sell access to its slopes to the smaller operator even at full retail prices.[72] The holding in *Aspen Skiing* was later limited by the Court in *Trinko* as applying when a firm is willing "to forsake short-term profits to achieve an anticompetitive end."[73] In any event, courts have limited *Aspen Skiing* to situations where a firm with market power has terminated a "prior course of dealing" with a competitor in a way that evidences a predatory intent through the sacrifice of short-term profits.[74]

Moreover, the question raised here is not an easy one because it closely resembles the facts of *Eastman Kodak Co. v. Image Technical Services*,[75] in which the Supreme Court held that a company which discontinued the sale of parts to its competitors in the market for servicing its machines could be held liable for violating Section 2 of the Sherman Act, which prohibits monopolization and attempts to monopolize.

Kodak sold photocopiers and microfilm equipment for which it also provided repair services. The market for this equipment was highly competitive, as there were several other companies that produced competing equipment. A number of independent companies (called "Independent Service Organizations" or "ISOs") competed with Kodak to repair Kodak's machines. Kodak's machines were unique in that Kodak's parts could not be used for other companies' machines, and vice versa. Kodak manufactured and sold some repair parts, and it purchased

---

72.   Although it is not illegal, standing alone, to be a monopolist, Section 2 prohibits "the willful acquisition or maintenance of [monopoly] power as distinguished from growth or development as a consequence of a superior product, business acumen, or historic accident." United States v. Grinnell Corp., 384 U.S. 563, 570-71 (1996). Thus, a Section 2 violation can be established by proving two elements: (1) the possession of monopoly power; (2) which is acquired, maintained, or enhanced by the use of "exclusionary" or "predatory" conduct. *Id.; see also Trinko*, 540 U.S. at 407.

73.   *Trinko*, 540 U.S. at 409.

74.   MetroNet Servs. Corp. v. Qwest Corp., 383 F.3d 1124, 1134 (9th Cir. 2004) ("*MetroNet* does not fall within the *Aspen Skiing* exception to the general 'no duty to deal' rule, because Qwest's switch to per location pricing does not entail a sacrifice of short-term profits for long-term gain from the exclusion of competition . . . ."); *see also In re Elevator*, 502 F.2d at 52 ("[B]ecause plaintiffs do not allege that defendants terminated any prior course of dealing – the sole exception to the broad right of a firm to refuse to deal with its competitors – the allegations are insufficient to state a unilateral-monopolization claim.").

75.   Eastman Kodak Co. v. Image Technical Servs., 504 U.S. 451 (1992).

others from independent companies, which also sold their parts to the ISOs. After a number of years, Kodak stopped selling parts to the ISOs and persuaded the independent manufacturers to stop also. In response, the ISOs sued Kodak, arguing that Kodak had violated the antitrust laws by, among other things, using its market power in the parts market to eliminate the ISOs as competitors and thus attain market power in an after-sale service market.

The ISOs' claims required a showing that Kodak had market power in a parts market. Kodak argued that the ISOs' claims failed as a matter of law because Kodak did not have market power in the market for photocopiers and microfilm equipment (the "primary" market) and so could not have market power in the parts (or service) "aftermarket." Said differently, Kodak asserted that the primary market and parts aftermarkets were not separate markets because competition in the primary market among photocopier suppliers prevented Kodak from raising prices above competitive levels in the parts aftermarkets since consumers would stop buying its equipment in the first place.[76]

The Supreme Court disagreed. First, the Court found that where it is costly for consumers to obtain information about a product's total "lifecycle cost," including parts and service, the existence of competition in the primary market might not affect pricing in the aftermarkets.[77] Second, the Court noted that where there were significant costs for consumers to change from one product to another, consumers were "locked in" and would accept price increases in the aftermarkets before switching products.[78] These two factors led the Court to conclude that the primary market and aftermarkets were separate markets, and that competition in one did not eliminate the risk of monopoly in the other.[79]

Following *Kodak*, a company in Kodak's position should consider the following questions:

---

76. Kodak also argued that as a matter of law a single brand could never be a relevant market under the Sherman Act. The Court disagreed, explaining that "[b]ecause service and parts for Kodak equipment are not interchangeable with other manufacturers' service and parts, the relevant market from the Kodak equipment owner's perspective is composed of only those companies that service Kodak machines." *Kodak*, 504 U.S. at 481-82.

77. *Id*. at 473-76.

78. *Id*. at 476-77.

79. *Id*. at 477-78.

- *Does the company have a dominant share of the relevant aftermarket?* In defining the aftermarket, the company should consider whether parts for its product are interchangeable with those sold by competitors. If there are other sources for parts, the company likely would not have the requisite market power in the aftermarket for parts to be held liable for refusing to sell the parts separately to competitors.

- *Do the consumers of the company's product have sufficient information about the lifecycle cost of the product at the time of purchase to make an informed decision?* In *Kodak*, the Court emphasized that Kodak had not presented sufficient evidence of what information its customers had about the total lifecycle costs of the product. If, in fact, customers are able to take total lifecycle costs into account when they make the initial purchase of equipment, then competition at the primary product level— which was acknowledged to be robust in the *Kodak* case—can prevent the exercise of market power in the aftermarket.

- *What is the cost for consumers to switch from the company's product to one sold by its competitors?* The Court in *Kodak* also noted that if the cost of switching from one service supplier to another is high, consumers are more likely to be locked in, which raises antitrust concerns if the aftermarket is dominated by one company. In contrast, if the cost of switching is low, even a dominant company likely cannot charge more than a competitive price, and there is less antitrust concern.

- *Does the company have a valid business justification that would support its refusal to sell to its competitors?* Kodak argued that it had business justifications for its refusal to sell, including promoting competition with other equipment producers, reducing inventory costs, and preventing ISOs from free riding on Kodak's investments in equipment, parts, and service. Although the Court did not find any of the proffered justifications to be sufficient to support summary judgment in Kodak's favor, it recognized that a valid business justification can be a defense to claims like those in *Kodak*.[80] Later courts have held that preventing competitors from free riding on a

---

80.   *Id.* at 483-86.

company's investments in research and development is a defense, though the inquiry is highly fact-specific.[81]

- *Does the company currently sell parts to its competitors, and would a refusal be a change in its historical practice?* Some later courts have interpreted *Kodak* as limited to situations where the manufacturer has terminated the ISOs' ability to obtain parts for its machines.[82] These courts have emphasized the fact that by purchasing Kodak equipment, Kodak's consumers made an investment that relied on the then-existing aftermarkets for parts and service.[83] This concern about a change in prior dealings reflects the Supreme Court's similar concern in *Aspen Skiing*. Thus, if a company has done business with its competitor in the past, its ability to terminate that relationship may be circumscribed by a limited duty to deal arising out of the prior relationship.[84]

In sum, a company's decision not to supply spare parts to a competitor in the business of providing service for the company's own

---

81. *See, e.g.*, Morris Commc'ns Corp. v. PGA Tour, 364 F.3d 1288 (11th Cir. 2004) (affirming summary judgment for professional golf tour where tour's refusal to continue providing a new live scoring product to plaintiff media company for free was justified to prevent the media company from free riding when reselling the information).

82. *See, e.g.*, SMS Sys. Maint. Servs. v. Digital Equip. Corp., 11 F. Supp. 2d 166 (D. Mass. 1998), *aff'd*, 188 F.3d 11 (1st Cir. 1999); Spahr v. Leegin Creative Leather Prods., 2008 WL 3914461 (E.D. Tenn. 2008).

83. *See, e.g.*, Schor v. Abbott Labs., 457 F.3d 608, 613-14 (7th Cir. 2006) ("What the Supreme Court held in [*Kodak*] is not that firms with market power are forbidden to deal in complementary products, but that they can't do this in ways that take advantage of customers' sunk costs.").

84. Aspen Skiing Co. v. Aspen Highlands Skiing Corp., 472 U.S. 585 (1985) (finding a Sherman Act violation where the owner of three ski areas canceled a joint ticket that had been offered in cooperation with a smaller ski operator and refused to sell to the smaller operator even at the retail price). The holding in *Aspen Skiing* was later explained in *Verizon Commc'ns v. Law Offices of Curtis V. Trinko, LLP*, 540 U.S. 398 (2004), where the Court stated: "The unilateral termination of a voluntary (*and thus presumably profitable*) course of dealing suggested a willingness to forsake short-term profits to achieve an anticompetitive end." *Id.* at 409 (emphasis in original); *see also In re* Elevator Antitrust Litig., 502 F.3d 47, 52 (2d Cir. 2007).

products is a difficult one under the antitrust laws that should be made with the advice of counsel after a review of all the facts.

## J. Where Can I Go For More Information?

### 1. The Key Principles

- Donald F. Turner, *The Definition of Agreement Under the Sherman Act: Conscious Parallelism and Refusals to Deal*, 75 Harv. L. Rev. 655 (1962);
- Julian O. Von Kalinowski, *Antitrust Laws and Trade Regulation* §§ 12.01, 16 (2d ed. 2012);
- William M. Hannay, *Corporate Compliance Series: Antitrust*, §§ 1:5, 1:12-:15 (Thomson Reuters 2011);
- U.S. Department of Justice, Antitrust Resource Manual: Elements of the Offense (2011), *available at* http://www.justice.gov/usao/ eousa/foia_reading_room/usam/title7/ant00007.htm;
- Federal Trade Commission, An FTC Guide to the Antitrust Laws (2010), *available at* http://www.ftc.gov/bc/antitrust/factsheets/ antitrustlawsguide.pdf;
- Federal Trade Commission & U.S. Department of Justice, Antitrust Guidelines for Collaborations Among Competitors (2000), *available at* http://www.ftc.gov/os/2000/04/ftcdojguidelines.pdf.

### 2. Social Interactions

- Larry Fullerton, *FTC Challenges to "Invitations to Collude,"* 25 *Antitrust* 30 (Spring 2011);
- Mike Murray et al., Presentation to the ABA Young Lawyers Division: Antitrust for Trade Associations (Dec. 19, 2007), *available at* http://apps.americanbar.org/antitrust/at-committees/at-yld/ppt/AntitrustforTradeAssociations.ppt;
- McCarthy Tetrault, Compliance Manual for Business Execs: United States Law, Ch. 3: How Do the Antitrust Laws Affect Relationships with Competitors?, *available at* http://www.mccarthy.ca/pubs/usch3.htm;
- Steven J. Fellman, *Antitrust Compliance: Trade Association Meetings and Groupings of Competitors: The Association's Perspective*, 57 *Antitrust L.J.* 209 (1988);

- William M. Hannay, *Corporate Compliance Series: Antitrust* § 1:24 (Thomson Reuters 2011);
- 1 ABA Section of Antitrust Law, *Antitrust Law Developments* 42-43, 121-23 (7th ed. 2012);
- Thomas V. Vakerics, *Antitrust Basics* § 6.13 (Law Journal Press 2006);
- Robert S. Chaloupka, *Trade Associations*, 167 *Antitrust Counselor* Article I (2008);
- 58 C.J.S. *Monopolies* § 169 (2012).

### 3. Competitor Complaints about Pricing

- Larry Fullerton, *FTC Challenges to "Invitations to Collude"*, 25 *Antitrust* 30 (Spring 2011);
- Susan S. DeSanti & Ernest A. Nagata, *Competitor Communications: Facilitating Practices or Invitations to Collude? An Application of Theories to Proposed Horizontal Agreements Submitted for Antitrust Review*, 63 *Antitrust L.J.* 93 (1995);
- U.S. Department of Justice, *Identifying Sherman Act Violations*, Antitrust Resource Manual, *available at* http://www.justice.gov/ usao/eousa/foia_reading_room/usam/title7/ant00008.htm.

### 4. Price Verification

- 1 ABA Section of Antitrust Law, *Antitrust Law Developments* 97-102 (7th ed. 2012);
- J. Thomas Rosch, Commissioner, Federal Trade Commission, Antitrust Issues Related to Benchmarking and Other Information Exchanges, Remarks before the ABA Section of Antitrust Law and ABA Center for Continuing Legal Education's Teleseminar on Benchmarking and Other Information Exchanges Among Competitors (May 3, 2011), *available at* http://www.ftc.gov/ speeches/rosch/110503roschbenchmarking.pdf;
- Thomas V. Vakerics, *Antitrust Basics* § 8.03[2] (Law Journal Press 2006).

5. *Copying a Competitor's Pricing Structure (or Meeting Its Price Increase*

- 1 ABA Section of Antitrust Law, *Antitrust Law Developments* 6-19 (7th ed. 2012);
- Rudolph J.R. Peritz, *Unfair Methods of Competition Under FTC § 5: Beyond the Sherman Act and an Ex Post Model of Enforcement*, 56 *The Antitrust Bulletin* 825 (Winter 2011), *available at* http://www.antitrustinstitute.org/~antitrust/sites/default/files/Peritz.FTC5_.ABulletin.pdf;
- William H. Page, *Communication and Concerted Action*, 38 *Loyola University Chicago Law Journal* 405 (2007), *available at* http://www.luc.edu/law/activities/publications/lljdocs/vol38_no3/Page.Online.4.0.pdf.

6. *Benchmarking and Information Exchanges*

- 1 ABA Section of Antitrust Law, *Antitrust Law Developments* 97-102 (7th ed. 2012);
- Brian R. Henry, *Benchmarking and Antitrust*, 62 *Antitrust L.J.* 483 (1994);
- James R. Loftis III, *Benchmarking and Statistical Data Exchanges: How to Do It Safely*, *Trade Associations and Antitrust – A Practical Guide*, ABA Section of Antitrust Law (June 28, 1996), *available at* http://apps.americanbar.org/antitrust/at-committees/at-ta/pdf/articles/safely.pdf;
- Price Surveys, Benchmarking and Information Exchanges: Remarks of Mary L. Azcuenaga, Commissioner, Federal Trade Commission, before the American Society of Association Executives (Nov. 8, 1994), *available at* http://www.ftc.gov/speeches/azcuenaga/ma11894.pdf.

7. *Competitive Intelligence*

- J. Thomas Rosch, Commissioner, Federal Trade Commission, Antitrust Issues Related to Benchmarking and Other Information Exchanges, Remarks before the ABA Section of Antitrust Law and ABA Center for Continuing Legal Education's Teleseminar on Benchmarking and Other Information Exchanges Among Competitors (May 3, 2011), *available at* http://www.ftc.gov/speeches/rosch/110503roschbenchmarking.pdf;

- William H. Page, *Communication and Concerted Action*, 38 *Loy. U. Chi. L.J.* 405 (2007);
- Anthony J. Dennis, *Assessing the Risks of Competitive Intelligence Activities Under the Antitrust Laws*, 46 *S.C. L. Rev.* 263 (1995);
- Brian R. Henry, *Benchmarking and Antitrust*, 62 *Antitrust L.J.* 483 (1994).

## 8. *Joint Lobbying Activities*

- 2 ABA Section of Antitrust Law, *Antitrust Law Developments* 1285-87 (7th ed. 2012);
- Exceptions and Immunities, *Noerr-Pennington* Doctrine, *available at* http://apps.americanbar.org/antitrust/at-committees/at-exemc/main-exemptions/noerr-pennington.shtml;
- Maureen K. Ohlhausen, *Enforcement Perspectives on the Noerr-Pennington Doctrine*, 21 *Antitrust* 49 (Spring 2007);
- Federal Trade Commission, FTC Staff Report 2006, *Enforcement Perspectives on the Noerr-Pennington Doctrine* (2006);
- Stephen Paul Mahinka, How to Preserve Your Antitrust Immunity for Lobbying and Obtaining State Actions, Morgan Lewis Trade Association Teleseminar Series (Mar. 17, 2004), *available at* http://www.morganlewis.com/pubs/MahinkaPaper2.pdf;
- Lisa Wood, *In Praise of the Noerr-Pennington Doctrine*, 18 *Antitrust* 72 (Fall 2003);
- M. Sean Royall & Seth M. M. Stodder, *Noerr Immunity for Sponsoring Litigation: From Burlington Northern to Baltimore Scrap*, 15 *Antitrust* 47 (Summer 2001);
- ABA Antitrust Section, *Monograph No. 19, The Noerr-Pennington Doctrine* (1993);
- William M. Hannay, *Corporate Compliance Series: Antitrust* §§ 1:57-:60 (Thomson Reuters 2011).

## 9. *Refusals to Supply a Competitor*

- 1 ABA Section of Antitrust Law, *Antitrust Law Developments* 260-69 (7th ed. 2012);

- Federal Trade Commission, An FTC Guide to the Antitrust Laws, Exclusionary or Predatory Acts: Refusal to Deal, *available at* http://www.ftc.gov/bc/antitrust/refusal_to_deal.shtm;
- John E. Lopatka & William H. Page, *Bargaining & Monopolization: In Search of the "Boundary of Section 2 Liability" between Aspen & Trinko*, 73 Antitrust L.J. 115 (2005);
- Glen O. Robinson, *On Refusing to Deal with Rivals*, 87 *Cornell L. Rev.* 1177 (2002);
- Kenneth L. Glazer & Abbott B. Lipsky, Jr., *Unilateral Refusals to Deal under Section 2 of the Sherman Act*, 63 *Antitrust L.J.* 749 (1995).

## CHAPTER II

# TRADE ASSOCIATIONS

## A. Should My Company Join a Trade Association?

The antitrust risks of participating in a trade association are generally manageable so long as they are understood and some basic best practices are followed.

Most trade association activities are either affirmatively procompetitive or competitively neutral. The procompetitive activities of an association may include (1) educating members on relevant new developments in the industry that may enable them to become more efficient, (2) providing product information that may enable sellers and purchasers to make more informed decisions, (3) performing standard-setting, accreditation, and certification functions that may instill confidence in the industry or promote the interoperability of complementary products, and (4) advising members on legal and regulatory constraints which govern their conduct. An association can also support or oppose legislative or regulatory initiatives of importance to its members.
[1] Finally, an association can simply be a way for people in the same field to meet one another and network.

Despite the many legitimate activities and objectives of trade associations, antitrust risks can arise in two fundamental ways.

First, trade associations may pursue activities that inherently raise a risk that their conduct could be viewed as violating Section 1 of the Sherman Act—such as organizing the exchange of price or cost information among members of the association or issuing standards for products or conduct that may have the effect of making it more difficult for some competitors to compete in the market. Those activities are discussed in greater detail below.

Second, although courts have repeatedly expressed the view that trade associations are not "walking [antitrust] conspirac[ies],"[2] they still

---

1.    *See* Chapter 1, Part H.

45

present opportunities for competitors to meet and thus, "opportunit[ies] to conspire" to fix prices or otherwise limit competition.[3] As a result, it is important to ensure that the individuals participating in these activities understand how to avoid creating even the appearance that they used participation in trade associations as an opportunity to reach an illicit, anticompetitive agreement with competitors. The best practices for avoiding the appearance of impropriety when dealing with competitors, during trade association activities or otherwise, are discussed in Chapter I, and employees involved in trade association activities should be familiar with them.

There are several preliminary steps that can be taken to minimize the antitrust risks of trade association activities so that a business can enjoy their full benefits without taking undue antitrust risks.

- Before joining a trade association, make sure that the objectives of the association and the activities it will undertake to achieve those objectives are clearly understood. If the association activities have clearly procompetitive objectives, do not involve competitively sensitive matters, or will be attended by companies that do not compete or persons who do not realistically have the ability to make anticompetitive agreements (or suggest them to competitors), the potential antitrust concerns may be minimal.

- If the trade association is likely to engage in activities that raise some antitrust risks (described below), it may be appropriate for the association to engage antitrust counsel to attend or monitor its activities. Not only can an attorney help guide the association through antitrust-sensitive issues; counsel's presence will go a long way toward dispelling any suggestion that the participants engaged in illegal conduct, or even inappropriate discussions, during meetings.

- Trade associations should have a written antitrust policy and rules that inform the members of specific conduct they are not

---

2.    Consolidated Metal Prods. v. Am. Petroleum Inst., 846 F.2d 284, 294 (5th Cir. 1988).

3.    *See, e.g.*, Capital Imaging Assocs. v. Mohawk Valley Med. Assocs., 996 F.2d 537, 545 (2d Cir. 1993) (explaining that, in the context of physician practice association, a "finding of a legal capacity to conspire does not resolve the issue of whether § 1 of the Sherman Act has been shown to be violated[, and t]he mere opportunity to conspire does not by itself support the inference that such an illegal combination actually occurred").

allowed to engage in and also provide guidance on how to conduct themselves in order to minimize antitrust risks. The trade association should take affirmative steps that would allow participating members and the association to establish, after the fact, that participants read and understood the policy—and confirm that they did not engage in any conduct that might have violated it. (Some trade associations routinely read their antitrust policy/rules at the start of all or certain types of meetings.)

- Each trade association meeting should have a detailed agenda, circulated in advance of the meeting, that clearly and specifically indicates what will be discussed (preferably not including, "any other business"). Participants should be instructed to stick to the agenda and not to engage in off-the-record, free-wheeling, or side discussions. Simply put, the documentation surrounding the association's activities should enable the participants to explain the legitimate reasons for their meeting if called upon to do so in a deposition held years after the events. For that same reason, minutes of the meeting should be taken and distributed to all participants.

- As mentioned earlier, member companies should educate their employees who participate in trade association activities about the topics that are inappropriate to discuss with competitors—regardless of whether these discussions occur in the context of or outside of trade association activities. These are addressed in Chapter I, Part B.

- Be sure that your client's representatives at trade association activities have been trained what to do if inappropriate proposals or discussions are raised during meetings. See Chapter I, Part B. Specifically, they should know that if this occurs, they should immediately make it clear that they will not participate in the discussion and if it continues, leave the room and insist that their departure be documented, preferably in the minutes of the meeting.

Some of the types of association activities that can raise significant antitrust risks are briefly discussed below.

## 1. *Price-Related Activities*

As discussed in Chapter I, a naked agreement among competitors on what price to charge customers is per se illegal under Section 1 of the

Sherman Act. Accordingly, any trade association activity that involves the discussion or exchange of information about prices, pricing structures, or terms and conditions—or any of the other sensitive topics described in Chapter I—requires very close scrutiny.

Any trade association activity that directly or indirectly dictates or suggests to its members what price to charge for their products or services is very likely to violate Section 1 of the Sherman Act. For example, a bar association rule setting minimum fee schedules for specific legal services has been found to violate the antitrust laws.[4] Likewise, any activity that even signals what price members should charge—or that suggests that members should raise, maintain, or even lower their prices—may provide the basis on which an enforcement agency or trier-of-fact may infer such an illegal agreement. For example, numerous medical associations have been prohibited by the Federal Trade Commission from distributing "relative value scales" that suggest what members should charge for their services.[5] Similarly, an association of health care providers that publicizes the payment level that it seeks for members would likely face an investigation or possibly, liability if members subsequently raised their fees to that level. In sum, any dissemination of future, projected, or recommended price by a trade association is considered highly suspect.[6]

Along the same lines, any association rule discouraging members from quoting a price to potential customers or types of customers is likely to violate Section 1.[7] Likewise, an "ethical standard" endorsed by a trade association that prohibited an architect from seeking a commission for which another architect had been selected, prior to the making of any final contract, was held to be anticompetitive because it limited competition among architects.[8]

The mere exchange of price information through an association can also raise difficult issues that are discussed in detail in Chapter I, Part F. On the one hand, trade associations often share historical, aggregated industry data (including pricing data) collected from their many

---

4.     Goldfarb v. Va. State Bar, 421 U.S. 773 (1975).
5.     *See, e.g.*, California Med. Ass'n., 105 F.T.C. 277 (1985).
6.     U.S. Dep't of Justice & Fed. Trade Comm'n, Statements of Antitrust Enforcement Policy in Health Care (1996) [hereinafter DOJ & FTC Health Care Guidelines], *available at* http://www.justice.gov/atr/public/guidelines/0000.htm.
7.     National Soc'y of Prof'l Eng'rs v. United States, 435 U.S. 679 (1978).
8.     Mardirosian v. Am. Inst. of Architects, 474 F. Supp. 628, 650-51 (D.D.C. 1979).

members. This data may enable members to compete more effectively by better understanding their industry, spotting trends, or assessing their own progress vis-à-vis their competitors. Such an exchange of data is generally considered consistent with the antitrust laws as it neither constitutes an agreement on price nor enables one competitor to predict confidently what price another is currently charging or in the future will charge to any specific customer; it therefore cannot reasonably support an inference that the members have reached an agreement with respect to price.[9]

On the other hand, an exchange of more recent or more specific price data among competitors, especially in a concentrated industry, may be found anticompetitive if it has the potential to chill price competition by enabling one competitor to predict with some confidence what another will charge specific customers.[10] As discussed in greater detail in Chapter I, Part F, the likelihood that an exchange of price information will have this effect depends on the structure of the industry and the nature of the data exchanged.[11]

## 2. *Exchanges of Cost Information, Including Compensation Surveys*

Just as the exchange of recent, current, or future price information among association members in a relatively concentrated industry may, in the right circumstance, chill price competition among members, the exchange of cost information can also raise antitrust concerns. First, an exchange of cost data could either facilitate an agreement on output prices or chill competition on output prices. That is, if competitors know each others' cost structures, lower cost competitors may be less inclined to lower prices, more secure in the expectation that higher cost competitors will not undercut them. Second, an exchange of cost information may stabilize prices for products that the members purchase as inputs to the goods and services they sell. The likelihood of such an effect on input prices is relatively low, for a variety of reasons, including that members of a trade association typically represent only a small portion of the buyers of the input and are therefore less likely to be able to affect the price of the input. Nonetheless, this issue must be assessed on a case-by-case basis.

---

9. *See* Maple Flooring Mfrs.' Ass'n v. United States, 268 U.S. 563 (1925) (upholding exchange of information regarding average costs and historical prices, without identifying individual sellers and buyers).
10. United States v. Container Corp. of Am., 393 U.S. 333 (1969).
11. United States v. U.S. Gypsum Co., 438 U.S. 422 (1978).

This issue sometimes arises in the context of compensation surveys for employees with relatively specialized skills. Especially if there are few companies who purchase those specialized skills in the labor market, an exchange of information on salaries to such employees may raise significant antitrust issues.[12] Specifically, the exchange of compensation information in these circumstances may limit the competition for the services of employees with specialized skills, depriving them of compensation they would receive absent the exchange of information. The exchange of compensation information is, however, subject to the same, presumptively lawful "safe harbor" that the Department of Justice and the Federal Trade Commission jointly described for the exchange of price information, i.e., such a compensation survey should be based on data at least three months old, and should include at least five survey participants, with no participant's data representing more than 25 percent of any disseminated statistic and no data identifiable by specific participants.[13]

### 3. *Rules Restraining Competition among Members*

Any association rule that restricts competition among members of the association may raise concerns under the antitrust laws—even if the rule is ostensibly designed to serve a legitimate purpose. For example, an FTC Order striking down an ethical rule of the American Medical Association that restricted truthful advertising by member physicians was upheld in *American Medical Ass'n v. FTC*,[14] even though the rule was designed to prevent patients from choosing doctors on the basis of advertising rather than quality.[15] Similarly, a work rule of a trade group of dentists forbidding members from submitting X-rays to dental insurers was held to violate the antitrust laws, despite its purpose of preventing unnecessary radiographs.[16] And an agreement among Detroit auto dealers to close on Sundays, purportedly to avoid labor unrest, was struck down as an antitrust violation.[17] In each case, the offending rule was not found to be per re illegal, but under a rule of reason test, the asserted benefits of the rule's restrictions on competition were found not to outweigh the anticompetitive harm flowing from those restrictions.

---

12.   *See* Todd v. Exxon Corp., 275 F.3d 191 (2d Cir. 2001).
13.   *See* DOJ & FTC HEALTH CARE GUIDELINES, *supra* note 6, at 63.
14.   American Medical Ass'n v. FTC, 638 F.2d 443 (2d Cir. 1980).
15.   *Id*.
16.   FTC v. Ind. Fed'n of Dentists, 476 U.S. 447 (1986).
17.   *In re* Detroit Auto Dealers Ass'n, 955 F.2d 457 (6th Cir. 1992).

## 4. *Boycotts of Competitors, of Members, or of Disfavored Entities*

Any agreement among association members not to deal with disfavored members or with others whose policies the association disagrees with also raises antitrust risks. In the case of *Fashion Originators' Guild v. FTC*,[18] for example, the Supreme Court invalidated a Guild policy forbidding members from dealing with so-called design pirates who infringed the copyrights of member firms. In *Radiant Burners, Inc. v. Peoples Gas Light & Coke Co.*,[19] the Supreme Court held that an agreement among members of the American Gas Association not to sell gas for products that did not meet its safety standards was unlawful.

Members of an association also risk antitrust exposure if they agree to boycott a third party until the party agrees to economic terms that the members seek. For example, the Supreme Court found a violation of Section 1 when the members of a trial lawyers association agreed not to provide legal services to the Superior Court until the Court raised their hourly pay.[20] Similarly, members of the Pima County Medical Association were indicted for threatening to withdraw from insurance plans that did not allow their member dentists to charge copayments that the dentists regarded as fair.[21]

On the other hand, boycotts that are deemed to be purely political in nature may be protected by the First Amendment, regardless of their competitive impact. In the leading case of *NAACP v. Claiborne Hardware Co.*,[22] the Supreme Court reversed a tort judgment against the NAACP for organizing a boycott of white-owned businesses which sought to advance a wide-ranging political agenda. Similarly, in *Missouri v. National Organization for Women*,[23] a boycott by the National Organization of Women against states that had not ratified the Equal Rights Amendment was found not to violate the antitrust laws.

---

18. Fashion Originators' Guild v. FTC, 312 U.S. 457 (1941).
19. Radiant Burners, Inc. v. Peoples Gas Light & Coke Co., 364 U.S. 656 (1961).
20. FTC v. Superior Court Trial Lawyers Ass'n, 493 U.S. 411 (1990).
21. United States v. A. Lanoy Alston, D.M.D., P.C., 974 F.2d 1206 (9th Cir. 1992); *see also* Michigan State Med. Soc'y, 101 F.T.C. 191 (1983) (finding that members of a state medical society could not collectively threaten to withdraw from the state Medicaid program to persuade the state to raise payment levels).
22. NAACP v. Claiborne Hardware Co., 458 U.S. 886 (1982).
23. Missouri v. Nat'l Org. for Women, 620 F.2d 1301 (8th Cir. 1980).

### 5. *Membership Rules That Restrict Competition*

As a general matter, associations are free to determine who will be permitted to join. Where, however, the membership rules of the association have the effect of suppressing competition, they may run afoul of the antitrust laws. For example, in *United States v. Realty Multi-List*,[24] the court struck down restrictions on membership in a multiple listing service after it concluded that a broker without access to the service could not compete effectively.

### 6. *Standard Setting and Product Certification*

Standard setting and product certification are generally regarded as procompetitive because these activities often provide useful information to purchasers, allow manufacturers to create interoperable, competing products, and encourage manufacturers to improve their products.[25] Accordingly, the antitrust laws generally permit these activities, even when the effect may be to exclude competitors who cannot meet standards or satisfy certification requirements. Indeed, even an erroneous denial of a valuable product certification, without more, does not constitute an unreasonable restraint of trade.[26] Where, however, a standard is deliberately skewed in a manner intended to suppress competition from qualified competitors, it has been found to violate the antitrust laws.[27] And where the procedures for formulating a standard are manipulated in order to protect existing or incumbent suppliers from new competition, the standard has been invalidated.[28] (Standard setting is discussed in greater detail later in this chapter. See Part B.)

### 7. *Accreditation Programs*

Association programs for accrediting institutions or programs are also generally viewed as promoting competition by encouraging

---

24. United States v. Realty Multi-List, 629 F.2d 1351 (5th Cir. 1980).
25. *See* Clamp-All Corp. v. Cast Iron Soil Pipe Inst., 851 F.2d 478 (1st Cir. 1988).
26. *See* Consolidated Metal Prods. v. Am. Petroleum Inst., 846 F.2d 284 (5th Cir. 1988).
27. *See* American Soc'y of Mech. Eng'rs v. Hydrolevel Corp., 456 U.S. 556 (1982).
28. *See* Allied Tube & Conduit Corp. v. Indian Head, Inc., 486 U.S. 492 (1988).

adherence to standards of quality and providing useful information to consumers that allows them to make informed purchase decisions. However, if the standards for accreditation are not directly related to promoting quality or serving some other procompetitive purpose, they may be viewed as unreasonably restraining competition if they serve mostly to protect incumbents from new or more innovative competitors.

Thus, in *United States v. American Bar Ass'n*,[29] the Antitrust Division successfully sued to invalidate a provision in the American Bar Association standards of accreditation for law schools that required accredited schools to pay faculty compensation that was "comparable" to compensation paid by law schools in their peer group. The government alleged that the standards were designed to increase faculty salaries and improve working conditions, rather than to serve their stated purpose of providing useful information to state bar officials and prospective law students regarding the quality of the education at a given school. This enforcement action was resolved by a consent decree that, among other things, prohibits the American Bar Association from conditioning the accreditation of a law school on the salaries, fringe benefits, or other compensation paid to its faculty or administrators.[30] Similarly, in *Bogus v. American Speech & Hearing Ass'n*,[31] a plaintiff was permitted to challenge a program in which certification of clinical competence was conditioned on membership in an association. (Accreditation activities are discussed in more detail later in this chapter.)

## 8. *Exchange of Non-Price Information*

Courts view exchanges of non-price information more favorably than those of price information. For example, in *Cement Manufacturers' Protective Ass'n v. United States*,[32] an exchange of information regarding the creditworthiness of buyers was held not to violate the antitrust laws because it was found to facilitate the prevention of buyer fraud. However, an exchange of non-price information may be unlawful if it facilitates anticompetitive conduct. In *Eastern States Retail Lumber Dealers' Ass'n v. United States*,[33] for example, circulation of the names of wholesalers who also sold directly to consumers was found unlawful

---

29. United States v. Am. Bar Ass'n, 934 F. Supp. 435 (D.D.C. 1996).
30. *Id.* at 436.
31. Bogus v. Am. Speech & Hearing Ass'n, 582 F.2d 277 (3d Cir. 1978).
32. Cement Mfrs.' Protective Ass'n v. United States, 268 U.S. 588 (1925).
33. Eastern States Retail Lumber Dealers' Ass'n v. United States, 234 U.S. 600 (1914).

because it was found to be a concerted effort by retails to prevent wholesalers from selling directly to consumers.

### 9. *Lobbying Efforts*

As discussed in greater detail in Chapter I, Part H above, pursuant to the *Noerr-Pennington* doctrine, the First Amendment protects the right of corporations, including competing corporations, to engage in joint lobbying of a legislature or regulatory agency, even if their objective is to obtain a statute or regulation that has the effect of restraining competition. Moreover, this right extends to pre-lobbying activities, including the discourse required to reach agreement among the corporations on the desired result and the tactics to achieve it. However, when the lobbying is a sham, i.e., conducted in bad faith to use the lobbying process to interfere with a competitor's relationships with others, it is not protected.[34] Nor can competitors engage in anticompetitive conduct, such as a boycott, in order to pressure government to take the action that they seek.[35]

### B. Our Trade Association Is Working on Some Industry Standards. Can We Participate?

The competitive benefits of standard setting are widely recognized. For example, by providing opportunities for industries to agree on technology standards, standard-setting organizations can increase interoperability of products, enhance efficiencies, and encourage follow-on innovation. In addition, industry safety certifications and similar standards can provide important information to consumers and improve product quality. Because of these widely recognized benefits, courts analyze antitrust challenges to standard-setting activities using a rule of reason analysis, which considers both the procompetitive benefits of setting the standard as well as the alleged harm to competition.[36]

Even under a rule of reason analysis, there are antitrust risks associated with participation in standard-setting organizations because they have the potential to cause competitive harm by excluding

---

34. *See* California Motor Transp. Co. v. Trucking Unlimited, 404 U.S. 508 (1972).
35. *See* FTC v. Superior Court Trial Lawyers Ass'n, 493 U.S. 411 (1990).
36. *See* Golden Bridge Tech. v. Nokia, Inc., 416 F. Supp. 2d 525, 530-33 (E.D. Tex. 2006).

competitors from the market, reducing consumer choice, diminishing price competition, or facilitating collusion.

As an initial matter, even though a standard-setting organization, like any trade association or collaboration among competitors, may have legitimate, procompetitive objectives, it still presents a so-called "opportunity to conspire" with competitors. The legitimate purposes of the organization do not immunize its activities from antitrust scrutiny. As such, the participants must conduct themselves so that they can defend against a future accusation that the organization has been used as a "sham to cloak naked price fixing" or other improper horizontal collusion.[37] Thus, participants in standard-setting organizations should be educated about the best practices, discussed in Chapter I, designed to protect against an unwarranted inference of collusion with competitors.

Second, manipulation of the standard-setting process that causes the resulting standard to have anticompetitive effects may be found to unreasonably restrain competition in violation of Section 1 or to perpetuate a monopoly through exclusionary conduct in violation of Section 2. Thus, in *Allied Tube & Conduit Corp. v. Indian Head, Inc.*,[38] producers of steel conduit packed a trade association meeting with paid supporters in order to defeat an amendment to the association's model fire code that would have approved the use of plastic conduit as an alternative to steel conduit. The Supreme Court found that, because many jurisdictions followed the model fire code, the ballot-stuffing by the steel conduit manufacturers unreasonably excluded plastic conduit manufacturers from the market and therefore violated the Sherman Act. Other courts have similarly found an antitrust violation for manipulation of standard-setting processes.[39]

In antitrust challenges to standard setting, courts often focus on whether there has been an abuse of the process rather than on the merits of the standards at issue. Courts often use procedure as a proxy for substance in making judgments about the competitive significance of a standard. The key to minimizing antitrust risks is therefore to ensure that

---

37. Business Review Letter from Thomas O. Barnett, Ass't Att'y Gen., U.S. Dep't of Justice, to Robert A. Skitol, Att'y, Drinker, Biddle & Reath, LLP (Oct. 30, 2006), *available at* http://www.usdoj.gov/atr/public/busreview/219380.pdf.

38. Allied Tube & Conduit Corp. v. Indian Head, Inc., 486 U.S. 492 (1988).

39. In *American Society of Mechanical Engineers v. Hydrolevel Corp.*, 456 U.S. 556 (1982), for example, a trade association was found liable where its processes permitted a member to manipulate a standard so as to exclude a rival's product for anticompetitive purposes.

safeguards are in place to prevent procedural abuses that have the effect of excluding rivals, whether through ballot-stuffing tactics as in *Allied Tube*, or through other tactics, such as manipulating the membership selection process.[40] As the Supreme Court stated in *Allied Tube*, standards promulgated by competitors are lawful if they are "based on the merits of objective expert judgments and [are selected] through procedures that prevent the standard-setting process from being biased by members with economic interests in stifling product competition."[41]

Participants in a standard-setting organization should also be careful to abide by the organization's intellectual property disclosure and licensing requirements. Standard-setting organizations often require participants to disclose to the organization and other participants all intellectual property relating to a proposed standard under consideration and/or to agree to license that intellectual property at fair, reasonable, and non-discriminatory (FRAND) rates, should it later be incorporated into the adopted standard. As discussed in greater detail elsewhere,[42] participants who do not disclose such standard-essential patents and/or do not license those patents at FRAND rates may be liable under Section 2 for obtaining or maintaining market power through exclusionary conduct.

### C. Our Trade Association Wants to Publish a Report on the Industry, and Has Asked Us for Information. What Information May We Provide?

Gathering and disseminating information about the competitors and the state of competition within an industry is a common trade association activity and frequently serves legitimate, procompetitive functions that promote demand for products and services and foster more efficient business decisions.[43] Those activities are not, however, immune from the antitrust laws, and in fact, are governed by the same principles as an exchange of information among competitors that occurs without the

---

40.  *See* Jennifer L. Gray, *Antitrust Guidelines for Participating in Standard Setting Efforts*, CORP. COUNSELING REP., Spring 2001, at 22, *available at* http://apps.americanbar.org/antitrust/at-committees/at-ta/pdf/articles/ standardsetting.pdf.
41.  *Allied Tube,* 486 U.S. at 501.
42.  *See infra* Chapter VI.D.
43.  *See In re* Citric Acid Litig., 191 F.3d 1090, 1098 (9th Cir. 1999); International Healthcare Mgmt. v. Haw. Coal. for Health, 332 F.3d 600, 608 (9th Cir. 2003).

involvement of a trade association. Those are discussed in Chapter I, Part F.

### D. At Our Trade Association Meeting Yesterday, a Competitor's Representative Proposed That All the Members Should Participate in a Joint Effort That I Am Uneasy About. What Should I Do?

The ultimate risk associated with participation in a trade association is the risk that your client and its participating employees are accused of entering an anticompetitive agreement with competitors during trade association activities. Accordingly, if any conversations or proposed activities of the trade association raise antitrust concerns, the employee and employer should, without undue delay, clearly and publicly disassociate themselves from the activity until the situation can be assessed and, if appropriate, the concern addressed.

Each employee involved in trade association activities should therefore be trained what to do if a suggestion is made at a trade association function that he knows or is reasonably confident would raise antitrust concern. For example, if the group proposes an "ethical rule" that would protect the members of the association from new or innovative competitors, your employee should state his discomfort to the group and disassociate himself and the company from the activity in a way that is clear to the other participants. Merely sitting silently and passively through the meeting, and not actively distancing oneself is not enough. Rather, the employee should state his objection or concern, ask that the conversation regarding the proposal or topic stop so that he can discuss it with counsel, and if it does not, leave the room and insist that his departure be noted in the minutes. He should then immediately consult with legal counsel as to the appropriate measures to take to minimize antitrust risk. If counsel concludes that the proposed joint effort raises substantial risk, the trade association should be advised of those concerns and, if they are not addressed to the company's satisfaction, the company should advise the association that it will not participate in the activity.[44]

---

44.  Similarly, if it occurs to your employee after a trade association meeting that a proposed activity discussed at the meeting may raise antitrust risks, he should immediately consult with counsel. If counsel concludes that the activity does in fact raise risks, she should advise the trade association in writing, documenting the company's position. If the association continues

## E. Our Trade Association Includes a Number of Representatives from Other Countries. Does That Present Any Issues to Be Aware of?

The fact that a trade association includes members or representatives from other countries does not suggest any change in the antitrust analysis or advice given in this chapter. Foreign companies that provide goods and services to U.S. consumers are therefore generally subject to U.S. law.

Foreign membership in a trade association also suggests that (1) some meetings might be held outside of the United States but concern trade and commerce with or within the United States (and elsewhere), and (2) meetings held in the United States (or outside the United States) may concern trade and commerce outside the United States. It is important to understand that the location of the meeting does not change the analysis or advice discussed in this chapter.

First, the mere fact that a trade association meeting is held outside the United States does not immunize the conversations and activities that occurred in that meeting from the U.S. antitrust laws. To the contrary, conduct occurring outside the United States will likely be subject to the U.S. antitrust laws if that conduct has an effect in the United States. The Foreign Trade Antitrust Improvement Act of 1982[45] allows the federal courts to exercise jurisdiction under the Sherman Act with respect to extraterritorial conduct where two jurisdictional prerequisites are met. First, the conduct must have a "direct, substantial, and reasonably foreseeable effect" on U.S. commerce. Second, the "direct, substantial and reasonably foreseeable effect" on domestic commerce must "give rise to" the Sherman Act claim.[46]

---

to pursue the activity in spite of these warnings (or otherwise fails to address counsel's concerns), counsel should be informed and the company should make it clear that it will not participate.

45.  *See* 15 U.S.C. § 6a.

46.  *See* F. Hoffman-La Roche Ltd. v. Empagran S.A., 542 U.S. 155 (2004). Note also that in 1995, the Department of Justice issued the *Antitrust Guidelines for International Operations* which provide useful background on the FTAIA and the various circumstances in which U.S. jurisdiction might be implicated. U.S. DEP'T OF JUSTICE & FED. TRADE COMM'N, ANTITRUST ENFORCEMENT GUIDELINES FOR INTERNATIONAL OPERATIONS (1995), *available at* http://www.justice.gov/atr/public/guidelines/internat.htm

While conduct occurring outside the United States does not always satisfy these two requirements, trade association activities occurring outside the United States often will. Accordingly, the best practice is to assume that ex-U.S. trade association activities that can be expected to affect U.S. markets will be subject to U.S. law. Moreover, employees active in foreign trade association activities should be informed that in recent years, the Antitrust Division has placed a very high priority on the prosecution of international cartels that affect U.S. markets and the incarceration of individuals who participated in those cartels, including the incarceration of foreign nationals.[47] The investigation and prosecution of international cartels have also led to very costly civil litigation, typically in the form of class actions brought on behalf of both direct and indirect purchasers. Even cases that do not result in significant settlements or judgments require the expenditure of significant resources simply to investigate and defend.

Employees participating in trade associations should also be made aware that most nations have enacted "competition" laws that include prohibitions very similar to those found in the Sherman Act. The European Commission has scrutinized cartel-like behavior, including such behavior organized through trade association activities, for many years and has in recent years imposed enormous fines in the billions of

---

47. Scott D. Hammond, Dep'y Ass't Att'y Gen., Recent Developments, Trends, and Milestones in the Antitrust Division's Criminal Enforcement Program, Remarks Before the ABA Section of Antitrust Law Spring Meeting (Mar. 26, 2008), *available at* http://www. usdoj.gov/atr/public/speeches/232716.htm. In May 2007, a Korean executive was sentenced to fourteen months in prison for participation in an international cartel regarding Dynamic Random Access Memory (DRAM). In November 2007, two French nationals pleaded guilty and agreed to fourteen months in prison for participation in an international cartel regarding marine hose, and in December 2007, three British nationals pleaded guilty and agreed to prison sentences for participation in the same cartel. *Id.* In November 2008, the DOJ secured three guilty pleas and fines totaling $585 million, including the second-highest fine levied in an antitrust case, arising from an international cartel regarding TFT-LCD panels. *See* Press Release, U.S. Dep't of Justice, LG, Sharp, Chunghwa Agree to Plead Guilty, Pay Total of $585 Million in Fines for Participating in LCD Price-Fixing Conspiracies (Nov. 12, 2008), *available at* http://www.justice.gov/atr/public/press_releases/ 2008/239349.htm. In total, since May 1999, thirty-one foreign defendants have served, or are serving, U.S. prison sentences for antitrust violations or obstructing an antitrust investigation. Hammond, *supra*.

Euros for violations.[48] In addition, China enacted an Anti-Monopoly Law that became effective in 2008. In fact, nearly all large countries with market economies now have competition laws that include very significant sanctions against cartel behavior.

Moreover, an investigation by an antitrust or competition law enforcement agency in one country typically leads to investigations in multiple other jurisdictions. Such international investigations have proliferated as more countries promote leniency programs designed to encourage the voluntary disclosure of cartal behavior. In addition, the International Competition Network's (ICN) Cartel Working Group encourages greater international cooperation among antitrust enforcement agencies, identifies "best investigative techniques and policy approaches" from around the world, and promotes "real-time coordination among enforcers conducting parallel investigations of the same cartel" across jurisdictions.[49] Finally, like many other countries, the United States has entered into bilateral agreements on antitrust cooperation with, among others, Germany, the European Commission, Canada, Israel, Japan, and Mexico.[50]

---

48.    Neelie Kroes, European Comm'n for Competition Policy, Competition Policy Objectives, Address Before Economic and Monetary Affairs Committee, European Parliament (Mar. 26, 2008), *available at* http://europa.eu/rapid/pressReleasesAction.do?reference=SPEECH/08/15 2&format=HTML&aged=0&language=EN&guiLanguage=en;    Neelie Kroes, European Comm'n for Competition Policy, Competition Policy Objectives, Lessons Learned from the Economic Crisis, Address Before Committee on Economic and Monetary Affairs, European Parliament (Sept. 29, 2009), *available at* http://europa.eu/rapid/ pressReleasesAction.do?reference=SPEECH/09/420&format=HTML&ag ed=0&language=EN&guiLanguage=en. In addition, the European Parliament adopted a Resolution regarding private damages for violations of Articles 81 and 82 of the EC Treaty on March 26, 2009. The likely consequence of this measure will be to increase the ability of private parties in the European Union to obtain compensation for antitrust violations.

49.    Scott D. Hammond, Dep'y Ass't Att'y Gen., The Evolution of Criminal Antitrust Enforcement Over the Last Two Decades, Address at ABA Criminal Justice Section, Nat'l Inst. on White Collar Crime Annual Meeting (Feb. 25, 2010), *available at* http://www.justice.gov/atr/ public/speeches/255515.htm.

50.    *See* 2 ABA SECTION OF ANTITRUST LAW, ANTITRUST LAW DEVELOPMENTS 1254 (7th ed. 2012).

In short, the involvement of trade association members or representatives from other countries should cause association participants to be careful (1) not to violate U.S. antitrust laws through conduct occurring overseas, and (2) to be sensitive to the competition laws of other countries.[51]

## F. Where Can I Go For More Information?

### 1. *Joining a Trade Association*

- 1 ABA Section of Antitrust Law, *Antitrust Law Developments* 40-42 (7th ed. 2012);
- Thomas V. Vakerics, *Antitrust Basics* § 6.13 (Law Journal Press 2006);
- Federal Trade Commission Guide to the Antitrust Laws, Dealings with Competitors: Spotlight on Trade Associations, *available at* http://www.ftc.gov/bc/antitrust/trade_associations.shtm;
- Hogan Lovells, *Competition Law for Trade Associations* (2009), *available at* http://www.hoganlovells.com/files/Publication/0de5d3e0-1597-4f36-957f-7a8bdf5fc03e/Presentation/PublicationAttachment/eb6aca14-d41f-49f7-8659-801b4f07ecb4/res42D3DA2275F7456183BAD01DDE0D79F3.pdf;
- David H. Evans & Benhamin D. Bleiberg, *Trade Associations: Collaboration, Conspiracy & Innovations to Collude, Antitrust Rev. Am.*, 2011, at 40 *available at* http://www.chadbourne.com/files/Publication/3637676f-39a5-472e-bdcd-afe08fd28fbc/Presentation/PublicationAttachment/1ef6ebel-4578-46d4-835b-bb43f10ee8f2/Evans%20Trade%20Associations%20reprint%209%2010.pdf.

---

51. There are a variety of resources available that can assist counsel in becoming generally familiar with the antitrust laws of specific nations and regions. For example, The Asia-Pacific Economic Cooperation (APEC) web site (http://www.apec.org) contains a wealth of information about the competition laws of member countries, which include the United States, Canada, Australia, Japan, the People's Republic of China, Russia, Mexico, and other countries. Information about European Union competition laws can be found at http://www.europa.eu. Also, the web site of the Organization for Economic Co-operation and Development (OECD) (http://www.oecd.org) contains information about the competition laws of its members.

## 2. Trade Associations and Industry Standards

- 1 ABA Section of Antitrust Law, *Antitrust Law Developments* 121-23 (7th ed. 2012);
- Thomas V. Vakerics, *Antitrust Basics*, § 6.12 (Law Journal Press 2006);
- Herbert Hovenkamp, *Standards Ownership & Competition Policy*, 48 *B.C. L. Rev.* 87 (Jan. 2007);
- Timothy M. Biddle et al., *Industry Standards As a Source Of Liability For Trade Associations & Association Members*, Crowell & Moring Publications (Oct. 2002), *available at* http://www.crowell.com/documents/DOCASSOCFKTYPE_AR TICLES_506.pdf;
- Jeffrey S. Tenenbaum, *Association Certification & Accreditation Programs Minimizing the Liability Risks*, The Center for Association Leadership (May 2002), *available at* http://www.asaecenter.org/Resources/whitepaperdetail.cfm?Item Number=12198;
- Marina Lao, *Discrediting Accreditation?: Antitrust & Legal Education*, 79 *Wash. U. L. Q.* 1035 (2001), *available at* http://digitalcommons.law.wustl.edu/lawreview/vol79/iss4/2/;
- Susan Dorm & Kristin Becker, Legal Update: *Current Issues Affecting Accrediting Bodies*, Council on Licensure, Enforcement & Regulation (2000), *available at* http://www.clearhq.org/resources/97-2.htm.

## 3. Trade Associations and Information Sharing

- 1 ABA Section of Antitrust Law, *Antitrust Law Developments* 97-102 (7th ed. 2012);
- Philip C. Larson et al., CLE presentations in conjunction with Strafford Webinar: Antitrust Pitfalls for Trade Associations and Members, 14 (Feb. 7, 2012), *available at* http://media.straffordpub.com/products/antitrust-pitfalls-for-trade-associations-and-members-2012-02-07/presentation.pdf;
- *Too Much Information? The Antitrust Implications of Price Signalling & Information Exchanges*, ABA International Antitrust Law Committee (June 28, 2011), *description available at* http://www.shearman.com/too-much-information-the-antitrust-implications-of-price-signalling-and-information-exchanges-06-28-2011/, *full audio available at*

http://www.americanbar.org/content/dam/aba/multimedia/interna tional_law/mp3/20110628_too_much_information.mp3;

- *Information Exchanges*, *Corporate Counsel Quarterly*, Jan. 2010, at article 2;
- Hogan Lovells, *Competition Law for Trade Associations* 2 (2009), *available at* http://www.hoganlovells.com/files/ Publication/0de5d3e0-1597-4f36-957f-7a8bdf5fc03e/ Presentation/PublicationAttachment/eb6aca14-d41f-49f7-8659- 801b4f07ecb4/res42D3DA2275F7456183BAD01DDE0D79F3.p df;
- William Randolph Smith et al., *Trade Associations & Other Information Exchange Programmes in the US: What Enforcers Prohibit, What They Require*, Crowell & Moring Publications (2007), *available at* http://www.crowell.com/document/ DOCASSOCFKTYPE_ARTICLES_364.pdf;
- Thomas V. Vakerics, *Antitrust Basics* § 6.07 (Law Journal Press 2006);
- Corby C. Anderson & Ted P. Pearce, *The Antitrust Risks of Information Sharing*, *Franchis L.J.*, Summer 2003, at 17.

## 4. *Trade Associationsand Joint Conduct*

- *The Practical Aspects of Corporate Antitrust Compliance Programs*, 1436 *PLI/Corp* 691, 693;
- William M. Hannay, *Corporate Compliance Series: Antitrust* §§ 3:36-:42 (Thompson Reuters 2011);
- Larry Fullerton, *FTC Challenges to "Invitations to Collude"*, 25 *Antitrust* 30 (Spring 2011);
- Richard Liebeskind et al., *FTC to Associations: Lack of Antitrust Compliance Can Facilitate Coordination & Violate the FTC Act*, Pillsbury Client Alert (Mar. 16, 2009), *available at* http://www.pillsburylaw.com/sitefiles/publications/316b8c28226 ccad15501a8a2bf7b4569.pdf;
- Barry J. Lipson, *Adopting an Effective Antitrust Compliance Program: The Trade Association Connection*, 3 No. 16 *Lawyers J.* 5 (2001).

## 5. *Trade Associations and International Members*

- *Too Much Information? The Antitrust Implications of Price Signalling & Information Exchanges*, ABA International

Antitrust Law Committee (June 28, 2011), *description available at* http://www.shearman.com/too-much-information-the-antitrust-implications-of-price-signalling-and-information-exchanges-06-28-2011/, *full audio available at* http://www.americanbar.org/content/dam/aba/multimedia/international_law/mp3/20110628_too_much_information.mp3;

- Rachel Bradenburger, Special Advisor, Antitrust Division, U.S. Dep't of Justice, Remarks at the International Bar Association Midyear Conference: The Many Facts of International Cooperation at the Antitrust Division (June 15, 2012), *available at* http://www.justice.gov/atr/public/speeches/284239.pdf;
- Rachel Bradenburger, Twenty Years of Transatlantic Antitrust Cooperation: the Past and the Future, U.S. Dep't of Justice Antitrust Division's International Program (Oct. 14, 2011), *available at* http://www.justice.gov/atr/public/articles/279068.pdf;
- Thomas O. Barnett, Assistant Attorney General, Antitrust Division, U.S. Department of Justice, Address at the Georgetown Law Global Antitrust Enforcement Symposium: Global Antitrust Enforcement (Sept. 26, 2007), *available at* http://www.justice.gov/atr/public/speeches/226334.htm.

CHAPTER III

# MERGERS AND JOINT VENTURES

## A. We Are Contemplating Merging with or Acquiring Another Company. What Sort of Antitrust Approvals Will We Need? What Are the Procedures for Obtaining These Approvals in the United States?

In the United States mergers and acquisitions are reviewed by one of two federal agencies, the Federal Trade Commission (FTC) or the Antitrust Division of the Department of Justice (DOJ). Which agency receives "clearance" to review a particular transaction will generally depend upon the agencies' relative expertise with respect to the industry (or industries) at issue.

Worldwide, close to one hundred jurisdictions have enacted merger control regimes, which, in many cases, require notification and approval before a transaction may be closed.

Below, we discuss three separate questions: (1) in what jurisdictions will a merger notification be required?; (2) what are the U.S. merger notification rules?; and (3) if U.S. approval is required, what is the process for the federal government's review of the notified transaction?

### 1. In What Jurisdictions Will a Merger Notification Be Required?

The jurisdictions where antitrust approvals must be sought will depend on the nature of the transaction and the jurisdictions in which the merging parties derive revenues.

a. The United States

In the United States the premerger notification process is governed by the Hart-Scott-Rodino Antitrust Improvements Act of 1976 (HSR

Act).[1] The HSR Act and regulations provide criteria and exemptions that determine whether a filing is required.[2]

For transactions that must be reported, the HSR Act imposes an "initial waiting period" for agency review before the transaction can be completed. For most acquisitions the initial waiting period is thirty days. For cash tender offers and certain acquisitions subject to bankruptcy approval the initial waiting period is fifteen days. During the initial waiting period the FTC or the DOJ will analyze the proposed transaction's likely effects on competition under Section 7 of the Clayton Act, which prohibits transactions that may have "the effect" of "substantially [lessening] competition, or [tending] to create a monopoly."[3] In practice agencies consider under the *Horizontal Merger Guidelines* whether the parties will have the ability and incentive to take anticompetitive actions after the merger.[4] The agency then decides whether to permit the transaction to proceed without further investigation. The waiting period can be extended if the reviewing agency issues a request for additional information, typically referred to as a "Second Request." See part A.3 of this chapter for a more detailed discussion of the merger review process in the United States, including an overview of the information that must be included in the HSR filing (HSR Filing).

The parties also should consider whether they are required to seek approval from other federal agencies that regulate transactions in specific industries, such as the Federal Communications Commission, the

---

1.    Hart-Scott-Rodino Antitrust Improvements Act of 1976, Pub. L. No. 94-435, § 201, 90 Stat. 1383, 1390 (1976) (codified as amended at 15 U.S.C. § 18a), amending the Clayton Antitrust Act of 1914, Pub. L. No. 63-212, 38 Stat. 730 (1918). The regulations adopted by the FTC to implement the HSR Act appear at 16 C.F.R. §§ 801–803. The FTC is charged with administering the HSR premerger notification process, although filings are made to both the FTC and the DOJ, and both agencies are responsible for substantive reviews of proposed transactions, although in any particular transaction only one of the agencies conducts the investigation.

2.    *See* part A.2 of this chapter for a more in-depth discussion of these criteria and exemptions.

3.    15 U.S.C. § 18.

4.    U.S. DEP'T OF JUSTICE & FED. TRADE COMM'N, HORIZONTAL MERGER GUIDELINES (2010) [hereinafter 2010 HORIZONTAL MERGER GUIDELINES], *available at* http://www.justice.gov/atr/public/guidelines/hmg-2010.html.

Department of Transportation, or the Federal Reserve. Although in-depth discussion of these agencies' reporting requirements is beyond the scope of this book, many agencies include competition issues in their analysis of whether to approve specific transactions within their substantive jurisdiction.

b. Outside of the United States

To date nearly one hundred jurisdictions worldwide have enacted merger review laws or created merger notification regimes, or both.[5] These jurisdictions differ with respect to critical issues such as the revenue or other thresholds sufficient to trigger merger review, when filings must be made, whether a party may close a transaction prior to obtaining regulatory approval, fines or other penalties for failing to notify, the substantive standards used to assess a transaction, the remedies employed to address competition concerns, and the degree to which each jurisdiction seeks to coordinate with the merger review process in other countries.[6] Many jurisdictions impose mandatory

---

5.  In addition to the European Union, the list includes: Albania, Argentina, Australia, Austria, Belarus, Belgium, Bolivia, Bosnia & Herzegovina, Brazil, Bulgaria, Canada, Chile, China, Colombia, Croatia, Cyprus, Czech Republic, Estonia, Faroe Islands, Finland, France, Germany, Greece, Hong Kong, Hungary, India, Indonesia, Ireland, Israel, Italy, Japan, Kenya, Korea, Latvia, Liechtenstein, Lithuania, Luxembourg, Macedonia, Malta, Mexico, Namibia, Netherlands, New Zealand, Nigeria, Norway, Poland, Portugal, Romania, Russia, Saudi Arabia, Serbia, Singapore, Slovakia, Slovenia, South Africa, Spain, Sweden, Switzerland, Taiwan, Thailand, Turkey, Ukraine, United Kingdom, United States, Uruguay, Venezuela, and Zambia. *See* GLOBAL COMPETITION REVIEW, MERGER CONTROL 2013 (2012) [hereinafter MERGER CONTROL 2013].

6.  *See* ABA SECTION OF ANTITRUST LAW, MERGER REVIEW PROCESS, Chapter II, "Representing Parties in Mergers Subject to Multijurisdictional Review" (2012) [hereinafter MERGER REVIEW PROCESS] for in-depth commentary on the specific concerns at issue in multijurisdictional clearance and procedures in certain key jurisdictions; *see also* MERGER CONTROL 2013, *supra* note 5, for commentary on the procedural and substantive features of each international jurisdiction with a transaction control regime. In addition, the website of the International Competition Network includes useful links to foreign transaction control laws at http://www.internationalcompetitionnetwork.org/working-groups/current/merger/templates.aspx.

notification regimes, whereas notification is voluntary in others.

Each jurisdiction has its own timetable, system, and procedures for review. These differences should be considered carefully in planning the schedule for a transaction. Delays from reviews by foreign agencies can be considerable.

In the European Union the data provided to the European Commission can be significantly more voluminous and more substantive than what must be provided to the United States authorities with the initial HSR Filing. The European Commission technically reaches an initial "Phase I" determination within twenty-five days of the effective date of the initial notification. If the European Commission determines that the transaction raises "serious doubts" as to whether it could impede effective competition, the agency can open an in-depth "Phase II" investigation (typically lasting ninety days in the first instance). In practice, however, due to the European Commission's ability to reject filings for incompleteness or require more detailed information the review process can last substantially longer.

Procedures and timetables for reporting to merger control authorities vary from one jurisdiction to another, and antitrust counsel should be consulted regarding when and how to notify authorities. For example, in China, the Ministry of Commerce (MOFCOM) regulates merger control, imposing a thirty-day "Phase I" period followed by the ministry's ability to extend review in a "Phase II" investigation by ninety days (or, in practice, possibly longer).

Antitrust enforcement authorities in relevant jurisdictions may cooperate or coordinate among one another to greater or lesser degrees. The European Union and the United States have developed extensive practices for coordinating merger reviews and in 2011 entered into an agreement updating those practices. The 2011 agreement provides expanded detail about how companies can work with agencies to coordinate merger review and emphasizes coordination between agencies at the final stage of investigation, when the agencies consider potential remedies to preserve competition.

The Chinese antimonopoly agencies similarly entered into an agreement with the FTC and the DOJ in 2011 to promote communication and cooperation between the agencies when conducting merger reviews. Other jurisdictions such as Switzerland, South Africa, and Venezuela, however, do not have formal mechanisms for coordinating merger reviews with foreign jurisdictions, although they may cooperate informally.

Even if two jurisdictions have a formal agreement in place for coordination, the substantive analysis, and even final determination, can differ from one jurisdiction to another. For example, in May 2001 ,the United States cleared General Electric's merger with Honeywell subject to certain divestitures, but in July 2001 the European Union's antitrust agency blocked the same transaction.

In sum, if the transaction requires notification in multiple international jurisdictions counsel should carefully assess the different procedural and substantive standards in play and adjust the strategy for clearing the transaction accordingly.

## 2. *What Are the U.S. Pre-Merger Notification Rules?*

In the United States the HSR Act and related regulations set the standards for when transacting parties must notify the federal government of their transaction.

The HSR Act applies both to the acquisition of assets (including certain types of exclusive licenses) and to voting securities. The acquisition of a controlling interest (50 percent or more) of an unincorporated entity such as a partnership or LLC is considered to be the acquisition of the assets held by the entity, and may trigger a filing requirement. The acquisition of nonvoting securities, as well as most warrants and options, does not generally require an HSR Filing.

As a general matter, unless certain exemptions apply parties must make an HSR Filing if the transaction meets three threshold tests: (1) the *commerce* test, (2) the *size-of-transaction* test, and, where applicable, (3) the *size-of-person* test.

- *The Commerce Test.* A transaction meets the commerce test if either party is engaged in commerce or in any activity affecting commerce.[7] This typically is not a significant hurdle.
- *The Size-of-Transaction Test.* An HSR Filing is required only if the value of the assets or voting securities held as a result of the acquisition is $50 million or more (as adjusted on an annual basis).

---

7.    15 U.S.C. § 18a(a)(1).

### The Size-of-Transaction Test

| Value of Transaction Provided by Statute | 2013 Adjusted Values[8] | HSR Filing? |
|---|---|---|
| Under $50 million (as adjusted annually) | Under $70.9 million | Not required |
| $50 million-$200 million (as adjusted annually) | $70.9 million-$286.3 million | Required if the size-of-person test is satisfied and no exemptions apply |
| Over $200 million (as adjusted annually) | Over $286.3 million | Required if no exemption applies |

- *The Size-of-Person Test.* If a transaction is valued at between $50 million and $200 million (as adjusted in 2012 to between $70.9 million and $286.3 million), as a general matter, the parties must file a premerger notification form only if (1) at least one of the parties had $100 million (as adjusted in 2012 to $141.8 million) or more in fiscal year net sales or total assets, *and* (2) the other party had $10 million (as adjusted in 2012 to $14.2 million) or more in fiscal year net sales or total assets.[9] If the transaction is valued at greater than $200 million (as adjusted in 2012 to $286.3 million), the size-of-person test is inapplicable and an HSR Filing is required. The key sources of data for applying the size-of-person test are likely to be the most recent, regularly prepared balance sheet and the most recent annual statement of income and expense.[10]

---

8.   *See* Press Release, Fed. Trade Comm'n, FTC Announces Revised Thresholds for Clayton Act Antitrust Reviews for 2013 (Jan. 10, 2013), *available at* http://www.ftc.gov/opa/2013/01/clayton.shtm; *see also* Revised Jurisdictional Thresholds [for Section 7A] of the Clayton Act, 78 Fed. Reg. 2406-07 (Jan. 11, 2013) [hereinafter Revised HSR Thresholds].
9.   15 U.S.C. § 18a(a)(2)(B)(ii); *see* FED. TRADE COMM'N, PREMERGER NOTIFICATION OFFICE, TO FILE OR NOT TO FILE: WHEN YOU MUST FILE A PREMERGER NOTIFICATION REPORT FORM (2008), *available at* http://www.ftc.gov/bc/hsr/introguides/guide2.pdf; *see also* Revised HSR Thresholds, *supra* note 8.
10.   16 C.F.R. § 801.11(c)(1)-(2).

The HSR Act and accompanying regulations provide a number of often complex exemptions. For example, acquisitions of goods and realty made "in the ordinary course of business" are exempt, and other exemptions include certain acquisitions of voting securities made "solely for the purpose of investment," certain acquisitions of real estate, and certain transactions involving foreign persons, assets, or voting securities.[11] Counsel should consider carefully whether any exemptions apply to the transaction.

In addition, the form of the transaction can be important in determining whether an HSR Filing is required. For example, the acquisition of $100 million of voting securities in a corporation may trigger an HSR Filing requirement in a situation in which the same investment in an LLC would not.

There are several useful sources for further guidance regarding the HSR Act. A particularly helpful resource is a monograph published by the American Bar Association Section of Antitrust Law that provides a thorough review of the entire merger review process.[12] Formal and informal interpretations of the HSR regulations by the FTC's premerger notification staff are available online and in the ABA Antitrust Section's *Premerger Notification Practice Manual*.[13] In addition, the staff of the FTC Premerger Notification Office is available to provide informal and confidential guidance by letter, e-mail, or telephone.

Failure to comply with the HSR requirements can lead to significant penalties of up to $16,000 per day.[14]

It is important to keep in mind, however, that the United States antitrust authorities may still review transactions that need not be notified under the HSR Act, applying the same substantive standards to assess the likely effects on competition. Those standards are explored further in part B, below.

---

11.　16 C.F.R. §§ 802.1-2, 802.9, 802.50-53.
12.　MERGER REVIEW PROCESS, *supra* note 6.
13.　FED. TRADE COMM'N, HSR INFORMAL INTERPRETATIONS, *available at* http://www.ftc.gov/bc/hsr/informal/index.shtm; ABA SECTION OF ANTITRUST LAW, PREMERGER NOTIFICATION PRACTICE MANUAL (4th ed. 2007).
14.　15 U.S.C. § 18a(g)(1); 16 C.F.R. § 1.98.

### 3.  What Is the Process for the Federal Government's Review of Our Merger or Acquisition?

a.  Filing the HSR Form

*(1)  The Fee and the Form*

There is no deadline for making an HSR filing. The parties cannot consummate a transaction, however, until they make all required filings under the HSR Act and observe all required waiting periods. An HSR Filing can be made any time after the signing of an agreement, or even of a memorandum of understanding or letter of intent, as long as the acquiring party submits an affidavit confirming a good faith intention to proceed with the acquisition.[15] In some cases, even the mere intention to acquire control on the open market is enough to permit a filing.

Under the HSR regulations the buyer is responsible for paying the HSR Filing fee, though the parties are free to come to a different arrangement by private agreement. In 2012, the filing fee was $45,000 for transactions valued in excess of $68.2 million but less than $136.4 million, $125,000 for transactions valued between $136.4 million and $682.1 million, and $280,000 for transactions valued at $682.1 million or more.[16] The FTC's website lists the current thresholds and corresponding filing fees.

In completing the HSR form, the ultimate parent entities of both parties must submit information about their companies, including information about their United States operations. Much of the information that the form requires can be collected independent of a particular transaction, and as a matter of practice a company may wish to have this data ready and available if it plans to engage in future acquisitions. For example, Item 5 of the HSR form requires parties to disclose certain revenue information and products sold during the most recent year using product codes of the North American Industrial Classification System (NAICS). Item 6 requires disclosure of a filing party's subsidiaries and large shareholders as well as minority investments in businesses related to a target.

Other parts of the HSR form require parties to disclose information specific to the transaction. As an example, Item 3(a) requires parties to provide a brief description of the transaction, including the names and

---

15.     16 C.F.R. § 803.5.
16.     *See* Fed. Trade Comm'n, *Filing Fee Information* (Feb. 27, 2012), *available at* http://www.ftc.gov/bc/hsr/filing2.shtm.

addresses of the parties, the consideration received by each party, and the expected dates of major events required to consummate the transaction (such as shareholders' meetings, certain public filings, or terminations of tender offers). Item 7 (regarding geographic markets in which both parties report revenue) and Item 8 (regarding other recent acquisitions by the acquirer in industries related to the target) also relate to information specific to the particular merging parties.

An affidavit from an officer of each party that his or her company intends in good faith to consummate the transaction must accompany the form. In addition, an officer or director must certify under oath that the information provided in the notification form is true, correct, and complete.[17]

### (2) Enclosures with the Form

The parties are required to include a number of key documents with the HSR filing. Those documents often contain the information most relevant to the agencies' review of the transaction.

Item 3(b) requires the parties to submit all documents that constitute the agreement(s) between the parties. Items 4(a) and 4(b) require submission of certain documents typically filed with the United States Securities and Exchange Commission.

Most significantly, Item 4(c) requires the submission of "all studies, surveys, analyses and reports which were prepared by or for any officer(s) or director(s) . . . for the purpose of evaluating or analyzing the acquisition with respect to *market shares, competition, competitors, markets, potential for sales growth or expansion into product or geographic markets.*"[18] Additionally, Item 4(d), added to the filing requirements in August 2011, requires the submission of documents "evaluating or analyzing synergies and/or efficiencies" and certain other materials that are not always captured by Item 4(c), such as confidential information memoranda and materials prepared by third-party advisors.[19] As a general matter, the DOJ and FTC pay close attention to Item 4(c)

---

17. Notification and Report Form for Certain Mergers and Acquisitions, *available at* http://www.ftc.gov/bc/hsr/hsr_form_ver_101.pdf.

18. FED. TRADE COMM'N, ANTITRUST IMPROVEMENTS ACT NOTIFICATION AND REPORT FORM FOR CERTAIN MERGERS AND ACQUISITIONS: INSTRUCTIONS, at V, Item (4)(c) (effective Aug. 18, 2011), *available at* http://www.ftc.gov/bc/hsr/ hsrform-instructions1_0_0.pdf (emphasis added).

19. *Id.* at V, Item 4(d).

and 4(d) documents because they may reveal the parties' motivations for entering into the transaction and their assessments of the competitive impact of the transaction. Item 4(c) permits filers to invoke attorney-client privilege as the basis for not producing a privileged document. Any invocation of the privilege must identify each document by its author, recipients, present location, date, and subject matter, as well as state who has control of the document. See part D of this chapter for more discussion of Item 4(c) and 4(d) documents.

In preparing the HSR filing, the parties should carefully search the files of any personnel likely to possess documents responsive to Items 4(c) or 4(d). Failure to produce all required documents can substantially delay the transaction. If such documents are discovered during the course of the initial waiting period or in the course of a Second Request, the agency may require the parties to file new HSR forms, thus sending the transaction back to square one with a new thirty-day waiting period.

Neglecting to produce the required documents also can lead to financial penalties. For example, in one case, the FTC imposed a civil penalty of $4 million as a result of a filer's failure to include all Item 4(c) documents and its failure to include a list of such documents withheld on claims of privilege.[20] In another case the DOJ independently initiated an inquiry about the lack of Item 4(c) documents in a transaction between two competing companies and ultimately sought and obtained a $550,000 civil penalty for an HSR Act violation despite also concluding that the transaction itself posed no competitive threat.[21] In a third case, the DOJ charged a merchant bank and the general partner who signed the bank's HSR certification with violating the HSR Act by failing to submit several Item 4(c) documents.[22] The bank agreed to pay a penalty of almost $3 million and, for the first time, HSR penalties (amounting to $50,000) were imposed upon the individual who signed the HSR certification.

Unless the parties agree otherwise, the contents of notification forms and accompanying documents are kept confidential by the FTC and the DOJ and are generally exempt from disclosure to private parties and other government agencies.[23] Except for certain circumstances (e.g., a

---

20.   United States v. Hearst Trust, 2001-2 Trade Cas. (CCH) ¶ 73,451 (D.D.C. 2001).

21.   United States v. Iconix Brand Grp., 2007-2 Trade Cas. (CCH) ¶ 75,900 (D.D.C. 2007).

22.   United States v. Blackstone Capital Partners II Merch. Banking Fund, 1999-1 Trade Cas. (CCH) ¶ 72,484 (D.D.C. 1999).

23.   15 U.S.C. § 18a(h).

lawsuit in which HSR filing documents are introduced in court), even the fact that a filing has been made is kept confidential. However, if the parties request in their HSR filings that the agencies grant "early termination" of the waiting period before the parties can complete their transaction and their request is granted, the grant of early termination will be made public by the FTC through publication in the Federal Register. In addition, HSR materials may be disclosed to Congress or in any administrative or judicial proceeding to which the FTC or DOJ is a party.

b.   Initial Thirty-Day Waiting Period

Once the agencies receive the parties' filings and the fee, the agencies typically have thirty days (or fifteen days in the case of a cash tender offer or a sale in bankruptcy) to make an initial determination as to whether there are any likely adverse competitive effects that would result from the transaction. This thirty-day period is known as the "initial waiting period."

The two agencies first engage in a "clearance process" to determine which agency will investigate the transaction. Usually, the transaction will "clear" to the agency with the greater experience with the industries or parties involved in the transaction. In some cases, both agencies seek to lead the investigation resulting in a "clearance dispute" that is resolved through an internal liaison process. Parties should consult with antitrust counsel about the potential consequences of clearing to one agency as opposed to the other and how the clearance process will affect plans to complete the transaction.

Second, the reviewing agency will use some or all of the initial waiting period to consider whether the parties might undertake anticompetitive actions following the merger. The agency may make informal voluntary requests for additional information or documents to assist in the initial review. The agency also might make factual inquiry, make particular requests regarding information contained in Item 4(c) documents, or consult with third parties affected by the transaction such as customers, competitors, or other agencies that regulate the industry.

The initial waiting period generally will end in one of three ways: (1) the agency can allow the thirty-day period to expire or grant "early termination" during the thirty-day period, thus permitting the parties to conclude the transaction, (2) the parties may decide it is in their interests to "pull and refile" their HSR forms in order to give the agency an extra thirty days to review the transaction if they believe that additional time will increase the chances of clearance (which the parties may do once without repaying the filing fee), or (3) the agency may issue a Request for Additional Information and Documentary Material, commonly known as a "Second Request."

c.  Second Requests

Issuance of a Second Request indicates that the reviewing agency has antitrust concerns about the transaction, and that it has not been able to resolve those concerns during the initial thirty-day waiting period (or a second thirty-day waiting period after pulling and refiling).

A Second Request is a detailed set of questions and document and data requests that are designed to give the agency insight into whether the parties could raise prices or otherwise substantially lessen competition posttransaction. The agency may seek information regarding, for example, the rationale for the transaction, the market structure, and the ability of other companies to enter the market and compete with the merging companies. Second Requests often are highly comprehensive in nature, involving extensive requests for documents, written questions, and interviews or sworn testimony.[24] The agencies have implemented reforms intended to reduce the burden of complying with a Second Request (including limiting the scope of initial document requests and the number of employees required to provide information), but the process still can be extremely costly and time-consuming. If faced with a Second Request, counsel likely will seek to negotiate narrowing the scope of the agency's request.

Depending on the nature of the industry and the scope of the Second Request, it can take several months or more for the parties to comply with the inquiries and demands of a Second Request. Once the parties have "substantially complied" with the Second Request, the parties then must observe another thirty-day waiting period (fifteen in the case of cash tender offers and acquisitions subject to bankruptcy court approval) before they can close the transaction. The agencies may contest whether a party has "substantially complied" with the Second Request, which could further delay the final thirty-day waiting period. On the other hand,

---

24.    The agencies have made available a "model" Second Request that provides a good indication of the types of information commonly requested. *See* FED. TRADE COMM'N, PREMERGER NOTIFICATION OFFICE, MODEL REQUEST FOR ADDITIONAL INFORMATION AND DOCUMENTARY MATERIAL (SECOND REQUEST) (2010), *available at* http://www.ftc.gov/bc/hsr/introguides/ guide3.pdf.

an agency can grant "early termination" if it concludes prior to or after substantial compliance with the Second Request that further investigation is not required. The agency also could close its investigation even before the parties substantially comply if it determines there are no competitive concerns.

At the conclusion of the Second Request phase, the agency may simply permit the parties to proceed with the transaction. Alternatively, the parties and the agency often seek a voluntary settlement resolving the antitrust concerns. Indeed, it is common for such negotiations to begin well before there has been substantial compliance with the Second Request. Such a voluntary settlement could entail injunctive relief of some kind, whether the relief is a structural remedy (such as an agreement to divest a certain business) or a behavioral remedy (such as access conditions, information walls, or nondiscrimination provisions). That relief is then subject to the terms of a formal consent order approved by the FTC or, in the case of transactions reviewed by the DOJ, a consent decree approved by a federal district court.

Alternatively, the agencies have the option of filing suit to enjoin the transaction, as the DOJ did in August 2011 when it filed a civil lawsuit to block AT&T Inc. from acquiring T-Mobile USA, Inc., an acquisition that AT&T and T-Mobile subsequently abandoned. In a civil proceeding, the parties would have the opportunity to challenge the agency's assertion that consummating the transaction would violate the antitrust laws.

There is no formal process for premerger review by individual U.S. states, which have not enacted their own premerger notification statutes. The states, however, are able to subpoena documents pursuant to state antitrust statutes, effectively enabling states to participate in the merger review process.[25] The states have established a compact to disclose information to one another through the National Association of Attorneys General, with the goal of facilitating cooperation among states

---

25. Many states have enacted statues similar to the federal Sherman Act and Clayton Act. 1 ABA SECTION OF ANTITRUST LAW, ANTITRUST LAW DEVELOPMENTS 633-54 (7th ed. 2012).

investigating a transaction.[26] The states have also adopted guidelines to assess horizontal transactions.[27]

In addition, private parties including competitors[28] and customers[29] can challenge transactions, although those challenges occur less frequently than government challenges.

## B. One of Our Competitors Is for Sale. We Would Like to Acquire Them, but the Acquisition Would Give Us the Lion's Share of the Market. Can We Do It?

The short answer is: it depends. The question for the agencies is not limited to a company's pastmerger share of the market but also covers what kind of market power a company has and the likelihood that the company could exercise that market power in a way that would be harmful to customers and to competition generally. By "harm," the agencies usually mean the ability to raise prices, reduce quality, reduce output, or diminish innovation.[30] Market shares are an important element of assessing market power, but the agencies' substantive analysis will be broader and more complex than evaluating market shares alone.

At the federal level in the United States, the FTC or DOJ will consider whether a transaction violates Section 7 of the Clayton Act, which prohibits transactions that may have "the effect" of "substantially [lessening] competition, or [tending] to create a monopoly."[31] In this

---

26.   Resolution, Nat'l Ass'n of Att'ys Gen., Revisions to the National Association of Attorneys General Pre-Merger Disclosure Compact (March 20-22, 1994), *available at* http://www.naag.org/assets/files/pdf/200612-antitrust-voluntary-premerger-disclosure-compact.pdf.

27.   NAT'L ASS'N OF ATT'YS GEN., HORIZONTAL MERGER GUIDELINES (1993), *available at* http://www.naag.org/assets/files/pdf/at-hmerger_guidelines.pdf.

28.   *See* Sprint Nextel Corp. v. AT&T, 2011 WL 3891692 (D.D.C. 2011) (competitor Sprint challenged the proposed AT&T/T-Mobile transaction); Complaint, Cellular South, Inc. v. AT&T, 2011, No. 1:11-cv-01690, ECF No. 1 (Sept. 19, 2011) (competitor Cellular South doing the same).

29.   *See* Blessing v. Sirius XM Radio Inc., 775 F. Supp. 2d 650 (S.D.N.Y. 2011) (approving settlement in consumer class action challenging the completed Sirius and XM transaction).

30.   2010 HORIZONTAL MERGER GUIDELINES, *supra* note 4, at Section 1.

31.   15 U.S.C. § 18. Section 7 of the Clayton Act applies to *all* mergers and acquisitions, not only those notifiable under HSR rules. Consequently, the DOJ and the FTC have the authority to, and do, investigate and challenge transactions that are not reportable under HSR rules.

analysis, the agencies are focused on the effect on customers and on competition, but not on the effect on competitors. During the waiting period, the parties will attempt to show the agency why the transaction will not result in a substantial lessening of competition and, therefore, why the agency should not seek to delay, modify, or block a transaction.

Here, we consider the analysis that agencies use specifically for "horizontal" transactions, that is, transactions involving competitors at the same level in the supply chain.[32] See part C of this chapter for a discussion of the substantive analysis that agencies use for non-horizontal transactions, such as transactions between a company and a supplier or distributor.

The agencies frequently review horizontal transactions. In fact, the agencies have revisited their guidelines for reviewing horizontal mergers three times in the last twenty years alone: in 1992,[33] again in 1997,[34] and yet again in 2010.[35] By contrast, the agencies last updated their non-horizontal guidelines nearly thirty years ago, in 1984.[36] The agencies' guidelines do not have the force of law, but nonetheless they are strong authority that guides courts' analyses of transactions, and they provide a useful framework for presenting arguments to the agency in support of the transaction. In addition to the agencies' general horizontal guidelines, the parties and their counsel also should consider any industry-specific guidance from the agencies, such as the agencies' 1996 health care guidelines[37] or any speeches or prior decisions on the relevant industry

---

32. The process used by the federal agencies to consider whether a proposed transaction violates Section 7 is detailed in the 2010 *Horizontal Merger Guidelines*, issued jointly by the DOJ and the FTC. 2010 HORIZONTAL MERGER GUIDELINES, *supra* note 4.

33. U.S. DEP'T OF JUSTICE & FED. TRADE COMM'N, HORIZONTAL MERGER GUIDELINES (2002), *available at* http://www.ftc.gov/bc/docs/horizmer.shtm.

34. U.S. DEP'T OF JUSTICE & FED. TRADE COMM'N, HORIZONTAL MERGER GUIDELINES (1997), *available at* http://www.justice.gov/atr/public/guidelines/hmg.htm.

35. 2010 HORIZONTAL MERGER GUIDELINES, supra note 4.

36. U.S. DEP'T OF JUSTICE & FED. TRADE COMM'N, NON-HORIZONTAL MERGER GUIDELINES (1984) [hereinafter NON-HORIZONTAL MERGER GUIDELINES], *available at* http://www.justice.gov/atr/public/guidelines/2614.htm.

37. U.S. DEP'T OF JUSTICE & FED. TRADE COMM'N, STATEMENTS OF ANTITRUST ENFORCEMENT POLICY IN HEALTH CARE (1996) [hereinafter DOJ & FTC HEALTH CARE GUIDELINES], *available at* http://www.justice.gov/atr/public/ guidelines/0000.htm.

by FTC or DOJ officials.

The agencies conduct a horizontal merger analysis to understand the likely effects of the proposed transaction on competition in the relevant market. Under the Clayton Act the agencies may challenge transactions where "the effect [may be to] substantially lessen competition, or tend to create a monopoly." In practice, the agencies often use the *Horizontal Merger Guidelines* to assess whether the parties will have the ability and incentive to undertake anticompetitive actions postmerger. In so doing, the agencies consider two major kinds of anticompetitive "effects": (1) the potential that the transaction will unlawfully give the combined entity power to raise price or reduce competition single-handedly (so-called "unilateral effects"), (2) the transaction's potential to increase the possibility of tacit collusion or coordination among rivals (so-called "coordinated effects")[38], or both.

To assess the competitive effects of the transaction, the first step that the government takes may be to define the relevant market in which the transaction is taking place. We say that this "may be" the first step because, as we explain below, the agencies have begun to shift away from a market-centric analysis. In defining the market, the agencies generally consider both the relevant *product market* (what group of products is relevant for antitrust purposes?) and the relevant *geographic market* (i.e., is this market local? national? is it defined by the location of suppliers or the location of customers?).[39] The agencies employ a test, known as the hypothetical monopolist test, to determine what other options customers could turn to if the merged entity were to impose a profitable "small but significant nontransitory increase in price" (or SSNIP).[40]

Once the agencies identify the relevant product and geographic markets, they then identify the competitors in that market, that is, entities currently competing for business as well as "potential competitors" that are positioned to enter into the market and compete.[41] The agencies

---

38.  2010 HORIZONTAL MERGER GUIDELINES, *supra* note 4, §§ 6 (Unilateral Effects), 7 (Coordinated Effects).

39.  *See id.* §§ 4.1 (Product Market Definition), 4.2 (Geographic Market Definition).

40.  *See id.* § 4.1.

41.  The 2010 *Horizontal Merger Guidelines* explain that firms currently without revenue in the relevant market can be considered market participants if the firm has committed to entering the market in the near future. Market participants would also include firms that "would very

consider the relative market shares of the merging companies and their competitors (usually measured by annual revenues in the relevant market), and they analyze how concentrated the market currently is and how concentrated it will be as a measure of the effect of the transaction on competition.[42] The agencies employ the Herfindahl-Hirschman Index (HHI) to assess market concentration; the HHIs provide a numerical method for assessing how concentrated a market is as well as how the transaction will affect concentration.[43]

In a traditional analysis, then, the government assesses the competitive effects of a transaction with a method that is focused around market definition: determining the relevant product and geographic markets, assessing the market shares of competitors in the market, and understanding the degree of concentration of the market as a proxy for the effect of the transaction on competition generally.

However, the agencies' 2010 joint guidelines deemphasize a market-focused analysis and provide the agencies with other tools to assess competitive effects.[44] These tools focus more directly on the likely effects of a transaction by looking at firm-specific evidence. That evidence includes, for example, analysis of win/loss records and other such evidence that can be used to assess the likely "upward pricing pressure" of the transaction. The agencies also will engage in direct comparison with analogous transactions in similar markets.[45]

In addition, there are a number of factors other than market structure that the agencies may consider in analyzing a horizontal transaction. For example, the reviewing agency might consider issues such as the ease with which companies can enter into the market and compete, the degree

---

likely provide rapid supply responses with direct competitive impact in the event of a SSNIP, without incurring significant sunk costs." *Id.* § 5.1.

42. *See generally id.* § 5.

43. The HHI is calculated by isolating competitors in a market, squaring each of their market shares, and adding the squares. Under the current guidelines, a market characterized by an HHI under 1500 is considered unconcentrated; a market with an HHI of 1500-2500 is considered to be moderately concentrated and a market with an HHI above 2500 is deemed highly concentrated. The agency also will calculate the change in HHI posttransaction, and depending upon the results, the agency may presume that the transaction raises competitive concerns. That presumption, however, may be rebutted by evidence that the transaction is unlikely to cnhance market power. *See id.* § 5.3.

44. 2010 HORIZONTAL MERGER GUIDELINES, *supra* note 4.

45. *See id.* §§ 6.1 (win/loss reports, diversion ratios, and upward pricing pressure), 2.1.2 (comparison with analogous mergers).

to which competitors' pricing is transparent to the market, and how powerful the merging companies' customers are in negotiating with the merging companies (i.e., so-called power buyers could prevent even a seller with high market share from exercising market power).[46] Ease of entry into the market is an especially important factor, because if it is easy for new firms to enter into the relevant market and compete, and if such entry is likely, it would be difficult for the merging companies to leverage market power in an anticompetitive way, for example by raising prices on consumers who have no other alternative than to stay with the company.[47]

Crucially, the agencies not only will assess the potential harms that may arise from a transaction; they also will consider the procompetitive benefits that could arise, such as cost-saving efficiencies or the potential for innovation.[48] Those procompetitive benefits in some instances can be a powerful means for countering agency doubts about a transaction. For example, some transactions can create significant efficiencies that are transaction-specific, that is, efficiencies that could not have been accomplished without the transaction.[49] Transactions also may create a potential for innovation that would not exist without the transaction, such as new or improved products possible solely by combining the enterprises.[50] While procompetitive benefits will not rescue a clearly anticompetitive transaction, they can be very helpful in ambiguous cases in which the parties can make a clear, credible case that customers will benefit from the transaction.[51]

---

46.    *See id.* § 8 (Powerful Buyers).

47.    *See id.* § 9 (Entry); *see, e.g.*, Complaint, United States v. AT&T, No. 1:11-cv-01560 (D.D.C. Aug. 31, 2011) (challenging the proposed AT&T/T-Mobile transaction because, *inter alia*, entry into the relevant market would be difficult and unlikely to thwart the competitive harm resulting from proposed acquisition).

48.    *See* 2010 Horizontal Merger Guidelines, *supra* note 4, § 10 (Efficiencies).

49.    *See id.*

50.    *See id.*; *cf. id.* § 6.4 (Innovation and Product Variety) (raising potential competitive concerns about the potential for transactions to stymie innovation).

51.    *See, e.g.*, Press Release, Dep't of Justice, Statement of the Department of Justice's Antitrust Division on its Decision to Close its Investigation of the Merger of Delta Air Lines Inc. and Northwest Airlines Corporation (Oct. 29, 2008), *available at* http://www.justice.gov/atr/public/press_releases/2008/238849.htm (allowing the transaction between Delta

## C. We Want to Merge with or Acquire a Company That Is a Supplier or a Customer of Ours. Can We Do It?

The short answer is that most transactions of this type do not raise significant antitrust concerns. There are, of course, exceptions. In some recent cases the antitrust agencies have required the parties to provide assurances that they will not foreclose others from access to key suppliers or customers.

Transactions between firms that operate at different levels in the chain of production, and thus do not compete with each other, are considered "vertical" or non-horizontal transactions. Common examples include a transaction between a distributor and a manufacturer or a transaction between two manufacturers, one which produces an end product and the other which produces a component used to make that end product.

Antitrust agencies have issued far fewer challenges to vertical transactions than to horizontal. As a general matter, vertical transactions are viewed as less likely to harm competition because they do not reduce the number of competing firms.[52] Vertical transactions also may result in procompetitive efficiencies such as lowered transaction costs, economies of scale, and various types of synergies.

The federal antitrust agencies addressed vertical transactions in their 1984 *Non-Horizontal Merger Guidelines*,[53] but those guidelines have not been updated and are considered by many practitioners, and at least one former FTC chairman, to be out of date.[54] After 1984, all merger guidelines issued by the FTC and the DOJ have focused only on horizontal transactions.

---

Air Lines and Northwest Airlines to close after a six-month investigation, citing procompetitive benefits).

52. *See* Michael A. Salinger, Director, Fed. Trade Comm'n, Bureau of Econ., Is It Live or Is It Memorex? Models of Vertical Mergers and Antitrust Enforcement, Remarks Before the Association of Competition Economics Seminar on Non-Horizontal Mergers (Sept. 7, 2005), *available at* http://www.ftc.gov/speeches/salinger/050927isitlive.pdf.

53. NON-HORIZONTAL MERGER GUIDELINES, *supra* note 36.

54. Robert Pitofsky, A Conversation with Tim Muris and Bob Pitofsky, Discussion for the FTC 90th Anniversary Symposium (Sept. 22, 2004), *available at* http://www.ftc.gov/ftc/history/transcripts/040922transcript 003.pdf ("[M]y guiding principle in deciding which challenges to initiate was to ignore the vertical merger guidelines. They are hopelessly out of date, and they ought to be revisited.").

Antitrust agency concerns about vertical transactions typically focus on the potential risks of "foreclosure" or information sharing that may harm competition. Foreclosure refers to the ability to limit competitors' access to important sources of supply or demand, which in turn can inhibit competition. For example, a manufacturer acquiring a retailer could make it more difficult or expensive for competing manufacturers to sell their products through that retailer. Similarly, a retailer acquiring a manufacturer could make it difficult or expensive for competing retailers to obtain the manufacturer's product. These concerns tend to be significant only when there are relatively few alternative manufacturers or suppliers. Where reasonable and competitively viable alternatives exist, the risk of such foreclosure should not be meaningful.

Antitrust agencies also may be concerned that vertical transactions could serve to facilitate horizontal collusion by removing obstacles to effective coordination. An upstream supplier might be able to learn proprietary information about its rivals by merging with a customer that buys from several suppliers, and a downstream customer could similarly learn about its own competition by merging with a supplier. This ongoing access to competitors' current price information could allow a party to monitor other market participants and help enforce a cartel. Alternately, access to competitor information could enable a party to underbid its competitors using their pricing and bidding data or else to decrease individual incentives to innovate by providing access to rivals' proprietary technology information.

As described above, antitrust agencies have not offered recent guidance as to what type of vertical transactions are of particular concern. Several factors that appear to make an investigation and/or challenge more likely include the following:

- Merging suppliers or customers with large market shares, where there is more risk of increased costs to rivals from any potential foreclosures. This could include transactions with either a single dominant party in one market, or significant market shares by both upstream and downstream parties;

- Vertical transactions in industries with higher structural entry barriers, such as the defense or pharmaceutical industries, where there may be fewer market participants;

- Vertical transactions in industries subject to close antitrust scrutiny because of their importance to the economy or the interest of the agencies, e.g., the health care or telecommunications industries; and

- Credible complaints from either party's rivals or consumers.

When antitrust agencies do take action in response to a vertical transaction, rather than blocking the transaction they often will impose narrower "remedies designed to prevent conduct that might harm consumers while still allowing the efficiencies" from the vertical transaction.[55] The transaction may be permitted to continue, but the merged firm may be prohibited from denying competitors access to necessary manufacturing inputs or distribution outlets, or the agencies may establish a "firewall" to prevent companies from gaining access to a rival's competitively sensitive information.

For example, in 2011 the DOJ and the FCC permitted a transaction between Comcast (a distributor) and NBCUniversal (a content provider), subject to certain conditions.[56] The DOJ consent decree required NBCUniversal to make video content available to online video distributors without discrimination, a condition designed to protect the potential development of online rivals to Comcast. The FCC imposed similar online video distribution provisions and also established an arbitration process for resolving disputes between NBCUniversal and cable and satellite companies. The FCC determined that the combination created efficiencies serving the public interest, including synergies from increased economies of scale and reduced transaction costs from coordinating content with distribution.

Also in 2011 the DOJ permitted Google's acquisition of the travel search engine company ITA Software, subject to certain restrictions.[57] Google agreed to continue to license ITA's search engine technology to Google's competitors without discrimination, establish a firewall to prevent Google employees from accessing confidential competitive information, maintain ITA's R&D spending at its pretransaction level, and to resolve licensing fee disputes with Google's competitors through a

---

55.   U.S. DEP'T OF JUSTICE, ANTITRUST DIVISION POLICY GUIDE TO MERGER REMEDIES § I.B.2 (2011), *available at* http://www.justice.gov/atr/public/guidelines/272350.pdf.

56.   Final Judgment, United States v. Comcast Corp., No. 11-cv-00106 (RJL) (D.D.C. Sept. 1, 2011), *available at* http://www.justice.gov/atr/cases/f274700/274713.pdf; Memorandum Opinion & Order, Comcast Corp., MB Docket No. 10-56 (F.C.C. Jan. 20, 2011), *available at* http://hraunfoss.fcc.gov/edocs_public/attachmatch/FCC-11-4A1.pdf.

57.   Final Judgment, United States v. Google Inc., No. 11-cv-00688 (RLW) (D.D.C. Oct. 5, 2011), *available at* http://www.justice.gov/atr/cases/f275800/275897.pdf.

special arbitration process. It is worthy of note that antitrust authorities do not always require these types of conduct remedies when approving high-profile vertical transactions. For instance, Google's next major vertical transaction, its 2012 acquisition of Motorola Mobility (the manufacturer of smartphones for which Google provided the operating system), was approved by both U.S. and European antitrust agencies without any conditions.

### D. We Are Preparing to Present a New Transaction to the Board of Directors. What Should We Keep in Mind While Drafting That Presentation?

The most important consideration in preparing a presentation for the Board of Directors is, of course, ensuring that the document provides the Board with accurate, useful information that is required for an informed business decision.

In the United States parties should assume that Board presentations and similar high-level documents analyzing the transaction will be provided to the government as part of the transaction clearance process.[58]

The FTC and DOJ likely will review such documents closely in reviewing the transaction. The parties should carefully consider how they characterize the market and their competitors, because the presentation may shape the government's view of their transaction. The parties also may wish to discuss with management and their counsel how to present information to the Board on issues such as the relevant markets and market shares, their competitors' relative strengths and similarities to their company, how their competitors set prices, the effects of the transaction on consumer prices and on profit margins, and the effect of

---

58.    *See supra* part A.3.a.2 of this chapter; *see also* FED. TRADE COMM'N, ANTITRUST IMPROVEMENTS ACT NOTIFICATION AND REPORT FORM FOR CERTAIN MERGERS AND ACQUISITIONS: INSTRUCTIONS, *supra* note 18, at V, Item 4(c). Note that while parties may technically redact or withhold eligible documents containing legal advice as privileged communications, the government requires a statement of reasons for withholding the documents and details about the documents withheld. *See id.*; *see also* 16 C.F.R. § 803.3(d). Before asserting privilege over such documents, the parties may wish to confer with their antitrust counsel about strategies for cooperation with the government. For further commentary on these submissions, *see* STEPHEN M. AXINN ET AL., ACQUISITIONS UNDER THE HART-SCOTT-RODINO ANTITRUST IMPROVEMENTS ACT: A PRACTICAL ANALYSIS OF THE STATUTE & REGULATIONS § 8.05[11] (3d ed. 2011).

the transaction on innovation in the market. All of these factors, among others, may affect how the government analyzes the transaction, and ill-considered statements early in the process could constrain the parties and their counsel in arguing a different viewpoint to the government later during the review process.

Of course, this is not meant to suggest that parties should avoid preparing documents and presenting facts to the Board and senior management. And it certainly is not meant to suggest that the parties should be anything other than candid and accurate in such documents. The point is to ensure, to the extent possible, that documents are carefully prepared and accurate to avoid unnecessarily complicating antitrust review of the transaction.

## E. We Are Going Forward with a Merger or an Acquisition. What Can We Talk about during Due Diligence?

Antitrust authorities and courts have recognized that companies contemplating a transaction in good faith may sometimes need to share sensitive information so that the acquiring party (or both parties in the event of a merger) can determine the value of what is being acquired. Where required, and so long as parties observe certain limits and safeguards, some information can be safely exchanged during the negotiation and due diligence phases.[59] It is the role of legal counsel to help minimize the antitrust risks of such information sharing.

As a practical matter the analysis of such questions, which depend on the specific context and the type of information in question, can involve a sliding scale. To the extent that the information has little competitive significance, such as traditional information technology or human resources information, there generally is more leeway to exchange information even if there is not a critical need for it prior to closing. On the other hand, the more competitively sensitive the information is, the greater will be the burden on the merging parties to demonstrate that the information must be shared at a particular point during the due diligence or integration planning processes in order for the transaction to proceed.

---

59. *See, e.g.*, U.S. DEP'T OF JUSTICE & FED. TRADE COMM'N, COMMENTARY ON THE HORIZONTAL MERGER GUIDELINES (2006), at 59, *available at* http://www.ftc.gov/os/2006/03/CommentaryontheHorizontalMergerGuid elinesMarch2006.pdf ("The Agencies are mindful of the parties' need to provide sensitive efficiencies-related information and, in that vein, the Agencies note that the antitrust laws are flexible enough to allow the parties to adopt reasonable means to achieve that end lawfully.").

There are certain categories of information that have been identified as being particularly competitively sensitive.[60] Exchanges of this type of information raise the most significant issues in deals involving parties with a competitive overlap:

- Current prices; proposed price changes; price ranges; pricing strategies or formulas;
- Customer-specific or product-specific pricing; discounts; contract terms;
- Actual production levels for specific customers; plans to increase or decrease production;
- Costs or profit margins for specific products; supplier data;
- Wages; salaries; benefits;
- Customer lists;
- Strategic plans; new services; future bid proposals; research and development efforts; capital investment plans; and
- Detailed marketing strategies.

Generally speaking, there are certain categories of information that are less sensitive and present lower risks where sharing is necessary during transaction discussions, although companies should consult their legal counsel to review particular questions as they arise:

- Historical pricing information that is outdated or not indicative of current competitive pricing;
- Aggregated financial information by business or country (not by product) useful for defining synergies;
- General business descriptions; information about manufacturing facilities; general corporate overhead costs;
- Organizational charts; internal information technology systems; accounting methods; other information useful for integration of the organizations;

---

60.    *See generally* ABA SECTION OF ANTITRUST LAW, PREMERGER COORDINATION: THE EMERGING LAW OF GUN JUMPING AND INFORMATION EXCHANGE (William R. Vigdor ed., 2006); William Blumenthal, *The Scope of Permissible Coordination Between Merging Entities Prior to Consummation*, 63 ANTITRUST L.J. 1 (1994); Ilene Knable Gotts & Michael B. Miller, *Information Sharing and Joint Activities in the Pre-Consummation Context: How to Plan for the Post-Transaction Entity*, ANTITRUST REPORT 2 (March 1999).

- Human Resources information; employee personnel lists; performance reviews;
- Real estate information; environmental risks; pending legal claims; safety records; and
- Any information that is publicly available.

In *Omnicare, Inc. v. UnitedHealth Group*,[61] a federal appellate court confirmed that competitors may exchange competitively sensitive information where there is a legitimate business need to do so and where the parties apply appropriate limits and safeguards. The court in *Omnicare* explained that a premerger information exchange between competing health insurers did not violate the antitrust laws because the shared price information was aggregated and did not contain specific pricing strategies because such information was shared with only a small group of high-level executives less than a month before the signing of the merger agreement, because such information was legitimately necessary to value the transaction, and because the information exchanges were monitored by antitrust counsel.

In the absence of such business necessities and safeguards, antitrust agencies have taken action against merging parties for sharing competitively sensitive information prior to the closing period. For instance, in *Insilco Corp.*,[62] after an acquisition involving two major aluminum tube manufacturers in the United States, the FTC charged that prior to the closing of the transaction the companies improperly exchanged customer-specific price information, price formulas, and current and future pricing plans and strategies. Because the two companies were significant competitors in a concentrated industry, the government alleged that the information exchange had the potential to injure competition. While the transaction was ultimately consummated, the FTC and the parties entered into a consent agreement, that, in part, prohibited the parties from sharing certain sensitive information in future acquisitions unless aggregated by a third party.

Finally, counsel should keep in mind that the extent of information sharing permitted during the due diligence process may in some cases actually be greater than the amount of information sharing allowed after signing the purchase or merger agreement. In due diligence, there may be

---

61. Omnicare, Inc. v. UnitedHealth Grp., 629 F.3d 697, 710-11 (7th Cir. 2011).

62. Insilco Corp., No. C-3783 (F.T.C. Jan. 30, 1998), *available at* www.ftc.gov/os/caselist/c3783.htm.

certain business necessities for sharing competitively sensitive information so that parties can make correct valuation judgments. Those business justifications may no longer be valid after the agreement is signed, although there may be other justifications for exchanging information that is necessary for integration planning.

In general, counsel can reduce antitrust risks by using precautions such as the following:

- *Historical and aggregated information.* Counsel should consider whether it is feasible to limit the exchange of sensitive information to include only: (1) historical information that is outdated or not indicative of current competitive pricing, (2) aggregated data in which no specific products or customers can be identified, and (3) data which has been filtered and aggregated by third parties.
- *Clean teams.* When competitively sensitive information is shared, it is generally prudent to limit disclosure only to individuals who are not directly involved with any competitive business activities. This can be done either by creating internal company firewalls limiting information to a small group of personnel involved in transaction discussions, or by giving sensitive information only to outside accountants or investment bankers under strict confidentiality obligations.
- *Confidentiality agreements.* It is typical for companies to use confidentiality agreements to confirm that competitively sensitive information will be used solely for purposes of due diligence and integration planning.
- *Document recovery agreements.* Counsel should have a plan for how to handle due diligence documents if the deal fails. One commonly used approach involves marking all shared documents. The parties agree that if negotiations end without a closed transaction, all shared materials will be returned to their original source and all copies will be destroyed. It is also increasingly common to enforce strict security procedures to regulate access to electronic data "rooms" and to restrict dissemination of materials accessed electronically.
- *Business necessity.* As discussed above, the parties' flexibility to exchange competitively sensitive business information is enhanced to the extent there is a business necessity to share such information with certain select individuals in order for the transaction to proceed. Before agreeing to exchange such

information, parties should articulate and discuss with antitrust counsel the business reasons for exchanging the information and whether it is possible to defer exchanging such information until (or nearer to) the closing. Ideally, exchanges of competitively sensitive information can proceed "stepwise" so that, as parties come closer to closing the transaction, progressively more detailed and sensitive disclosures can be made as necessary.

## F. We Have Agreed to Acquire Another Company. What Measures Can We Take to Plan for Integration or to Ensure That the Seller Does Not Diminish the Value of the Business Before Closing?

During the period between signing and closing there are two separate questions to consider. First, are the parties doing anything that could be viewed as one party effectively taking ownership of the other, or the merged enterprise, before HSR clearance has been obtained?[63] This is referred to as "gun-jumping." Second, are the parties coordinating the businesses in a way that could violate the antitrust laws, whether such coordination occurs before or after HSR clearance?

The antitrust enforcement agencies recognize that some preclosing coordination activities are beneficial, and even necessary, for successful deal implementation.[64] Acquirers often are concerned that the value of

---

63.　The HSR Act requires parties to wait at least thirty days (fifteen days in the case of a cash tender offer or acquisitions subject to bankruptcy court approval) before consummating their transaction unless the waiting period is terminated earlier. *See supra* part A of this chapter. The purpose of the HSR Act is to maintain the competitive status quo while the agencies are given an opportunity to review prospective transactions for possible competitive problems and to decide whether to challenge them or to require some corrective action (such as asset divestitures) to be taken prior to clearance.

64.　*See, e.g.*, Paul Pautler, *The Effects of Mergers and Post-Merger Integration: A Review of Business Consulting Literature* (Jan. 21, 2003), *available at* http://www.ftc.gov/be/rt/businesreviewpaper.pdf (reviewing literature supporting the conclusion that early planning for integration is a critical component for successful transactions); William Blumenthal, The Rhetoric of Gun-Jumping, Remarks Before the Association of Corporate Counsel Greater New York Chapter Annual Antitrust Seminar (Nov. 10, 2005), *available at* http://www.ftc.gov/speeches/blumenthal/ 20051110gunjumping.pdf ("[W]e are mindful that many forms of premerger coordination are reasonable and even necessary and that care

the business being purchased may be lost or diminished between signing and closing, when the current owner of the asset may have different incentives than its future owner. Acquirers also often want to perform preclosing integration planning so as to be able to "hit the ground running" on the day of closing.

As a general rule, until the transaction is closed and the parties lose their separate identities they may plan for integration but may not stop competing against one another. Finding the proper balance between permissible preparatory activities and gun-jumping can involve difficult judgment calls. Listed below are some general principles,[65] although companies should consult their legal counsel to review particular questions as they arise.

- *Assumption of ownership.* Prior to receiving HSR approval, the acquiring company cannot assume "beneficial ownership" of the acquired business or assets. For example, the two parties should not hire or transfer substantial groups of each other's employees, and officers of one party should not be placed in a position of authority to approve or reject contractual terms of the other party's clients.
- *Price coordination.* Until closing the two parties should not coordinate or restrict prices or otherwise participate in activities that would be illegal if undertaken by separate entities. More detailed transition planning activities may be permitted in noncompeting business areas without horizontal overlaps, but counsel still should ensure that confidentiality agreements are signed to limit the use of any shared information to integration planning.
- *Ordinary course of business.* An acquirer generally can obligate the acquired entity to continue to operate in the ordinary course of business (e.g., not materially changing its business model) and maintain the corporate governance status quo (e.g., not increasing the compensation of directors or officers, transferring or acquiring assets, or settling material claims). The key is to ensure that restrictions are reasonable, in that they are necessary

---

needs to be taken not unduly to jeopardize the ability of merging firms to implement the transaction and achieve available efficiencies.").

65.    *See generally* William Blumenthal, *supra* note 64; Michael C. Naughton, *Gun-Jumping and Premerger Information Exchange: Counseling the Harder Questions,* ANTITRUST, Summer 2006, at 69.

to preserve the value of the business but do not enable the acquirer to exercise day-to-day control over the competitive operations of the acquired entity.

- *Joint courtesy calls.* The two parties generally can make joint courtesy calls to inform customers of the general benefits of the transaction and to answer any questions their customers might have. However, these joint courtesy calls should not curtail the current competition between the parties, for example, by coordinating their pricing or marketing. The parties can also convey information to the marketplace as to what the combined entity will look like following the closing, but the two parties should not hold themselves out as a single firm prior to closing.

- *Communication with employees.* Prior to HSR clearance and closing, the two generally can inform particular employees that they will be retained or released by the acquired company after closing, but it should be made clear to the target's employees that they are not reporting to the acquiring company's employees (or vice versa if the target's business will continue in operation).

- *Administrative departments.* The two parties generally can take steps to coordinate administrative functions to prepare for the postclosing environment, such as the two businesses' information technology systems, employee benefits, or human resources departments. However, these integration plans cannot actually be implemented prior to HSR clearance as this can raise issues of beneficial ownership where, for example, existing employees can be interviewed for postclosing positions but cannot actually be transferred from one business to the other.

The FTC and the DOJ have been particularly concerned about provisions giving one party what amounts to any pre-closing veto power over the business operations of another party. In 2010 the DOJ settled with Smithfield Foods for $900,000 after bringing a complaint alleging violations of the HSR Act in Smithfield's 2007 acquisition of Premium Standard Farms.[66] The DOJ alleged that in the period after a Second Request had been issued and prior to the closing date, Premium Standard had unlawfully transferred beneficial ownership to Smithfield by requiring Smithfield's consent before entering into new supply contracts,

---

66. Complaint, United States v. Smithfield Foods, No. 10-cv-00120 (D.D.C. Jan 21, 2010), *available at* http://www.justice.gov/atr/cases/f254300/254369.htm.

thereby prematurely giving Smithfield operational control over Premium Standard.

The Smithfield Foods case is not the only one in which the agencies have challenged acquirers that assume operational control over a target prior to closing. In 2006, the DOJ settled with Qualcomm for $1.8 million after alleging gun-jumping violations in Qualcomm's 2005 acquisition of Flarion Technologies.[67] The DOJ's complaint alleged that the merger agreement required Qualcomm to approve ordinary course licensing agreements, personnel decisions, and customer proposals, which effectively transferred operational control to Qualcomm in violation of the HSR Act.

Moreover, allegations of gun-jumping can rest upon strategic decisions beyond assumption of day-to-day operational control. In a 2003 gun-jumping settlement, Gemstar and TV Guide agreed to pay $5.7 million in civil penalties to settle charges asserted by the DOJ after their 2000 merger.[68] The DOJ's complaint alleged that, before the HSR waiting period had expired, the two companies had essentially combined their businesses by agreeing to allocate markets and customers between them and to fix prices and material terms offered to customers. The DOJ charged that this preclosing conduct violated both the gun-jumping concerns of the HSR Act and the general competition concerns of Section 1 of the Sherman Act.

Premerger coordination and information exchange issues do not lend themselves to bright line rules. Antitrust counsel must provide advice based on specific fact assessments. For more information, a comprehensive resource is the ABA Section of Antitrust Law's 2006 book, *Premerger Coordination: The Emerging Law of Gun Jumping and Information Exchange.*

### G. We Are Planning a Joint Venture or Strategic Alliance with Our Competitor. What Do We Need to Know?

The term "joint venture" is difficult to define. At one extreme, the Supreme Court has observed that an otherwise objectionable price-fixing

---

67.  Complaint for Civil Penalties for Violation of Premerger Reporting Requirements of the Hart-Scott-Rodino Act, United States v. Qualcomm Inc., No. 06CV00672 (D.D.C. Apr. 13, 2006), *available at* http://www.usdoj.gov/atr/cases/f215600/215608.htm.

68.  Complaint for Equitable Relief and Civil Penalties, United States v. Gemstar-TV Guide Int'l, No. 03CV00198 (D.D.C. Feb. 6, 2003), *available at* http://www.justice.gov/atr/cases/gemstar0.htm.

agreement among independent companies could be lawful where accurately characterized by the parties as a joint venture.[69] At the other extreme, a complete merger of two independent businesses into a combined business could be referred to as a joint venture. Most arrangements commonly referred to as joint ventures or strategic alliances fall somewhere between these two extremes and involve some form of cooperative behavior designed to create a new product or business or to enhance the efficiency of existing businesses, short of a full merger.

Courts and antitrust agencies conduct fact-specific analyses of the competitive risks of joint ventures. The FTC and the DOJ have recognized that joint ventures can create procompetitive effects, such as lower costs from economies of scale, synergies allowing more efficient research and development, and risk diversification.[70] At the same time, the courts and agencies also recognize that joint ventures can reduce competition that otherwise would exist between the parties, may increase the likelihood of collusion, or may foreclose competitors from access to resources or markets.[71]

## 1. General Overview

a. Applicable Statutes

Joint ventures are evaluated under several different provisions of the federal antitrust laws.

Section 1 of the Sherman Act prohibits "contracts" and "conspiracies" in restraint of trade.[72] A joint venture might raise issues under Section 1 both because the formation of the venture involves a "contract" and because the ongoing operations of the venture can require the joint action and agreement of the parties. As to the latter, certain joint ventures involve such a complete integration of the parties' economic interests, akin to a merger of the businesses, that the ongoing activities of the venture may be considered to be the activities of a single enterprise and thus outside the scope of Section 1. For example, the Supreme Court has held that a jointly owned and operated refiner and seller of gasoline

---

69. Arizona v. Maricopa Cnty. Med. Soc'y, 457 U.S. 332 (1982).
70. *See* Thomas A. Piraino, Jr., *Antitrust Aspects of Joint Ventures*, 66-2nd CORP. PRACTICE SERIES, at A-1, A-2 (2010).
71. *See id.*
72. Sherman Antitrust Act § 1, 26 Stat. 209 (codified as amended at 15 U.S.C. § 1).

constituted a single entity for antitrust purposes and thus its activities, including setting prices for the venture's outputs, were outside the scope of Section 1.[73] On the other hand, the Court found in another case that the National Football League was not acting as a single entity when it chose an exclusive licensee for team apparel, because the thirty-two teams in the league were separate and independent economic actors with respect to the licensing of their own intellectual property and the league's activities thus were subject to scrutiny under Section 1.[74]

While Section 1 of the Sherman Act governs concerted action, a joint venture also might be analyzed under Section 2 of the Sherman Act if the formation or operation of the joint venture empowers members to act as a single party and creates or threatens to create a monopoly.[75]

Depending on the corporate form used (e.g., corporation, partnership), a joint venture's formation may require notification under the HSR Act if it involves the acquisition of assets or voting securities.[76] Notice to the European Commission under the merger regulations also may be required.[77]

A joint venture or strategic alliance that results in the creation of a new entity may be subject to Section 7 of the Clayton Act which prohibits transactions that may have "the effect" of "substantially [lessening] competition, or [tending] to create a monopoly."[78] In making that assessment the agencies may consider, under the FTC's *Guidelines for Collaborations Among Competitors*, whether the parties are likely to undertake anticompetitive actions pursuant to the collaboration.

Finally, Section 5 of the FTC Act prohibits unfair methods of competition and also may be applicable to the formation or operation of joint ventures.[79]

We recommend that parties consult with their antitrust counsel to determine which of these statutes is relevant in a particular case.

---

73.    Texaco Inc. v. Dagher, 547 U.S. 1 (2006).

74.    American Needle, Inc. v. NFL, 130 S. Ct. 2201 (2010).

75.    15 U.S.C. § 2; *see, e.g.*, United States v. Am. Airlines, 743 F.2d 1114, 1122 (5th Cir. 1984) (noting "if . . . the firm proposing [the merger or joint venture] acts with a specific intent to monopolize, then we see no reason why § 2 liability should not attach").

76.    15 U.S.C. § 18(a); *see supra* part A of this chapter for a more in-depth discussion of the HSR notification analysis.

77.    Council Regulation (EC) No. 139/2004, 2004 O.J. (L24) 1.

78     15 U.S.C. § 18.

79.    15 U.S.C. § 45.

b.   Enforcement Agency Guidelines

In 2000 the FTC and the DOJ jointly issued their *Guidelines for Collaborations Among Competitors.*[80] The guidelines explain that many joint ventures among competitors can be procompetitive. On the other hand, ventures that principally restrict or eliminate competition, such as price-fixing or output agreements, bid rigging, or market allocation from dividing customers, suppliers, territories, or lines of commerce, all are likely to raise significant concerns and be considered to be per se unlawful by the antitrust agencies. For a third group of joint ventures that are not per se illegal, but that the reviewing agency believes are likely to have anticompetitive effects, the agency will consider whether the parties have offered credible procompetitive justifications.

If parties to a joint venture or strategic alliance can identify a credible and procompetitive justification, the agency likely would undertake a rule of reason analysis. This analysis involves defining relevant markets, measuring any creation of market power, examining the competitive effects of potential new entrants, and balancing the joint venture's potential anticompetitive effects against any offsetting procompetitive benefits. Parties to the transaction should be prepared to describe to the antitrust agencies the procompetitive efficiencies of the joint venture and to explain how their proposed joint venture is necessary to achieve those benefits. After concluding these analyses, the reviewing agency will then decide whether or not to challenge the joint venture in court, or in some cases to work with the parties to identify conditions on which the venture can proceed without challenge.

c.   Collateral Restraints

Joint venture participants sometimes agree to restrict or eliminate competition between the venture and its participants or between the participants themselves. Such restrictions may include geographic or product market limitations, agreements on the price or output of the venture's products, restrictions on advertising and the like. Courts and antitrust agencies have recognized that, although such agreements might create significant antitrust concerns outside the context of a joint venture, certain restraints may be permissible where they are reasonably

---

80.   FED. TRADE COMM'N & U.S. DEP'T OF JUSTICE, ANTITRUST GUIDELINES FOR COLLABORATIONS AMONG COMPETITORS (2000) [hereinafter GUIDELINES FOR COLLABORATIONS], *available at* http://www.ftc.gov/os/2000/04/ftcdojguidelines.pdf.

necessary (or "ancillary") to achieve the joint venture's procompetitive benefits, such as lower prices or enhanced quality and efficiency.[81] In determining whether a restraint is reasonably ancillary to a legitimate joint venture, courts and antitrust authorities may consider not only the extent to which the restraint is necessary to achieve the venture's goals, but also whether there were less restrictive alternatives that would provide the same or similar benefits without unduly limiting competition.[82] It is therefore important that all aspects of a joint venture, including such collateral restraints, be examined by antitrust counsel.

d.   Information Sharing

Joint venture participants must take precautions when exchanging competitively sensitive information. Antitrust agencies may infer an improper pricing or output agreement between collaborating competitors from any unnecessary sharing of detailed price or cost information. For that reason, competitors in a joint venture should limit their exchange of such competitively sensitive information to that which is essential to the joint venture.

## 2.  *Specific Types of Joint Ventures*

Because joint ventures can vary so widely, it is worth noting that different types of collaborations may be treated differently by the antitrust authorities.

a.   Research and Development Joint Ventures

R&D joint ventures generally are treated favorably by antitrust agencies because they often create procompetitive efficiencies through economies of scale, the pooling of complementary technologies and

---

81.   *See id.*; *see also* DOJ & FTC HEALTH CARE GUIDELINES, *supra* note 37 (requiring that collateral agreements contained in certain joint ventures be "reasonably necessary" to achieve stated efficiencies); U.S. DEP'T OF JUSTICE & FEDERAL TRADE COMM'N ANTITRUST GUIDELINES FOR THE LICENSING OF INTELLECTUAL PROPERTY (1995) [hereinafter INTELLECTUAL PROPERTY GUIDELINES] (considering whether "restraint in a licensing arrangement" is "reasonably necessary to achieve procompetitive benefits")      ,       *available       at* http://www.justice.gov/atr/public/guidelines/558.htm.

82.   *See* GUIDELINES FOR COLLABORATIONS, *supra* note 80.

knowledge, and the sharing of costs and risks. A specific statute limits antitrust liability to single, as opposed to treble, damages where the federal agencies are notified of the R&D venture.[83]

However, R&D joint ventures may raise antitrust concerns if they have the potential to slow the pace of innovation or if they are used as a "contract or conspiracy, in restraint of trade" in violation of Section 1 of the Sherman Act.[84] In particular, antitrust agencies may scrutinize R&D joint ventures where the participants stop competing with one another in the market in which the venture operates, where one of the joint venture participants already possesses significant market power over an existing product, or where preexisting requirements, such as the need for FDA approval, may make it more difficult for new entrants to "catch up" to the joint venture.

### b.  Joint Purchasing Arrangements

Joint purchasing arrangements are in many instances viewed favorably by antitrust agencies because joint purchasing can reduce costs and improve efficiencies to the benefit of consumers. However, the FTC and the DOJ may become concerned about such competitor arrangements when they account for a large percentage of the purchasing market and can yield significant buying power. The government may be concerned that these ventures will drive prices below competitive and sustainable levels, thus potentially causing competitive injury in the sellers' market.

### c.  Joint Selling or Marketing Arrangements

Joint selling or marketing arrangements between competitors generally receive heightened scrutiny by antitrust agencies, particularly those that prevent participants from selling outside of the venture and provide for coordinated pricing and output decisions. Concerns about anticompetitive effects, such as the elimination of comparative advertising, might be reduced if the joint venture also has procompetitive benefits. For example, if a joint venture generates efficiencies such as the ability to market a product that the participants could not have otherwise sold independently, then the joint venture's procompetitive virtues may outweigh its anticompetitive risks.

---

83.  *See* National Cooperative Research and Production Act of 1993, 15 U.S.C. §§ 4301-4305.
84.  *See* INTELLECTUAL PROPERTY GUIDELINES, *supra* note 81.

d.  Accountable Care Organizations

Under the Patient Protection and Affordable Health Care Act of 2010,[85] health care providers are encouraged to form integrated organizations known as Accountable Care Organizations (ACOs) to offer joint services in order to coordinate treatment, reduce costs, and improve the quality of patient care. ACOs are not immune from the antitrust laws. Although the FTC and the DOJ have recognized ACOs' benefits, they have also explained that these competitor collaborations may raise certain concerns, such as the potential for collusion outside of the ACO's operations or the potential for the tying of ACO services to the purchase of those providers' non-ACO services.[86]

e.  Fully Integrated Joint Ventures

Joint ventures that completely integrate all aspects of two businesses are evaluated similarly to horizontal mergers.[87] Antitrust agencies likely will focus on any reduction of competition in a given market, the potential exclusion of competitors from access to the joint venture's participants, and the potential for reduced output or higher prices for downstream customers.

## H.  Where Can I Go for More Information?

### 1.  *Regulatory Approvals of Transactions*

- ABA Section of Antitrust Law, *Merger Review Process* (2012);
- ABA Section of Antitrust Law, *Premerger Notification Practice Manual* (4th ed. 2007);
- Global Competition Review, *Merger Control 2013* (2012);
- Federal Trade Commission, *Antitrust Improvements Act Notification and Report Form for Certain Mergers and Acquisitions: Instructions*, at V, Item (4)(c) (effective Aug. 18,

---

85.  Pub. L. No. 111-148, 124 Stat. 119 (2010).
86.  *See* Statement of Antitrust Enforcement Policy Regarding Accountable Care Organizations Participating in the Medicare Shared Savings Program, 76 Fed. Reg. 67, 026 (Oct. 28, 2011), *available at* http://www.justice.gov/atr/public/health_care/279568.pdf.
87.  This means that the merger analysis of Section 7 of the Clayton Act discussed earlier applies. *See supra* part A of this chapter; *see also* 15 U.S.C. § 18.

2011), *available at* http://www.ftc.gov/bc/hsr/hsrform-instructions1_0_0.pdf;

- Press Release, Federal Trade Commission, *FTC Announces Revised Thresholds for Clayton Act Antitrust Reviews for 2013* (Jan. 10, 2013), *available at* http://www.ftc.gov/opa/2012/01/clayton.shtm.

## 2. Acquisition of a Competitor

- U.S. Department of Justice & Federal Trade Commission, *Horizontal Merger Guidelines* (2010), *available at* http://www.justice.gov/atr/public/guidelines/hmg-2010.html;
- U.S. Department of Justice & Federal Trade Commission, *Statements of Antitrust Enforcement Policy in Health Care* (1996), *available at* http://www.justice.gov/atr/public/guidelines/0000.htm.

## 3. Acquisition of a Supplier

- U.S. Department of Justice & Federal Trade Commission, *Non-Horizontal Merger Guidelines* (1984), *available at* http://www.usdoj.gov/atr/public/guidelines/2614.htm.

## 4. Presentation of a New Transaction to the Board of Directors

- Stephen M. Axinn et al., *Acquisitions Under the Hart-Scott-Rodino Antitrust Improvements Act* § 8.05[11] (3d ed. 2011);
- Federal Trade Commission, *Antitrust Improvements Act Notification and Report Form for Certain Mergers and Acquisitions: Instructions*, at V, Item (4)(c) (effective Aug. 18, 2011), *available at* http://www.ftc.gov/bc/hsr/hsrform-instructions1_0_0.pdf.

## 5. Due Diligence

- ABA Section of Antitrust Law, *Premerger Coordination: The Emerging Law of Gun Jumping and Information Exchange* (William R. Vigdor ed., 2006);
- U.S. Department of Justice & Federal Trade Commission, *Commentary on the Horizontal Merger Guidelines* (2006),

*available        at*        http://www.ftc.gov/os/2006/03/
CommentaryontheHorizontalMergerGuidelinesMarch2006.pdf.

## 6. Integration Planning

- ABA Section of Antitrust Law, *Premerger Coordination: The Emerging Law of Gun Jumping and Information Exchange* (William R. Vigdor ed., 2006);
- William Blumenthal, *The Rhetoric of Gun-Jumping*, Remarks Before the Association of Corporate Counsel Greater New York Chapter Annual Antitrust Seminar (November 10, 2005), *available        at*        http://www.ftc.gov/speeches/blumenthal/20051110gunjumping.pdf.

## 7. Joint Ventures and Strategic Alliances with Competitors

- U.S. Department of Justice & Federal Trade Commission, *Antitrust Guidelines For Collaborations Among Competitors* (2000), *available        at*        http://www.ftc.gov/os/2000/04/ftcdojguidelines.pdf;
- Thomas A. Piraino, Jr., *Antitrust Aspects of Joint Ventures*, 66-2nd *Corporate Practice Series* (2010);
- ABA Section of Antitrust Law, *Antitrust Law Developments* (7th ed. 2012);
- ABA Section of Antitrust Law, *Joint Ventures: Antitrust Analysis of Collaborations Among Competitors* (2006).

## CHAPTER IV

# PRICING

## A. We Want to Create and Implement a New Price Discount Scheme for Our Customers That Gives Some Customers Better Prices Than Others. What Antitrust Principles Do We Need to Keep in Mind?

Section 2 of the Clayton Act,[1] as amended by the Robinson-Patman Act,[2] is the principal federal statute addressing price discrimination. The Robinson-Patman Act prohibits the sale of two products of like grade and quality at different prices to two different buyers where the price difference may result in injury to competition.

A prima facie case of discrimination under the Robinson-Patman Act is established when the following elements are satisfied:

- The goods involved in either the sale to the "favored customer" or the sale to a competing "disfavored customer" are "in commerce"—meaning they cross a state line.[3]
- The buyers pay different prices.[4] "Price" under Section 2(a) is the ultimate purchase price, net of all discounts, rebates, allowances, payment terms, and credits.[5]
- A single seller makes at least two completed sales to different

---

1. Clayton Antitrust Act of 1914, Pub. L. No. 63-212, 38 Stat. 730 (1914) (codified at 15 U.S.C. § 13).
2. Pub. L. No. 74-692, 49 Stat. 1526 (1936) (codified at 15 U.S.C. §§ 13–13b, 21a). Section 1 of the Robinson-Patman Act generally amended Section 2 of the Clayton Act.
3. *See, e.g.*, Gulf Oil Corp. v. Copp Paving Co., 419 U.S. 186, 194-95 (1974).
4. *See, e.g.*, FTC v. Anheuser-Busch, Inc., 363 U.S. 536, 549 (1960).
5. *See, e.g.*, Conoco Inc. v. Inman Oil Co., 774 F.2d 895, 901–02 (8th Cir. 1985).

purchasers.[6]

- The products are of "like grade and quality." Products meet this test if they have the same (or similar) physical and performance characteristics. Differences in brand name, packaging, or labeling of the products do not sufficiently distinguish them for purposes of the Act.[7]

- The "products" in question are tangible goods, not intangible items such as services.[8] Mixed transactions involving goods and services are considered tangible goods if the goods component of the package "predominates," i.e., the tangible goods composed "the crux of the transaction" and were not merely "incidental" to the purchase of a service.[9] When a contract includes both the right to distribute a commodity and the purchase of the commodity itself, the product purchase satisfies the tangible goods element.[10]

- The transactions must involve the *sale* of products. The Act does not apply to leases, consignments, or product swaps.[11]

- The price differential threatens to injure competition. Competitive injury can occur at the "primary line" of the distribution chain (where the alleged victim is a competitor of the seller) or at the "secondary line" of the distribution chain (if the injured party is a competitor of the favored buyer). In a primary-line case, the evidence must show injury to competition (as opposed to a single competitor) due to

---

6.   The two completed sales also must be reasonably contemporaneous in time. *See, e.g.*, Airweld, Inc. v. Airco, Inc., 742 F.2d 1184, 1191 (9th Cir. 1984).

7.   *See, e.g.*, FTC v. Borden Co., 383 U.S. 637, 639–47 (1966).

8.   *See, e.g.*, Metro Commc'ns Co. v. Ameritech Mobile Commc'ns, 984 F.2d 739, 745 (6th Cir. 1993) (cellular telephone service not a commodity); *see also* Ambook Enters. v. Time Inc., 612 F.2d 604, 609–10 (2d Cir. 1979) (sale of retail newspaper advertising not a commodity).

9.   *See, e.g.*, First Comics, Inc. v. World Color Press, 884 F.2d 1033, 1037–38 (7th Cir. 1989).

10   Innomed Labs v. ALZA Corp., 368 F.3d 148, 156–61 (2d Cir. 2004) (Robinson-Patman Act applies to sale of patented pharmaceuticals sold with exclusive distribution rights).

11.  *See, e.g.*, Export Liquor Sales v. Ammex Warehouse Co., 426 F.2d 251, 252 (6th Cir. 1970) (leases); Rebel Oil Co. v. Atl. Richfield Oil Co., 146 F.3d 1088, 1094 (9th Cir. 1998) (swaps).

predatory pricing by the seller.[12] Proof of injury in a secondary-line case requires a showing of competition between the favored and disfavored buyers.[13] Thus, there can be no secondary-line injury where the two buyers compete for different sets of customers or in different geographic markets.[14] The courts of appeal are split on whether proof of injury to a single competitor of a favored buyer establishes prima facie injury to competition in a secondary-line case or whether injury to competition more broadly is required at the secondary-line level.[15] An inference of injury to competition may be established by proof of "a substantial price discrimination between competing purchasers over time."[16]

Even if a prima facie case of price discrimination is established, a company alleged to have engaged in a Robison-Patman Act violation has numerous potential defenses. For example, the scheme may be defensible if the discounted price was offered in order to "meet competition," i.e., a seller was acting to meet, but not beat, a competitor's price; is justified based on cost-savings; resulted from "changing market conditions," i.e., changing conditions that affect the

---

12.  *See, e.g.*, Brooke Grp. v. Brown & Williamson Tobacco Corp., 509 U.S. 209, 221–22 (1993).

13.  Shell Co. (P.R.) v. Los Frailes Serv. Station, 605 F.3d 10, 25 (1st Cir. 2010).

14.  *See, e.g.*, Volvo Trucks N. Am. v. Reeder-Simco GMC, Inc., 546 U.S. 164, 178–79 (2006) (no finding of competitive injury because purchasers did not compete for the same retail customers).

15.  *Compare* George Haug Co. v. Rolls Royce Motor Cars, 148 F.3d 136, 143–44 (2d Cir. 1998) (injury to individual competitor sufficient to establish secondary-line competitive injury), Chroma Lighting v. GTE Prods. Corp., 111 F.3d 653, 658 (9th Cir. 1997) (same), Coastal Fuels of P.R. v. Caribbean Petroleum Corp., 79 F.3d 182, 189 (1st Cir. 1996) (same), J.F. Feeser, Inc. v. Serv-A-Portion, Inc., 909 F.2d 1524, 1535 (3d Cir. 1990) (same), *and* Alan's of Atlanta, Inc. v. Minolta Corp., 903 F.2d 1414, 1418 n.6 (11th Cir. 1990), *reh'g denied*, 929 F.2d 704 (11th Cir. 1991) (same), *with* Boise Cascade Corp. v. FTC, 837 F.2d 1127, 1144 (D.C. Cir. 1988) (injury to competition required for secondary-line violation), Richard Short Oil Co. v. Texaco, Inc., 799 F.2d 415, 420 (8th Cir. 1986) (same), *and* Motive Parts Warehouse v. Facet Enters., 774 F.2d 380, 393-95 (10th Cir. 1985) (same).

16.  *See, e.g.*, Falls City Indus. v. Vanco Beverage, 460 U.S. 428, 435 (1983) (citing FTC v. Morton Salt Co., 334 U.S. 37, 46, 50-51 (1948)).

marketability of a good or the market for a good when setting prices; or was "functionally available" to all competing customers. Those potential defenses are discussed in more detail in Questions B and C below.

## B. Under What Circumstances Can We Offer Our Large Customers Discounts That We Don't Make Available to Our Small Customers? If It Is Cheaper for Us to Sell to Our Large Customers, Can We Offer the Large Customers a Special Discount?

Volume discounts are not a defense to price discrimination under the Robinson-Patman Act unless they are justified by differences in the cost of manufacture, sale, or delivery resulting from the differing methods or quantities in which the goods are sold or delivered, or the discount is functionally available, as a practical matter, to all customers.[17]

An "availability" defense can be asserted if the lower price offered to the favored buyer is, as a practical matter, available to the disfavored buyer, but that buyer fails to take advantage of it. A discount is functionally available to a disfavored buyer if the disfavored buyer knows about the offer, and the lower price is actually, not just theoretically, available to the disfavored purchaser.[18] "Share of shelf space"[19] discounts normally meet these conditions. A volume discount program might not be actually available to a purchaser if the latter is unable to purchase enough volume to earn the discount.[20] However, a minimum purchase requirement well

---

17.  *See* 15 U.S.C. § 13(a); FTC v. Morton Salt Co., 334 U.S. 37, 42-43 (1948).

18.  *See, e.g.*, Smith Wholesale Co. v. R.J. Reynolds Tobacco Co., 477 F.3d 854, 872 (6th Cir. 2007) (discount program based on market share goals was functionally available to all customers).

19.  *See id.* (discount program based on the amount of buyer's share of its retail shelf space dedicated to seller's products, as compared to products of seller's competitors, was functionally available to all buyers).

20.  *Morton Salt*, 334 U.S. at 42-43 (quantity discount was not functionally available to individual customers that could not purchase enough volume to qualify for the quantity discounts enjoyed by larger customers).

within the means of the average dealer may not be considered discriminatory.[21]

A "cost-justification" defense to price discrimination is available where the seller can show that the discount it provided to the favored buyer was not greater than the savings the seller enjoyed because the buyer purchased certain quantities of product or purchased through certain methods.[22] Volume discounts thus may only qualify for the cost-justification defense if the seller can establish that the additional volume purchased allowed it to reduce its manufacturing, selling, or delivery costs.[23] For example, a customer that agrees to pick up a purchased product at the seller's factory or to receive full carload deliveries may be eligible for a discount, provided that the discount is equal to or less than the delivery costs avoided by the seller.[24] Where a plaintiff has established a prima facie case, the seller has the burden of proving the cost-justification defense through a prediscount cost study that demonstrates actual cost savings that would be generated by the sale to the favored purchaser; cost-justification defenses constructed after the discrimination occurs face a relatively high standard of proof.[25] This rigorous cost study requirement has limited the utility of the cost-justification defense.

The seller need not account for the cost justification on a customer-by-customer basis, but must group customers based on similarities "as to make the averaging of the cost of dealing with the group a valid and reasonable indicium of the cost of dealing with any specific group member."[26] Within these tailored cost groups, the seller must show legally cognizable cost savings that fully justify the price discount.[27] Many types of cost differentials can be used to support a cost-justification defense, including differences in

---

21. *See* Bouldis v. U.S. Suzuki Motor Corp., 711 F.2d 1319, 1326 (6th Cir. 1983) (minimum of four to eight motorcycles).

22. 15 U.S.C. § 13(a).

23. *See, e.g.*, Acadia Motors v. Ford Motor Co., 844 F. Supp. 819, 831 (D. Me. 1994), *aff'd in part and rev'd in part on other grounds*, 44 F.3d 1050 (1st Cir. 1995).

24. *See Morton Salt*, 334 U.S. at 48.

25. *See, e.g.*, Philadelphia Carpet Co., 64 F.T.C. 762, 776 (1964) ("when, as here, the cost justification defense is constructed post complaint . . . the proponent . . . must be held to a relatively high standard of proof"), *aff'd* 343 F.2d 994 (3d Cir. 1965).

26. United States v. Borden Co., 370 U.S. 460, 469 (1962).

27. *See id.* at 468-71; *Morton Salt*, 334 U.S. at 48.

manufacture, sale, or delivery costs.[28] The cost justification must be based on actual costs and documented in sufficient detail to show the passing on of cost savings.[29]

A lower price also may be justified by proof that the large buyer performed a "function" that relieved the seller of costs or raised the buyer's costs. Like the cost-justification defense, the functional discount defense allows the seller to pass along cost savings generated by a buyer that performs certain functions for the seller, as long as the savings and the discount are reasonably related. The functional discount defense may, for example, justify the grant of a lower price to a wholesaler than to a retailer of the same product based on a reasonable reimbursement of the wholesaler's higher costs.[30] To succeed, the seller must show that the discount to the favored buyer was reasonably related to the cost or value of services performed by the buyer.[31]

## C. Can We Charge One of Our Best Customers a Lower Price? Every Other Competitor Is Offering Them a Discount.

Charging the "best" customer a lower price may result in prima facie price discrimination. However, this question raises a possible "meeting competition" defense (other potential defenses may be available as well). The "meeting competition" defense permits a seller to offer discriminatory discounts to meet the "equally low price of a competitor."[32] The defendant has the burden of proving it had a *good faith* basis[33] for meeting the competitive offer, but not beating

---

28.    15 U.S.C. § 13(a); Morton v. Nat'l Dairy Prods. Corp., 414 F.2d 403, 406 (3d Cir. 1969).

29.    Texaco Inc. v. Hasbrouck, 496 U.S. 543, 561 n.18 (1990); *Borden*, 370 U.S. at 469.

30.    *Hasbrouck*, 496 U.S. at 561. For guidelines on using functional discounts as a defense to a Section 2(a) claim, see David G. Hemminger, *Cost Justification—A Defense With New Applications*, 59 ANTITRUST L.J. 827, 846–48 (1991).

31.    *See Hasbrouck*, 496 U.S. at 562.

32.    15 U.S.C. § 13(b).

33.    United States v. U.S. Gypsum Co., 438 U.S. 422, 453-55 (1978) (indicia of good faith to meet competition include: (1) whether the seller "had received reports of similar discounts from other customers"; (2) whether the seller "was threatened with a termination of purchases if the discount were not met"; (3) whether the seller made "[e]fforts to corroborate the reported discount by seeking documentary evidence or by appraising its

it.[34]

A successful meeting competition defense requires a factual showing that would allow a "reasonable and prudent person" to find that the granting of the disparate price would in fact meet the equally low price of a competitor.[35] The seller must receive information about the competitive offer from a reliable source, typically the customer to whom the offer was made.[36] (Note, however, that attempts by the seller to verify a price through direct contact with a competitor may be construed as evidence of a price-fixing agreement and can therefore lead to liability under Section 1 of the Sherman Act and should thus be avoided.[37]) As a consequence, a seller wishing to meet a competitor's offer should make specific inquiries to the customer to determine key terms of the competitive offer, such as the identity of the competitor, the nature of the product, the price or discount offered, and the duration of the offer. The seller should try to get this information in writing, and if not available, contemporaneously record this information (including its source) in preparation for a possible challenge to its differential price.[38]

A seller may respond to a competitor's price across an entire geographic area, such as a state or region.[39] The defense may be used to retain an existing customer or to gain a new one. The seller's price may be reduced to meet the competitor's price, but not to beat it. In some unusual situations, an equal price may in fact "beat" the competitor's price, once quality differences are considered.[40] Finally,

---

reasonableness in terms of available market data"; and (4) whether the seller had "past experience with the particular buyer in question").

34. Falls City Indus. v. Vanco Beverage, 460 U.S. 428, 446 (1983).

35. *See* FTC v. A. E. Staley Mfg. Co., 324 U.S. 746, 759−60 (1945).

36. *See* Great Atl. & Pac. Tea Co. v. FTC, 440 U.S. 69, 84 (1979).

37. *United States Gypsum Company*, 438 U.S. at 451−58.

38. *See* Reserve Supply Corp. v. Owens-Corning Fiberglass Corp., 971 F.2d 37, 40−48 (7th Cir. 1992).

39. *Falls City Industries*, 460 U.S. at 442.

40. *See* Power Replacements Corp. v. Air Preheater Co., 356 F. Supp. 872, 890, 898 (E.D. Pa. 1973) (manufacturer's price, though nominally higher than those of its competitors, could beat its competition because the manufacturer's product commands a premium); *see also* Porto Rican Am. Tobacco Co. v. Am. Tobacco Co., 30 F.2d 234, 237 (2d Cir. 1929) (manufacturer-of-premium-brand-cigarettes' price reduction to the level of manufacturer of poorer quality cigarettes was designed to beat the competitor in violation of Section 2 of the Clayton Act).

the defense is available even if the seller elects to meet competing offers to some customers, but not others.[41]

### D. We Want to Offer a "Loss Leader"—a Product That We Are Willing to Price Below Our Costs Because It Will Get Customers Interested in Our Entire Product Line. Can We Do That?

While price reductions can be procompetitive and benefit consumers, a "loss leader" or other pricing strategy resulting in below-cost pricing can give rise to a claim of predatory pricing—i.e., "pricing below an appropriate measure of cost for the purpose of eliminating competitors in the short run and reducing competition in the long run."[42] Unlawful predatory pricing consists of two elements: pricing below an appropriate measure of costs; and eventual probable recoupment of losses via supracompetitive prices.[43] However, "loss leaders" involving below-cost pricing without the intent to recoup losses through supracompetitive prices are not sufficient to sustain a predatory pricing claim under the Robinson-Patman Act or Section 2 of the Sherman Act.[44]

There is no Supreme Court precedent or consensus among courts or commentators as to the correct measure of "cost" to be used in assessing potential predatory pricing. Some commentators have advocated the use of marginal cost as the appropriate cost measure,[45] but due to the difficulties of measuring marginal cost, courts instead

---

41.   *Falls City Industries*, 460 U.S. at 445.
42.   Cargill, Inc. v. Monfort of Colo., Inc., 479 U.S. 104, 117 (1986).
43.   *See* Pacific Bell Tel. Co. v. Linkline Commc'ns, 555 U.S. 438, 451 (2009); Brooke Grp. v. Brown & Williamson Tobacco Corp., 509 U.S. 209, 222–24 (1993). In a primary-line Robinson-Patman Act case, a plaintiff need show only that the defendant had a "reasonable prospect" of recoupment; Section 2 of the Sherman Act requires a "dangerous probability" of recoupment. *Brooke Group*, 509 U.S. at 224.
44.   *See, e.g.*, Parish Oil Co. v. Dillon Cos., 523 F.3d 1244, 1254 (10th Cir. 2008) (distinguishing loss leaders from predatory pricing and noting that loss leaders can have legitimate economic purposes and effects—e.g., the loss on the "leader" may be offset by gains in customer goodwill and loyalty as well as the sale of other items at regular or inflated prices).
45.   *See, e.g.*, Phillip Areeda & Donald F. Turner, *Predatory Pricing & Related Practices Under Section 2 of the Sherman Act*, 88 HARV. L. REV. 697 (1975).

tend to use average variable cost.[46] However, average variable cost is not the sole potential measure of appropriate cost,[47] and even prices above average variable cost have the potential to be found predatory.[48]

The second element of a predatory pricing case, recoupment, requires a showing that the below-cost pricing is capable of causing a rival to exit the market, and that following this forced exit, the market would be susceptible to sustained monopoly pricing, i.e., pricing at a level higher than in a competitive market.[49] Temporary promotional discounts typically do not raise predatory pricing or other anticompetitive concerns because there is little risk that the limited promotional price will drive competition from the market and allow for recoupment.[50]

Certain state antitrust statutes separately address the issue of sales below cost and loss leaders. Such statutes are state specific, but typically include a requirement of anticompetitive intent.[51]

---

46.  *See, e.g.*, Spirit Airlines v. Nw. Airlines, 431 F.3d 917, 938 (6th Cir. 2005) (pricing below average variable cost establishes a prima facie case of predation); Stearns Airport Equip. Co. v. FMC Corp., 170 F.3d 518, 532 (5th Cir. 1999) (same); Morgan v. Ponder, 892 F.2d 1355, 1360 (8th Cir. 1989) (same); Kelco Disposal v. Browning-Ferris Indus. of Vt., 845 F.2d 404, 407 (2d Cir. 1988) (same), *aff'd*, 492 U.S. 257 (1989).

47.  *See, e.g.*, United States v. AMR Corp., 335 F.3d 1109, 1120 (10th Cir. 2003) (declining to dictate a definitive cost measure for all cases).

48.  *See, e.g.*, Transamerica Computer Co. v. IBM, 698 F.2d 1377, 1388 (9th Cir. 1983) (cost categories may be used to allocate burden of proof, but prices above average variable cost or even average total cost may be shown to be predatory).

49.  Brooke Grp. v. Brown & Williamson Tobacco Corp., 509 U.S. 209, 224–26 (1993).

50.  *See, e.g.*, Taylor Publ'g Co. v. Jostens, Inc., 216 F.3d 465, 479 n.8 (5th Cir. 2000) (limited promotion presented no risk of driving competitor from the market and allowing seller to recoup the allegedly predatory discounts). *But see* Multistate Legal Studies, Inc. v. Harcourt Brace Jovanovich Legal & Prof'l Publ'ns, 63 F.3d 1540, 1551 (10th Cir. 1995) (promotional marketing program linking product giveaway to monopoly power in a separate market is not a legal marketing method, absent showing of legitimate business rationale).

51.  ABA SECTION OF ANTITRUST LAW, STATE ANTITRUST PRACTICE AND STATUTES (4th Ed. 2009), Section 13.a.10 of state outlines.

### E. We Want to Package Several Products Together and Offer Them at a Discount Over What They Would Cost Separately. Are There Antitrust Issues? What If We Want to Sell a Product Only If It Is Bought Together with a Different Product?

While bundled discounts often are procompetitive and result in lower prices, bundling and similar incentive schemes by a monopolist also have potential anticompetitive foreclosure effects. Like volume discounts or other rebate schemes, bundled pricing by a monopolist may harm competition if the bundled discount cannot be matched by an equally efficient rival, for example by permitting the monopolist to gain market power in an adjacent market. A firm with market power potentially may "foreclose portions of the market to a potential competitor who does not manufacture an equally diverse group of products and who therefore cannot make a comparable offer."[52] Bundled discounts and similar incentive schemes with the potential for both procompetitive and anticompetitive effects typically are evaluated under a Section 2 rule of reason analysis.

The courts have not reached a consensus for determining when a bundled discount program by a monopolist is exclusionary for purposes of a monopolization or attempted monopolization claim under Section 2 of the Sherman Act. The Third Circuit has found a monopolist's bundled discounts unlawful where there is direct evidence of anticompetitive exclusionary effects absent a procompetitive rationale, without regard to whether prices are below the seller's costs[53] for the competitive product. The Ninth Circuit has declined to follow the Third Circuit, finding instead that bundled discounts by a monopolist are not exclusionary unless they result in an effective price that is below an appropriate measure of the seller's costs[54] for the competitive product.

---

52.    LePage's Inc. v. 3M, 324 F.3d 141, 155 (3d Cir. 2003) (bundled pricing of branded and private label transparent tape and office products was unreasonably exclusionary in violation of Section 2 of the Sherman Act).

53.    *See LePage's*, 324 F.3d at 155 (below-cost pricing not required to find monopolist's bundled discount scheme exclusionary and illegal).

54.    *See* Cascade Health Solutions v. Peacehealth, 515 F.3d 883, 903 (9th Cir. 2008) (bundled discounts are not illegal under Section 2 of the Sherman Act "unless the discounts result in prices that are below an appropriate measure of the defendant's costs").

Tying arrangements are similar to bundled discounts in that they seek to influence the customer to purchase multiple products from the seller. However, in a tying arrangement, the seller is not merely providing a pricing incentive; rather, the sale of one product [the tying product] is *conditioned* upon the buyer also purchasing another product [the tied product].[55]

Tying arrangements historically have been subject to per se condemnation, but in the past few decades, such schemes increasingly have been subjected either to a modified per se rule or a full rule of reason analysis.[56]

Tying arrangements challenged under Section 1 of the Sherman Act are treated as per se unlawful if several elements are satisfied: (1) two separate products or services are affected; (2) the sale or agreement to sell one product or service is conditioned on the purchase of another; (3) the seller has sufficient market power in the market for the tying product or service to permit it to restrain trade in the market for the tied product; and (4) the tie affects a "substantial volume of commerce" in the tied product.[57]

Despite the per se prescription against tying arrangements that meet these elements, some courts have considered competitive effects in the tied product market[58] and/or justifications for the tying arrangements in evaluating these arrangements.[59] Further, many

---

55. Northern Pac. Ry. Co. v. United States, 356 U.S. 1, 5-6 (1958).

56. Illinois Tool Works v. Indep. Ink, 547 U.S. 28, 35 (2006) ("Over the years, . . . this Court's strong disapproval of tying arrangements has substantially diminished.").

57. *See, e.g.*, Fortner Enters. v. U.S. Steel Corp., 394 U.S. 495, 498-99 (1969); *Northern Pacific Railway*, 356 U.S. at 5-6; E & L Consulting v. Doman Indus., 472 F.3d 23, 31-32 (2d Cir. 2006); Gordon v. Lewistown Hosp., 423 F.3d 184, 214 (3d Cir. 2005); *In re* Visa Check/MasterMoney Antitrust Litig., 280 F.3d 124, 134 n.5 (2d Cir. 2001); Thompson v. Metro. Multi-List, Inc., 934 F.2d 1566, 1574 (11th Cir. 1991); Fox Motors v. Mazda Distribs. (Gulf), 806 F.2d 953, 957 (10th Cir. 1986); Digidyne Corp. v. Data Gen. Corp., 734 F.2d 1336, 1338 (9th Cir. 1984); Jefferson Parish Hosp. Dist. No. 2 v. Hyde, 6 U.S. 2, 29 (1984).

58. Princo Corp. v. Int'l Trade Comm'n, 616 F.3d 1318, 1338 (Fed. Cir. 2010), *cert. denied*, 131 S. Ct. 2480 (2011); *E & L Consulting*, 472 F.3d at 32.

59. *See, e.g.*, International Salt Co. v. United States, 332 U.S. 392, 398 (1947); IBM v. United States, 298 U.S. 131, 139–40 (1936); Mozart Co. v. Mercedes-Benz of N. Am., Inc., 833 F.2d 1342, 1348–51 (9th Cir. 1987) (upholding verdict for defendant asserting quality control defense);

commentators have argued that tying arrangements should be evaluated under the rule of reason instead of subject to per se condemnation.[60]

If a plaintiff cannot demonstrate one or more of the elements for per se treatment, a tying arrangement still may be challenged as a violation of Section 1 of the Sherman Act under the rule of reason if a plaintiff can demonstrate an anticompetitive effect in the tied product market.[61]

### F. Can We Require Our Distributors to Agree Not to Discount Below Our Manufacturer's Suggested Retail Pricing? Isn't That What *Leegin Creative Leather Products v. PSKS, Inc.* Was All About?

Requiring distributors to adhere to a suggested minimum retail price is a form of resale price maintenance (a vertical price restraint). It has long been the case that a manufacturer can lawfully advertise a minimum retail price and *unilaterally* refuse to sell to retailers who do not follow the manufacturer's minimum advertised retail price.[62] However, a manufacturer's coercion of or agreement with a distributor or retailer to institute a minimum resale price may fall afoul of federal or state antitrust laws.

The Supreme Court's 2007 decision in *Leegin Creative Leather Products v. PSKS, Inc.*[63] overturned the long-standing precedent deeming minimum resale price maintenance agreements to be per se unlawful. The Court ruled that resale price maintenance agreements in which a manufacturer sets the minimum price level can have

---

Phonetele, Inc. v. AT&T, 664 F.2d 716, 738–39 (9th Cir. 1981) (tie may be justified by legitimate purpose).

60.  *See, e.g.*, Herbert Hovenkamp, FEDERAL ANTITRUST POLICY 432 (3d ed. 2005); *see also Jefferson Parish*, 466 U.S. at 35 (O'Connor, J., concurring, joined by Burger, C.J., Powell, J., and Rehnquist J.) (advocating that per se rule be reserved for "those few horizontal or quasi-horizontal restraints that can be said to have no economic justification whatsoever").

61.  *See* United States v. Microsoft Corp., 253 F.3d 34 (D.C. Cir. 2001) (en banc).

62.  This type of pricing is considered lawful pursuant to the *Colgate* doctrine, which recognizes that a unilateral policy is not an agreement in restraint of trade. *See* United States v. Colgate & Co., 250 U.S. 300, 307 (1919).

63.  Leegin Creative Leather Prods. v. PSKS, Inc., 551 U.S. 877 (2007).

procompetitive effects, and should thus be evaluated under the rule of reason standard—courts will weigh facts to determine whether the restriction on balance harms competition.[64]

Since the *Leegin* decision, sellers may (at least under federal law) require distributors to adhere to suggested minimum retail prices to promote procompetitive business purposes.[65] Resale price maintenance agreements nonetheless can be unlawful if the agreement raises price, limits consumer choice, enhances monopoly power, or facilitates cartel conduct.[66] For example, it may be unlawful for a manufacturer to adopt a minimum resale price agreement that is the result of a horizontal agreement between resellers seeking to maintain high resale prices, or a horizontal agreement between manufacturers to facilitate price fixing.[67] Resale price maintenance also can be illegal if it is used by a manufacturer or retailer with market power to forestall competition.[68]

Minimum resale pricing agreements also can be challenged under state laws.[69] *Leegin* did not address the status of resale price maintenance agreements under state law, and some states continue to treat such agreements as per se illegal.[70]

---

64. *Id.* at 889–900.
65. Minimum resale price agreements may promote interbrand competition, including incentivizing retailers to provide better customer service, knowledgeable staff, appealing stores, and other non-price benefits. *See, e.g.*, PSKS, Inc. v. Leegin Creative Leather Prods., 615 F.3d 412, 419 (5th Cir. 2010) (failure to plead plausible anticompetitive effect of minimum resale price agreement absent evidence of harm to interbrand competition).
66. *See Leegin*, 551 U.S. at 892–99.
67. *Id.* at 892–94.
68. *Id.*; *see also* Babyage.com v. Toys "R" Us, Inc., 558 F. Supp. 2d 575, 587 (E.D. Pa. 2008) (refusing to dismiss claims alleging that minimum resale price agreements aided dominant reseller in maintaining monopoly power).
69. *See, e.g.*, Complaint, People v. Bioelements Inc., No. 10011659 (Cal. Super. Ct., Riverside County 2010) (alleging manufacturer illegally fixed resale prices for its products in violation of state competition laws); Complaint, New York v. Herman Miller, Inc., No. 08-cv-2977 (S.D.N.Y. 2008) (alleging that furniture seller's suggested retail price policy sought to stabilize and raise retail prices in violation of state and federal laws).
70. Maryland was the first state to adopt "*Leegin* repealer" legislation aimed specifically to reject the application of *Leegin* to state antitrust law. MD.

## G. Where Can I Go for More Information?

### 1. Antitrust Issues Related to Pricing Generally

- 1 ABA Section of Antitrust Law, *Antitrust Law Developments* 497-566 (7th ed. 2012);
- ABA Section of Antitrust Law, *Antitrust Law and Economics of Product Distribution* 295-342 (2006);
- ABA Section of Antitrust Law, *Antitrust Handbook for Franchise and Distributions Practitioners* 72-92 (2008).

### 2. Discounting to Large Customers

- 1 ABA Section of Antitrust Law, *Antitrust Law Developments* 497-566 (7th ed. 2012).

### 3. Cost-Based Discounts

- 1 ABA Section of Antitrust Law, *Antitrust Law Developments* 497-566 (7th ed. 2012).

### 4. Discounting to Best Customers

- 1 ABA Section of Antitrust Law, *Antitrust Law Developments* 497-566 (7th ed. 2012);
- ABA Section of Antitrust Law, *Monograph No. 4, The Robinson-Patman Act: Policy and Law* (1980, 1983).

### 5. Resale Price Maintenance

- 1 ABA Section of Antitrust Law, *Antitrust Law Developments* 137-43 (7th ed. 2012);
- ABA Section of Antitrust Law, *State Antitrust Practice and Statutes* (4th ed. 2009), Section 5 of state outlines;
- Michael A. Lindsey, *Overview of State RPM*, *The Antitrust Source* (April 2011), *available at* http://www.americanbar.org

---

CODE ANN., COM. LAW § 11-204(a)(1) (2009) (providing that "a contract . . . that establishes a minimum price below which a retailer, wholesaler, or distributor may not sell a commodity or service is an unreasonable restraint of trade or commerce"). *Id.* § 11-204(b).

/content/dam/aba/publications/antitrust_law/source_lindsay_c
hart.authcheckdam.pdf.

## 6.  *Pricing and Bundling*

- 1 ABA Section of Antitrust Law, *Antitrust Law Developments* 173-209, 252-53, 256-59 (7th ed. 2012).

## CHAPTER V

# DEALING WITH CUSTOMERS AND SUPPLIERS

## A. Our Customer Offered to Give Us a Competitor's Price Quote. Is It Okay for Us to Accept It? Can We Use It in Reviewing Our Pricing Generally?

Courts have recognized that it is "common sense to obtain as much information as possible [about] the pricing policies and marketing strategies of one's competitors."[1] The gathering of information, including price information, about one's competitors can promote interbrand competition.[2] Simply obtaining information about a competitor's prices would not necessarily amount to a violation of any antitrust laws. Whether or not the receipt of such information might result in the violation of the antitrust laws depends in large part on the source of the competitor's price information and any actions taken in response to the information. The risk of an antitrust violation is much higher when competitors directly share information on current or future prices because such an exchange may be seen as facilitating (or even evidencing) a price-fixing agreement in violation of Section 1 of the Sherman Act. When that information comes from a customer, or publicly available sources, a seller's antitrust risk is significantly lower because such information sharing is more likely to be used for procompetitive purposes.[3] In other words, a customer is unlikely to share another supplier's prices with a particular supplier, unless the customer believes this would be in their own interest.

---

1. *In re* Baby Food Antitrust Litig., 166 F.3d 112, 126 (3d Cir. 1999).
2. United States v. U.S. Gypsum Co., 438 U.S. 422, 441 n.16 (1978) (recognizing that information exchanged between competitors may have procompetitive effects).
3. *See* U.S. Dep't of Justice Business Review Letter (BRL) 97-1, DataCheck, Inc. (Jan. 6, 1997) (explaining that any threat of harm to competition is "attenuated . . . where the prices at issue already are publicly available").

Because the antitrust risk varies with the source of the competitively sensitive information, it is usually wise to document how the information was obtained—and in particular that it came from legitimate and lawful sources, such as a customer.

That said, even the sharing of information directly among competitors can be accomplished consistently with the antitrust laws under certain circumstances. The Supreme Court has held that competitors do not violate Section 1 of the Sherman Act if they merely "openly and fairly gather and disseminate information" as to their costs, production volumes, actual prices in previous transactions, and inventory, so long as they do not reach or attempt to reach any agreement in restraint of competition with respect to such prices or other commercial terms.[4] Such legitimate benchmarking activities may include, for example, the open exchange of statistical information about past prices that do not identify particular customers.[5] As a general matter, it is advisable when entering into such an exchange with competitors, to properly document the procompetitive nature of the exchange and the specific source of information, to avoid any suggestion later that the exchange was used to facilitate an illegal agreement. It is also advisable to have legal counsel closely involved and monitoring the data that is exchanged. For more detail on the risks of benchmarking, please see Chapter 1.

## B.   Can a Supplier Offer to Give a Buyer Money to Be Used in the Buyer's Promotions of the Supplier's Products, in Exchange for Signing an Agreement Not to Sell the Products Distributed by the Supplier's Competitors?

Exclusive dealing arrangements, like the arrangement in this hypothetical, are generally considered as potentially beneficial to competition and thus do not necessarily amount to a violation of Section 1 of the Sherman Act or any other antitrust laws.[6] Such arrangements are

---

4.    Maple Flooring Mfrs.' Ass'n v. United States, 268 U.S. 563, 586 (1925).
5.    *Id.* at 567.
6.    *See* Fed. Trade Comm'n, An FTC Guide to the Antitrust Laws, Dealings in the Supply Chain: Exclusive Dealing or Requirements Contracts       1        (2008),       *available*       *at* http://www.ftc.gov/bc/antitrust/factsheets/ antitrustlawsguide.pdf ("Most exclusive dealing contracts are beneficial because they encourage marketing support for the manufacturer's brand.").

analyzed under the "rule of reason" standard.[7] Under the rule of reason, courts assess the facts and circumstances of particular conduct and balance the potential anticompetitive harms with the potential procompetitive benefits of the conduct. When this analysis is applied to exclusive dealing arrangements, courts often begin this balancing exercise by examining whether the restriction will prevent competitors from reaching an unduly significant proportion of the relevant market.[8]

In the past, courts focused almost exclusively on the percentage of the relevant market foreclosed to competing suppliers by the exclusive dealing arrangement. The vestiges of that focus are still present in today's exclusive dealing analysis[9] such that courts still consider market foreclosure as a significant factor in determining the potential anticompetitive effects of the arrangement.[10] Courts also generally consider how a supplier's exclusive dealing arrangements when examined together with its other competitive actions impact the downstream market, and how a supplier's arrangements work in concert with other market participants' exclusive dealing arrangements to foreclose the market and make entry more difficult.[11]

In assessing the antitrust risk of a proposed arrangement along the lines of that outlined in this hypothetical, the parties should begin by looking at the supplier's market share, its overall use of exclusive dealing

---

7.   *Id.*

8.   *See* JOE SIMS, KATHRYN M. FENTON, & DAVID P. WALES, ANTITRUST LAW ANSWER BOOK 2011-12 257 (Practising Law Institute 2011) (discussing vertical agreements generally).

9.   *See, e.g.,* ERNEST GELLHORN, WILLIAM E. KOVACIC, & STEPHEN CALKINS, ANTITRUST LAW & ECONOMICS IN A NUTSHELL 8 (5TH ED. 2004) (citing Standard Oil Co. v. United States, 337 U.S. 293 (1949)) (stating that "exclusive dealing has long been subject to a modified rule of reason approach that examines the effect of foreclosure on other sellers").

10.  *See* GELLHORN, KOVACIC, & CALKINS, *supra* note 9, at 8; SIMS, FENTON, & WALES, *supra* note 8, at 281; Jonathan M. Jacobson, *Exclusive Dealing, "Foreclosure," & Consumer Harm*, 70 ANTITRUST L.J. 311, 312 (2002) ("Increasingly, the courts are focusing on the effect of the challenged arrangement on the defendant's market power, rather than foreclosure as such, as the source of potential exclusive dealing liability.").

11.  *See* GELLHORN, KOVACIC, & CALKINS, *supra* note 9, at 8; SIMS, FENTON, & WALES, *supra* note 8, at 281; Standard Oil Co. v. United States, 337 U.S. 293, 314 (1949).

contracts, the buyer's share of the market, and the percentage of the market foreclosed by the prospective exclusive contract (as well as other exclusive contracts). In most cases, if the percentage of the market foreclosed is below 30 percent, the agreement is unlikely to be found anticompetitive.[12] However, there are no absolute rules; the question of whether an exclusive dealing contract is unreasonable under the antitrust laws will depend on the specific circumstances of each case.[13]

Second, the parties should consider whether the supplier's competitors have alternative distribution possibilities open to them such that they are still able to reach the ultimate consumers.[14] Even if the exclusive agreement between the supplier and a particular buyer affects a significant portion of the market, the supplier's competitors may still have other, sufficient ways of reaching the market and consumers so as to alleviate any competitive concern.

Third, the duration of an exclusive dealing arrangement may also have a significant impact on the analysis of its competitive effects. Courts have held that exclusive dealing arrangements that last for less than one year are less likely to be anticompetitive.[15] Longer exclusive

---

12.   *See* SIMS, FENTON, & WALES, *supra* note 8, at 282; *see also, e.g.*, Valley Prods. Co. v. Landmark, 128 F.3d 398, 402 n.3 (6th Cir. 1997) (federal courts "hav[e] repeatedly held that a 30% market share is insufficient to confer . . . market power"); Sewell Plastics v. Coca-Cola Co., 720 F. Supp. 1196, 1212-13 (W.D.N.C. 1989) (40 percent market share would not enable bottling cooperative to increase prices profitably above the competitive level), *aff'd*, 912 F.2d 463 (4th Cir. 1990); Gonzalez v. Insignares, 1985-2 Trade Cas. (CCH) ¶ 66, 701, at 63, 335 (N.D. Ga. 1985) (summary judgment for defendant where only 40 percent of consumers affected).

13.   *See, e.g.*, CDC Techs. v. IDEXX Labs., 186 F.3d 74, 77, 81 (2d Cir. 1999) (holding that 80 percent market share was insufficient in the absence of "other grounds" to believe that the challenged conduct injured competition); Omega Envtl. v. Gilbarco, Inc., 127 F.3d 1157, 1162-65 (9th Cir. 1997) (upholding exclusive dealing arrangements where company had 55 percent market share that foreclosed 38 percent of relevant market).

14.   *See* SIMS, FENTON, & WALES, *supra* note 8, at 281.

15.   *See* GELLHORN, KOVACIC, & CALKINS, *supra* note 9, at 8-9; SIMS, FENTON, & WALES, *supra* note 8, at 282; *see also, e.g.*, Thompson Everett, Inc. v. Nat'l Cable Adver., 57 F.3d 1317, 1326 (4th Cir. 1995) (upholding exclusive contracts that were "typically of short duration, usually terminable after a year"); Western Parcel Express v. United Parcel Serv. of America, 190 F.3d 974, 976 (upholding exclusive contract

dealing agreements pose greater risk but still might be found to be procompetitive on balance, depending on the facts of the case.[16]

Finally, the existence of entry barriers for a relevant market also affects the potential reasonableness of an exclusive dealing relationship.[17] Where market entry barriers are high, an exclusive dealing arrangement is likely to receive greater antitrust scrutiny.[18]

Any anticompetitive effects of an exclusive dealing arrangement must be weighed against the procompetitive benefits resulting from the relationship to determine if the restraint is reasonable on balance. Examples of compelling procompetitive justifications for an exclusive dealing arrangement include to "assure supply, afford protection against rises in price, enable long-term planning on the basis of known costs, and obviating the expense and risk of storage in the quantity necessary for a commodity having a fluctuating demand."[19] From the supplier's perspective, procompetitive justifications may include the fact that the contract "may make possible the substantial reduction of selling expenses, give protection against price fluctuations, and . . . offer the possibility of a predictable market."[20]

---

terminable "for any reason with very little notice" as not anticompetitive).

16. *See, e.g.*, Ferguson v. Greater Pocatello Chamber of Commerce, 848 F.2d 976, 982 (9th Cir. 1988) (upholding six-year lease); Barry Wright Corp. v. ITT Grinnell Corp., 724 F.2d 227, 236-38 (1st Cir. 1983) (upholding limit that extended for about two years over something less than defendant's expected requirements).

17. *See, e.g.*, R. J. Reynolds Tobacco Co. v. Philip Morris Inc., 199 F. Supp. 2d 362, 389 (M.D.N.C. 2002) ("[I]n addition to the foreclosure percentage, courts, including this court, consider the duration of the agreement, the ability of consumers to comparison shop, and their propensity to switch products, the existence of barriers to entry, and the availability of alternative channels of distribution. . . . The lower the foreclosure percentage, the more salient these factors become in determining whether there has been substantial foreclosure.") (citations omitted).

18. *Id.*

19. LAWRENCE A. SULLIVAN & WARREN S. GRIMES, HORNBOOK ON THE LAW OF ANTITRUST: AN INTEGRATED HANDBOOK 4 (2d ed. 2006) (quoting Standard Oil Co. v. United States, 337 U.S. 293, 306 (1949)).

20. *Standard Oil Co.*, 337 U.S. at 306-07.

One common procompetitive benefit of an exclusive dealing relationship is the reduction of "free riding."[21] Free riding may occur where one distributor of a product engages in promotional activities to help sell a supplier's products, but customers enticed by the promotional activities end up purchasing the same supplier's products from another distributor who did not incur the cost of the promotions.[22] In this scenario, free riding discourages distributors from engaging in promotional activities (and growing demand and output), since they bear the full costs of these activities but do not necessarily receive all of the benefits. An exclusive dealing relationship can eliminate free riding (as there are no other distributors who could free ride on a distributor's promotional activities) and encourage the distributor to run its promotions—thus growing demand and output. While intrabrand competition may thus be reduced as a result of an exclusive dealing arrangement, interbrand competition can be spurred as it allows dealers and suppliers to engage in promotional activities without the concern that others selling the same brands will free ride on their efforts.

As a practical matter, the parties should contemporaneously document the procompetitive benefits of any exclusive dealing arrangement to establish in any future review that the justifications were not merely pretextual.[23]

## C. Our Customers Are Telling Us That Our Distributor's Pricing and Advertising Are Wrecking the Marketplace. What Can We Do About It?

Under certain circumstances, a manufacturer may become concerned that a distributor's pricing and advertising methods are harming the competitiveness of the manufacturer's product.[24] For example, a low-price distributor may simply be free riding on the advertising or services provided by other distributors offering more comprehensive or higher-quality service.[25] Many manufacturers go to significant expense to

---

21.   *See* FED. TRADE COMM'N, Dealings in the Supply Chain: Exclusive Dealing or Requirements Contracts, *supra* note 6, at 1.
22.   *See* SIMS, FENTON, & WALES, *supra* note 8, at 280; SULLIVAN & GRIMES, *supra* note 19, at 4.
23.   *See* SIMS, FENTON, & WALES, *supra* note 8, at 282-83.
24.   *See* Leegin Creative Leather Prods. v. PSKS, Inc., 551 U.S. 877, 883 (2007) (discussing the manufacturer's belief that the retailer's discounting of the manufacturer's products had injured its reputation).
25.   *Id.* at 890.

encourage consumers to associate their products with superior quality, exceptional service, or both.[26] A distributor's low price or poor service levels may frustrate such efforts and ultimately tarnish a manufacturer's brand or reputation.[27]

A manufacturer's effort to more directly control a distributor's resale prices is covered in Chapter 4. In this Chapter we address cooperative advertising, another strategy that might be used to impact the decision-making of distributors.

Some manufacturers seek to limit certain price-based advertising by cooperatively advertising with distributors or offering programs that compensate a distributor for maintaining a minimum advertised price (MAP).[28] MAP programs may involve the manufacturer's subsidization of all or part of a distributor's advertising costs in exchange for a promise by the distributor not to advertise a product (or products) below a certain price.[29] MAP programs may, for example, take the form of rebates or allowances to a distributor.[30] They are generally less likely to be viewed as unreasonable restraints inconsistent with Section 1 of the Sherman Act than minimum resale price maintenance agreements.[31]

MAP programs are evaluated under the rule of reason. They are voluntary and do not restrict a distributor's freedom to *sell* a product below a certain suggested price, only to advertise it.[32] The Federal Trade Commission (FTC) has recognized that MAP programs often promote

---

26.   *Id*. at 890-91.
27.   *See also* Chapter 4 regarding resale price maintenance, *Leegin Creative Leather Products v. PSKS, Inc.*, and Colgate policies.
28.   J. Thomas Rosch, Comm'r, Fed. Trade Comm'n, Current Issues in Competition and Consumer Protection Enforcement in the Retail Sector, Remarks at the Retail Industry Leaders Association's Retail Law Conference (Nov. 10, 2010), at 21 (describing MAP programs), *available at* http://www.ftc.gov/speeches/rosch/101110roschretailerspeech.pdf.
29.   *Id*.
30.   *See* Brian R. Henry & Eugene F. Zelek, Jr., *Establishing and Maintaining an Effective Minimum Resale Price Policy: A Colgate How-To*, ANTITRUST 8, n.9 (discussing various forms of MAP programs).
31.   *Id*.
32.   *See* Lake Hill Motors v. Jim Bennett Yacht Sales, 246 F.3d 752, 757 (5th Cir. 2001) (holding that cooperative advertising programs are "analyzed under the rule of reason"); *see also* Campbell v. Austin Air Sys., 423 F. Supp. 2d 61, 68 n.6 (W.D.N.Y. 2005) (concluding in a case involving an Internet-based MAP program that the program must be judged according to the rule of reason).

competition by "channeling the retailer's advertising efforts in directions that the manufacturer believes consumers will find more compelling and beneficial."[33] MAP programs have been enjoined only in particularly egregious circumstances.[34] However, if a MAP program is unduly restrictive or appears to be part of a broader effort to impose resale price maintenance, it may be found to be unreasonable and in violation of Section 1 of the Sherman Act.[35]

## D. Our Purchasing Department Wants to Join Forces with the Purchasing Folks from Our Competitor to See If We Can Buy Office Supplies Jointly to Get a Better Deal. Is That Okay?

A joint purchasing agreement with a competitor to get better input pricing is generally considered under a rule of reason analysis.

Joint purchasing agreements and group purchasing associations are a common way for competitors to work together to achieve economic efficiencies, such as volume discounts and economies of scale, in obtaining supplies.[36] To the extent these benefits result in lower marginal costs and increased output and decreased prices, these arrangements are

---

33.    U.S. Pioneer Elecs. Corp., 115 F.T.C. 446, 456 (1992) (internal quotations omitted).

34.    *See* Analysis to Aid Public Comment, CD MAP, FTC File No. 971-0070 (May 10, 2000) (inviting public comment on a proposed consent order involving MAP programs between music distributors and retailers where "retailers seeking any [MAP] funds were required to observe the distributors' minimum advertised prices in all media advertisements, even in advertisements funded solely by the retailers," music distributors controlled 85 percent of the market, and there was evidence of interdependent activity by the distributors in adopting MAP programs), *available at* http://www.ftc.gov/os/2000/05/mapanalysis.htm.

35.    *See* Reebok Int'l, 120 F.T.C. 20 (1995) (consent order barring manufacturer from threatening sanctions for selling below a minimum price); Acquaire v. Canada Dry Bottling Co., 24 F.3d 401, 412 (2d Cir. 1994) (affirming injunctive relief barring manufacturer from withholding supply from the plaintiff dealer allegedly to enforce resale price maintenance).

36.    *See* Northwest Wholesale Stationers v. Pac. Stationery & Printing Co., 472 U.S. 284, 295 (1985) (discussing positive benefits of purchasing cooperative, including increasing economic efficiency, making markets more competitive, achieving economics of scale, and ensuring quicker access to goods).

viewed favorably.[37] Joint purchasing agreements, however, also can have anticompetitive effects, especially where the participants in the joint purchasing arrangements collectively have market power.[38]

It is prudent for businesses to analyze contemplated joint purchasing agreements with competitors under the "35/20" rule set out in the Department of Justice (DOJ) and FTC's Statement of Antitrust Enforcement Policy in Health Care.[39]

The DOJ first articulated the 35/20 rules in 1985.[40] A decade later, the DOJ and FTC issued a formal statement in 1996 that applies the 35/20 rules to health care providers.[41] The DOJ and FTC have indicated that the 20 percent rule will generally apply across the board "absent extraordinary circumstances" (although not if an agreement is per se illegal).[42] Though the DOJ and FTC have not issued a formal statement applying the 35 percent rule to other industries, the DOJ's Antitrust Division Business Review Letters over the last 16 years suggest that it uses the 35/20 rules across the board as the first and most important step in a rule of reason analysis involving joint purchasing.[43]

---

37.    *See* U.S. Dep't of Justice & Fed. Trade Comm'n, Antitrust Guidelines for Collaborations Among Competitors § 3.31(a) (2000) [hereinafter Guidelines for Collaborations] ("Many [joint purchasing agreements] do not raise antitrust concerns and indeed may be procompetitive."), *available at* http://ftc.gov/os/2000/04/ ftcdojguidelines.pdf; *see also* North Jackson Pharmacy v. Caremark RX, Inc., 385 F. Supp. 2d 740, 748 (N.D. Ill. 2005) ("[W]here . . . buyers join together in a productive venture, cooperative buying is rarely viewed as a per se unlawful restraint under Section 1 [of the Sherman Act] so long as it contributes to the productive enterprise.").

38.    *See* Mandeville Island Farms v. Am.Crystal Sugar Co., 334 U.S. 219, 223 (1948) (joint purchasing arrangement was unlawful where sugar refiners controlled relevant market); Jonathan M. Jacobson & Gary J. Dorman, *Joint Purchasing, Monopsony & Antitrust*, 36 Antitrust Bull. 1, 29 (1991).

39.    U.S. Dep't of Justice & Fed. Trade Comm'n, Statements of Antitrust Enforcement Policy in Health Care, (1996) [hereinafter DOJ & FTC Health Care Guidelines]., *available at* http://www.justice.gov/atr/ public/guidelines/0000.htm.

40.    *See* Jacobson & Dorman, *supra* note 38, at 36.

41.    *See* DOJ & FTC Health Care Guidelines, *supra* note 39, at Statement 7.

42.    Guidelines for Collaborations, *supra* note 37, § 4.2.

43.    *See* BRL 09-1, Memorial Health, Inc. and St. Joseph's/Candler Health System (Sept. 4, 2009); BRL 03-3, The National Cable Television

Under these rules, the agencies examine the buying and selling sides of the contemplated joint purchasing agreement. On the buying side, the agencies assess whether the purchasing parties have the power to depress output below competitive levels.[44] An absence of such power is presumed—and the analysis typically ends—if the buyers' collective purchases make up less than 35 percent of the relevant market for the purchased goods.[45] If the joint purchases would make up more than 35 percent of the relevant market, the agencies proceed to review other aspects of the proposed agreement, such as selling-side efficiencies.[46]

On the selling side, the agencies assess whether collusion is likely to result between the joint purchasers as a result of their cooperation in acquiring their supplies (and knowledge of each other's costs). If the jointly purchased supplies represent less than 20 percent of the final product price, the agencies will usually assume that anticompetitive effects in the end-product market are unlikely.[47] The agencies will nonetheless carefully review in all cases whether the joint purchasing forum could be used as a platform to discuss sensitive competitive information, such as prices.[48] Moreover, if the 20 percent level is exceeded, then the agencies will also consider other competitive factors.[49]

Businesses may also consider several prophylactic measures to minimize any potential anticompetitive effects of joint purchasing arrangements, especially if the 35/20 guidelines are exceeded.[50] The more directly businesses compete with each other, and the more market power a joint purchasing arrangement can wield, the more important these measures become.

---

Cooperative, Inc. (Oct. 17, 2003); BRL 00-5, Containers America LLC (Mar. 8, 2000); BRL 99-1, NSM Purchasing Association (Jan. 13, 1999); BRL 98-9, Textile Energy Association (Sept. 4, 1998); BRL 98-4, Armored Transport Alliance (Mar. 12, 1998). These BRLs are *available at* http://www.justice.gov/atr/public/busreview/letters.html.

44.   *See* GUIDELINES FOR COLLABORATIONS, *supra* note 37, § 3.31(a).
45.   Jacobson & Dorman, *supra* note 38, at 37. The number, 35 percent, was taken from the DOJ Merger Guidelines and represents the numerical point where the DOJ becomes concerned that a firm can unilaterally exercise market power. *Id.* at 37 n.90.
46.   *Id.* at 37.
47.   *Id.* at 37.
48.   *Id.* at 37 n.93.
49.   *Id.* at 37.
50.   *See* BRLs, *supra* note 43, for examples of these prophylactic measures.

- Businesses should articulate their procompetitive reasons for the arrangement, such as decreased informational and transactional costs, and volume discounts. Ideally, companies involved in joint purchasing arrangements should also demonstrate how these decreased costs will be passed on to consumers.

- Businesses also should consider creating a neutral third-party entity to act as the purchasing organization so as to reduce the amount of competitively sensitive information shared between competitors. This third-party entity should not share information between the joint purchasers and should receive information from the joint purchasers only as strictly necessary to achieve the legitimate purposes of the joint purchasing arrangement. Under such an arrangement, businesses should not share information directly with each other, and third-party agents should be truly independent from the joint purchasers. Formal, written contracts memorializing confidentiality safeguards may be advisable. It may also be advisable for the joint purchasing arrangement to give participants the freedom to make purchases outside the confines of the joint arrangement.[51]

- Companies involved in joint purchasing arrangements should further consider whether significant competitors will continue to be present that will not be part of the joint arrangement and that can therefore counteract any monopsony pressure the joint purchasers could otherwise place on suppliers.

- Finally, companies should also consider to what extent they are in direct competition with their potential joint purchasers. The more direct the competition and the more market purchasing power the joint arrangement would have, the greater the antitrust concern. The less direct the competition, the more leeway businesses will have to exceed the 35/20 guidelines.[52]

Because most joint purchasing arrangements, if challenged, will be analyzed under the rule of reason, developing a joint purchasing arrangement to withstand antitrust scrutiny is more art than science. If counsel determines a business' proposed joint purchasing arrangement to be borderline or risky, then the business may wish to have counsel seek a

---

51. *See* BRL 03-3, The National Cable Television Cooperative, Inc., *supra* note 43.

52. *Id. See also* BRL 00-5, Containers America LLC, *supra* note 43.

Business Review Letter from the Department of Justice in which the DOJ may, at its discretion, indicate whether it would intend to challenge the proposed arrangement under the antitrust laws.[53]

### E. This Customer Is More Trouble Than It's Worth. Can We Refuse to Do Business with It?

In most cases and for antitrust purposes only,[54] yes, a business can terminate or refuse to deal with a customer. This is true even for businesses with monopoly power.[55] Businesses have a long-recognized right to choose the customers with which they deal.[56] But this right carries some qualifications: termination of a customer or a refusal to deal in the first instance cannot be in furtherance of anticompetitive conduct designed to cripple or eliminate competition. The key question here is: *why* is this customer "more trouble than it's worth?"

A valid, procompetitive, business justification for refusing to deal or terminating a customer will eliminate most, if not all, antitrust concerns.[57] Procompetitive business reasons can include a failure to pay bills on time, unreasonable demands on the seller, efficiency gains, a personality conflict between buyer and seller, and similar reasons.[58]

---

53. *See* 28 C.F.R. § 50.6.
54. When terminating a customer or refusing to deal in the first instance, a business should also consider if its actions might violate state and federal non-discrimination laws. The business should further consider any regulatory schemes that apply to its industry, such as FCC regulations, which might displace the operation of the Sherman Act and other antitrust laws. *See e.g.*, Verizon Commc'ns v. Law Offices of Curtis V. Trinko, 540 U.S. 398, 404-06 (2004).
55. *See generally*, FED. TRADE COMM'N, AN FTC GUIDE TO THE ANTITRUST LAWS, Exclusionary or Predatory Acts: Refusal to Deal, *available at* http://www.ftc.gov /bc/antitrust/refusal_to_deal.shtm).
56. *See Trinko*, 540 U.S. at 408 (citing United States v. Colgate & Co., 250 U.S. 300, 307 (1919)); *see also* Aspen Skiing Co. v. Aspen Highlands Skiing Corp., 472 U.S. 585, 601 (1985) (noting the "cherished" and "high value" right to select customers and associates).
57. *See Aspen Skiing Company*, 472 U.S. at 604-05, 608-11.
58. For rationales for refusals to deal that courts have considered, and frequently upheld, see 1 ABA SECTION OF ANTITRUST LAW, ANTITRUST LAW DEVELOPMENTS 167-68 (7th ed. 2012) (collecting cases). Such rationales include the manufacturer's decision not to deal with a potential new distributor, an attempt to implement standards for distributors involving matters such as appearance, image, credit requirements, and

As discussed in Chapter 1, antitrust concerns may arise when a customer is also a competitor of the seller. In these situations, a lack of cooperation with a customer may reveal an illegal effort to gain or maintain monopoly power in a relevant market, which may raise antitrust risks under Section 2 of the Sherman Act.

If a business is a monopolist or oligopolist, has a significant market share, is in competition with its own customers, or has developed a uniquely special relationship with a customer or competitor and contemplates acting in a way that terminates that special relationship, then the risk that a refusal to deal or termination will be seen as anticompetitive is increased. If so, the business should have even stronger and better-documented procompetitive reasons for its actions.

## F. Can I Offer My Customers a Package Deal to Encourage Them to Buy More of Our Products?

As a general matter, suppliers may offer customers a package deal without violating the antitrust laws. "Tying" and "bundling" are generally permitted, but they can raise antitrust risks in certain circumstances, especially where the supplier has market power.

*Tying.* A tying arrangement occurs when a seller conditions a purchase of one product or service on the purchase of a second product or service. Tying may be unlawful under the Sherman Act where four factors are present:

- Two separate products or services are involved;
- The sale or agreement to sell one product or service is conditioned on the purchase of another;
- The seller has sufficient economic power in the market for the tying product (the product the buyer primarily wants) to enable it to restrain trade in the market for the tied product (the product the buyer is arguably being forced to take); and
- A "not insubstantial" amount of interstate commerce is affected.[59]

Tying law is still evolving. Historically, all tying relationships were evaluated under the per se rule and so automatically deemed

---

sales quotas, the manufacturer's effort to reduce costs and increase operating efficiency, and other similar rationales. *Id.*

59.   *See* Eastman Kodak Co. v. Image Technical Servs., 504 U.S. 451 (1992).

anticompetitive. Courts now recognize that tying relationships can be procompetitive and so judge tying agreements under either a modified per se rule or the rule of reason. Courts use the per se rule if they find market power by the seller in the market for the tying product.[60] Otherwise, courts use the rule of reason, which permits sellers to advance defenses in support of a tying arrangement, such as a procompetitive rationale or a business justification.[61]

Technological tying is viewed somewhat differently. A technological tie is achieved through integration of what could be viewed as two products. A manufacturer-seller engages in technological tying when it designs one product so that it functions only when used in conjunction with the manufacturer's own complementary products. For example, a manufacturer engages in technological tying when it designs its printers to be compatible with only that manufacturer's ink cartridges. This dependency between products may be a result of merely engineering a better product, or it may represent the manufacturer's attempt to foreclose competition. Courts generally view technological ties more leniently, applying the rule of reason rather than the per se approach.[62]

*Bundling and Bundled Discounts.* "Bundling is the practice of offering, for a single price, two or more goods or services that could be sold separately. A bundled discount occurs when a firm sells a bundle of goods or services for a lower price than the seller charges for the goods or services purchased individually."[63] Bundling is quite common, such as season tickets, fast food value meals, and all-in-one home theater systems. Despite its prevalence and permissibility, bundling has the potential to raise antitrust concerns where the supplier has market power.

Antitrust law regarding bundling is unsettled. Generally speaking, as long as no part of the bundle is discounted below cost or otherwise priced to implicate predatory pricing concerns, the practice will likely be considered acceptable under the antitrust laws. However, the law

---

60. *See* Jefferson Parish Hosp. Dist. No. 2 v. Hyde, 466 U.S. 2, 12 (1984).
61. *See* Cascade Health Solutions v. PeaceHealth, 515 F.3d 883, 894 (9th Cir. 2008).
62. *See* United States v. Microsoft Co., 253 F.3d 34, 95 (D.C. Cir. 2001) (rule of reason, not per se analysis, applies "where the tying product is software whose major purpose is to serve as a platform for third-party applications and the tied product is complementary software functionality"); Foremost Pro Color, Inc. v. Eastman Kodak Co., 703 F.2d 534, 542 (9th Cir. 1983) ("we decline to place such technological ties in the category of economic restrictions deemed per se unlawful").
63. *Cascade Health Solutions*, 515 F.3d at 894

currently varies by jurisdiction. For additional information regarding bundling, see Chapter 4.

## G. Where Can I Go for More Information?

- Brian R. Henry & Eugene F. Zelek, Jr., *Establishing and Maintaining an Effective Minimum Resale Price Policy: A Colgate How-To*, Antitrust 8 (Summer 2003);
- Daniel A. Sasse & Chahira Solh, *Has Resale Price Maintenance Counseling Changed Post-Leegin?*, The Price Point 1 (Winter 2010);
- Ernest Gellhorn, William E. Kovacic & Stephen Calkins, *Antitrust Law & Economics in a Nutshell* (5th ed. 2004);
- Federal Trade Commission, *FTC Guide to the Antitrust Laws, Dealings in the Supply Chain: Exclusive Dealing or Requirements Contracts, available at* http://www.ftc.gov/bc/antitrust/factsheets/antitrustlawsguide.pdf;
- Federal Trade Commission, *FTC Guide to the Antitrust Laws, Dealings with Competitors, available at* http://www.ftc.gov/bc/antitrust/dealings_with_competitors.shtm;
- Federal Trade Commission, *FTC Guide to the Antitrust Laws, Exclusionary or Predatory Acts: Refusal to Deal, available at* http://www.ftc.gov/bc/antitrust/refusal_to_deal.shtm;
- Federal Trade Commission & U.S. Department of Justice, *Antitrust Guidelines for Collaborations Among Competitors* (Apr. 2000), *available at* http://www.ftc.gov/os/2000/04/ftcdojguidelines.pdf;
- Frank M. Hinman & Sujal J. Shah, *Counseling Clients on Vertical Price Restraints*, Antitrust 23 (Summer 2009);
- Joe Sims, Kathryn M. Fenton & David P. Wales, *Antitrust Law Answer Book 2011-12* (Practising Law Institute 2011);
- Lawrence A. Sullivan & Warren S. Grimes, 8.4 *Hornbook on the Law of Antitrust: An Integrated Handbook* (2d ed. 2006);
- U.S. Department of Justice, Business Review Letters, *available at* http://www.justice.gov/atr/public/busreview/letters.html;
- U.S. Department of Justice, *Competition and Monopoly: Single-Firm Conduct Under Section 2 of the Sherman Act* (2008), *available at* http://www.usdoj.gov/atr/public/reports/236681.htm;

- Federal Trade Commission & U.S. Department of Justice, *Antitrust Guidelines for Collaborations Among Competitors* (2000), *available at* http://ftc.gov/os/2000/04/ftcdojguidelines.pdf;
- U.S. Department of Justice & Federal Trade Commission, *Statements of Antitrust Enforcement Policy in Health Care* (Aug. 1996), *available at* http://www.justice.gov/atr/public/guidelines/0000.pdf.

CHAPTER VI

# ANTITRUST AND INTELLECTUAL PROPERTY

## A. Introduction: Do Antitrust Laws Apply to Conduct Involving Patents?

The antitrust laws apply to conduct involving patents generally, with only limited exceptions. As a general matter, conduct involving a patent needs to be assessed under the antitrust laws in the same manner as conduct not involving a patent. Patents that contribute to or create market power are the most likely to raise significant antitrust issues, but patent holders can sometimes be affected by the antitrust laws even under circumstances that may not seem intuitively likely to be implicated by the antitrust laws.[1]

The issues raised by patent-related conduct may be better understood by briefly examining the intersection of patents and antitrust under U.S. law. Patent law and antitrust law are core components of U.S. law regulating competition between firms. Antitrust laws are intended to apply generally to competition and to ensure robust competition. In contrast, the patent grant provides an innovator with a limited respite from competition in exchange for the patent holder's investment in the invention and its contribution to the public domain by publishing the patent. A patent has the potential to restrict competition because it provides its holder with the right to exclude others, including competitors, from practicing the claimed invention.

The juxtaposition of patent and antitrust laws is sometimes referred to as presenting "tension" or "conflict" and often presents courts and antitrust enforcers with difficult questions. In those instances in which a patent right appears to conflict with antitrust law, it is sometimes not

---

1.    For ease of discussion, except where noted otherwise, this chapter addresses antitrust issues related to patents. Many of the topics discussed in this chapter also apply to copyrights, trademarks, trade secrets, and other forms of intellectual property protection, but a discussion of those laws lies outside the scope of this chapter.

easy to determine whether, or to what degree, certain conduct is protected from antitrust liability. The Supreme Court has provided only limited guidance in this area to date. Lower courts, the U.S. Department of Justice (DOJ), the Federal Trade Commission (FTC), and state attorneys general sometimes differ in how they treat specific antitrust issues that involve patents. Consequently, it often can be difficult to provide simple "rules of the road" in this area of law.

Depending on the circumstances, each stage in the life-cycle of a patent has the potential to present to the patent holder various antitrust risks, including the risk of an investigation or enforcement action brought by the DOJ, the FTC, state attorneys general, or private litigants, any of which may result in significant expense even if the patent holder is ultimately held not to have violated antitrust laws. Consequently, firms that are acquiring or enforcing patent rights should consider whether conduct that is contemplated will raise antitrust risks and, if so, whether there are appropriate means of reducing such risks while accomplishing bona fide business objectives.

In addition, the U.S. patent code[2] specifically addresses certain issues that may bear on potential application of the antitrust laws, such as the territorial scope of a patent license.[3]

Further, to the extent that certain uses of patents are treated as "immune" from antitrust law, such immunity is typically not available when the patent at issue has been procured through fraud or is being enforced through a "sham" action by a patent holder who knows that the patent is invalid or otherwise unenforceable.[4]

This chapter aims only to facilitate the identification of potentially significant antitrust issues that may be raised by conduct involving patents. To that end, it provides a brief, high-level overview of some of the more significant antitrust risks that may arise during the life-cycle of a patent. However, each of the topics addressed below merits detailed analysis based on the specific facts at issue.

## B.  We Are Going to Acquire a Patent. Could That Raise Antitrust Issues?

Yes, acquiring a patent or an exclusive right to a patent can raise both procedural and substantive antitrust issues.

---

2.      35 U.S.C. §§ 1-376.
3.      35 U.S.C. § 261.
4.      *See infra* part F of this chapter.

First, the acquisition of a patent or a patent license[5] that is exclusive as to all (including as to the patentee) may be reportable under the Hart-Scott-Rodino Antitrust Improvements Act of 1976, as amended (HSR), regardless of whether the acquisition raises substantive antitrust issues. While a detailed discussion of HSR rules lies outside the scope of this chapter, HSR may be implicated if the value of the patent(s) (or exclusive license) and other assets being acquired exceed $70.9 million (2013 threshold).[6] If an HSR filing is required, the acquisition cannot be closed prior to expiration of the applicable waiting period.[7]

Second, acquisitions of patents, exclusive licenses, and other assets can raise substantive antitrust issues. In particular, such acquisitions are subject to review under Section 7 of the Clayton Act, regardless of whether they are reportable under the HSR Act. Section 7 bars acquisitions of assets, including patents, where "the effect of such acquisition may be substantially to lessen competition, or to tend to create a monopoly."[8] For example, if two firms propose to merge and that merger would consolidate the only two types of patented technology to make a type of product, the parties would need to consider whether other products would sufficiently constrain their behavior postmerger, such that the combination would not lessen competition in a relevant market under Section 7.

Defining the relevant market that applies to the acquisition of a patent or an exclusive patent license can raise issues that are not well settled by existing case law. For example, while such a relevant market may include a traditional product market, the DOJ and the FTC (taken together, the "agencies") have taken the position that the relevant market may be defined as a so-called "technology market" that may be comprised only of patents or patented technology or an "innovation market" that involves only research and development relating to patents.[9]

---

5. For the antitrust implications of exclusive patent licensing, *see infra* part C.1.c of this chapter.

6. The "size-of-transaction" threshold is amended annually to reflect inflation and is announced by the FTC each January. Revised Jurisdictional Thresholds of the Clayton Act, 78 Fed. Reg. 2406, 2407 (Jan. 11, 2013).

7. Please see Chapter III for additional discussion of the HSR process.

8. 15 U.S.C. § 18.

9. *See, e.g.*, Cephalon Inc., 138 F.T.C. 583, 637 (2004) (analyzing the loss in innovation competition that would likely result from the merger of two manufacturers of brand-name pharmaceuticals); *see generally* U.S. DEP'T OF JUSTICE & FED. TRADE COMM'N, ANTITRUST GUIDELINES FOR THE

Third, the acquisition of a patent or exclusive patent license may provide the basis, in whole or part, for a claim of monopolization under Section 2 of the Sherman Act.[10] Such a claim may be in addition to a potential Section 7 claim. Given the lower threshold for proving a Section 7 claim, however, the incremental risk posed by a Section 2 claim in this context may not be material.

### C. If We Want to License Our Patent, What Antitrust Issues Should We Consider?

The antitrust issues raised by the licensing of patents differ depending on the context. As discussed below, under some circumstances it is relatively easy to conclude whether a proposed license would present antitrust concerns. However, other circumstances are more controversial and there is uncertainty as to whether certain licensing restrictions may present potential violations of the antitrust laws.

License agreements involving intellectual property, just like any other agreements, can be subject to Section 1 of the Sherman Act, which

---

LICENSING OF INTELLECTUAL PROPERTY § 3.2.3 (1995) [hereinafter INTELLECTUAL PROPERTY GUIDELINES], *available at* http://www.justice.gov/atr/public/guidelines/ 0558.pdf; Richard J. Gilbert, *Competition & Innovation*; ISSUES IN COMPETITION LAW & POLICY (Wayne Dale Collins ed., 2006), *available at* http://works.bepress.com/richard_gilbert/12/; J. Thomas Rosch, Comm'r, Fed. Trade Comm'n, Antitrust Regulation of Innovation Markets, Remarks Before the ABA Antitrust Intellectual Property Conference (Feb. 5, 2009), *available at* http://ftc.gov/speeches/rosch/ 090205innovationspeech.pdf; Dean V. Williamson, *Antitrust, Innovation, & Uncertain Property Rights: Some Practical Considerations*, 2010 DUKE L. & TECH. REV. 001, ¶¶ 24-30 (2010), *available at* http//www.law.duke.edu/journals/altr/articles/2010altr001.html.

10.    *See, e.g.*, Kobe, Inc. v. Dempsey Pump Co., 198 F.2d 416 (10th Cir. 1952) (finding a Section 2 violation where a dominant firm pursued a course of acquiring patents for competing technology and subsequently suppressing those technologies by both refusing to use the patent itself and refusing to license the patented technologies to others). *But see* SCM Corp. v. Xerox Corp., 645 F.2d 1195, 1206 (2d Cir. 1981) (holding that the acquisition of the patents at issue did not violate Section 2 where those acquisitions occurred "[years] prior to the existence of the relevant market and . . . [years] prior to the commercialization of the patented art").

prohibits unreasonable agreements in restraint of trade.[11] One important distinction for analyzing license agreements is the same inquiry that applies to other types of agreements: does the license run to a competitor or a non-competitor? If the latter, which may be referred to as a "vertical" license, it is less likely to raise antitrust issues. In contrast, when one competitor licenses another competitor (a "horizontal" transaction), such an agreement may raise substantive antitrust risks, just like any other agreement between competitors.

Except where noted, the discussion below focuses on bona fide licenses in which any restrictions relate to the specific patent being licensed. While the grant of a patent permits the holder to exclude others as to the claims covered by the patent, a patent generally does not enable its holder to restrict competition or coordinate terms of competition among competitors outside the scope of the patent grant.

## 1. Vertical Licenses

Vertical agreements are subject to review under the rule of reason, which requires a finding that the anticompetitive effects of the agreement outweigh any procompetitive effects to establish a violation of Section 1 of the Sherman Act.[12] Restrictions on intrabrand competition, such as territorial restrictions imposed on distributors by a manufacturer, are classic examples of vertical restrictions. Vertical agreements entered into by a monopolist are also potentially subject to a Section 2 claim.

Since *Continental T.V., Inc. v. GTE Sylvania Inc.*,[13] all vertical nonprice restrictions, including but not limited to those that involve patent rights, have been subject to rule of reason treatment.[14] Similarly, under federal law, all vertical maximum resale price agreements have been subject to rule of reason treatment since *State Oil Co. v. Khan*,[15]

---

11. Board of Trade of Chi. v. United States, 246 U.S. 231, 238 (1918) ("The true test of legality is whether the restraint imposed is such as merely regulates and perhaps thereby promotes competition or whether it is such as may suppress or even destroy competition.").

12. *See, e.g.*, NYNEX Corp. v. Discon, Inc., 525 U.S. 128 (1998). It should be noted that this discussion addresses only federal U.S. antitrust law. Vertical agreements may be subject to per se treatment under some state laws.

13. Continental T.V., Inc. v. GTE Sylvania Inc., 433 U.S. 36 (1977).

14. *Id.* at 58; Business Elecs. Corp. v. Sharp Elecs. Corp., 485 U.S. 717, 724 (1988).

15. State Oil Co. v. Khan, 522 U.S. 3, 19 (1997).

and all vertical minimum resale price agreements have similarly been analyzed under the rule of reason under federal law since *Leegin Creative Leather Products v. PSKS, Inc.*[16]

For a vertical agreement to violate antitrust law under the rule of reason, it must cause a marketwide anticompetitive effect.[17] To prove such an effect, a plaintiff typically must show that the firm imposing the vertical restriction has market power or control over some "upstream" input or "downstream" resource by which it can sufficiently disadvantage rivals and thus cause harm to competition in a relevant market.[18] Ostensibly vertical agreements that, in fact, facilitate horizontal collusion among competitors at either an upstream or downstream level also may violate U.S. antitrust law.[19]

Further, as discussed below, when a vertical agreement is based on a patent, the patent laws may provide additional protection against antitrust liability.[20] However, any protection provided by the patent laws generally is extinguished upon the "first sale" of the patented product.

Under the first-sale doctrine, also known as "patent exhaustion," a patent owner's first authorized sale of the patented product to a third party terminates the original owner's patent rights as to subsequent uses or sales of the product. For example, assume a patent owner licenses to a wholesaler the right to use a product covered by a patent and to sell the finished product to a retailer. Although the patent owner may dictate the terms by which the licensee uses and sells the product to the retailer (the first sale), the patent owner generally retains no such rights with respect to subsequent sales by the retailer to consumers.[21]

---

16. Leegin Creative Leather Prods. v. PSKS, Inc., 551 U.S. 877, 899-900 (2007).

17. *See generally* 1 HERBERT HOVENKAMP ET AL., IP & ANTITRUST: AN ANALYSIS OF ANTITRUST PRINCIPLES APPLIED TO INTELLECTUAL PROPERTY LAW § 20 (2d ed. 2011) [hereinafter IP AND ANTITRUST].

18. *Id.*

19. *Id. See also, e.g.*, Beltone Elecs. Corp., 100 F.T.C. 68, 96-97 (1982) (acknowledging that vertical exclusive dealing agreement may facilitate collusion but ultimately finding no evidence of collusion in the industry).

20. For example, certain territorial restrictions are expressly permitted under patent law. *See* 35 U.S.C. § 261 (A patent owner may "grant and convey an exclusive right under his application for patent, or patents, to the whole or any specified part of the United States.").

21. *See, e.g.*, IP AND ANTITRUST, *supra* note 17, § 24.1c.; United States v. Univis Lens Co., 316 U.S. 241, 250-52 (1942); Quanta Computer, Inc. v. LG Elecs., 553 U.S. 617, 625-38 (2008). In October 2012, the Supreme

a.   Tying a Patent to a Non-Patented Product

If a patent license is offered on the condition that the licensee purchase other unpatented goods, such a condition may be challenged as "tying." Although existing Supreme Court precedent holds that tying can be illegal per se, the test that courts use to assess such claims resembles a type of rule of reason analysis.[22] The elements of a "per se" claim under Section 1 of the Sherman Act or Section 3 of the Clayton Act[23] typically include (1) the sale of two separate products or services; (2) the conditioning of the sale of one product on the purchase of a second product; (3) the seller having sufficient economic power in the product for the tying product to enable it to restrain trade in the market for the tied product; and (4) a not insubstantial amount of interstate commerce in the tied product is affected.[24]

---

Court granted a petition for certiorari concerning patent exhaustion and self-replicating patented technology. The case is *Monsanto Co. v. Bowman*, 657 F.3d 1341, 1347-48 (Fed. Cir. 2011) (finding that patent exhaustion did not bar an infringement action where a farmer purchased and planted commodity seeds in order to replicate Monsanto's patented seed technology), *cert. granted*, 133 S. Ct. 420 (Oct. 5, 2012). The petitioner argues that the Federal Circuit erroneously refused to find that Monsanto's patent rights were exhausted even after an authorized sale. The Supreme Court scheduled oral arguments for February 19, 2013 and is expected to render an opinion this term.

22.   1 ABA SECTION OF ANTITRUST LAW, ANTITRUST LAW DEVELOPMENTS 173-78 (7th ed. 2012) [hereinafter ALD].

23.   Section 3 of the Clayton Act prohibits sales and leases:
> on the condition, agreement, or understanding that the lessee or purchaser thereof shall not use or deal in the goods, wares, merchandise, machinery, supplies, or other commodities of a competitor or competitors of the lessor or seller, where the effect of such lease, sale, or contract for sale or such condition, agreement, or understanding may be to substantially lessen competition or tend to create a monopoly in any line of commerce.

15 U.S.C. § 14.

24.   2 ALD, *supra* note 22, at 1099; *see, e.g.*, PSI Repair Servs. v. Honeywell, Inc., 104 F.3d 811, 815 n.2 (6th Cir. 1997) ("While PSI argues on appeal that Honeywell's tying arrangement is illegal under both per se and rule-of-reason analysis, these two theories have, in effect, merged in recent years.").

The law provides that a unilateral refusal to license or sell a patented product cannot be challenged as a tie.[25] If a patent license is offered, however, *on the condition* that the licensee purchase other unpatented goods, such a requirement may be challenged as a tie unless the patent license is also offered on "untied" terms that are reasonably economic such that the "tied" offer is not effectively forced onto the licensee.[26]

At present, the substantive analysis of a tying claim involving a patent, under either the per se or rule of reason standard, is similar to one that does not involve a patent. Historically, there had been a presumption that a patent conferred market power for purposes of a tying claim, but that presumption was eliminated by the Supreme Court in *Illinois Tool Works v. Independent Ink*.[27]

Courts that apply a rule of reason analysis to a tying claim typically demand proof of marketwide harm in the tied market and seek to balance the procompetitive and anticompetitive effects of ties that are based on plausible business justifications (e.g., quality control).[28]

b.   Package Licenses/Bundling

Patents are often licensed in bundles or packages for procompetitive reasons (e.g., reducing transaction costs and avoiding or resolving otherwise costly disputes regarding infringement claims).[29] Such package licenses may be challenged as a tie. Such arrangements generally do not

---

25.   2 ALD, *supra* note 22, at 1099; *see, e.g.*, Data Gen. Corp. v. Grumman Sys. Support Corp., 36 F.3d 1147, 1152 (1st Cir. 1994) (affirming district court decision that Data General's unilateral refusal to license its copyrighted software did not constitute an illegal tying arrangement).

26.   2 ALD, *supra* note 22, at 1101; *cf.* Monsanto Co. v. McFarling, 302 F.3d 1291, 1297-98 (Fed. Cir. 2002) (affirming that defendant was not likely to succeed on tying claim because Monsanto's license restriction on using its patented seeds to produce and replant new patented seeds did not require customers to buy new seeds from Monsanto).

27.   Illinois Tool Works v. Indep. Ink, 547 U.S. 28, 45-46 (2006)("Congress, the antitrust enforcement agencies, and most economists have all reached the conclusion that a patent does not necessarily confer market power upon the patentee. Today, we reach the same conclusion, and therefore hold that, in all cases involving a tying arrangement, the plaintiff must prove that the defendant has market power in the tying product.").

28.   *See, e.g.*, United States v. Microsoft Corp., 253 F.3d 34, 95-97 (D.C. Cir. 2001) (en banc).

29.   U.S. Philips Corp. v. Int'l Trade Comm'n, 424 F.3d 1179, 1192-93 (Fed. Cir. 2005).

violate antitrust law (or constitute patent misuse) where the licensee is not coerced or forced to accept the bundle.[30]

### c. Exclusive Dealing or Price Restrictions

The Patent Act states that a patent owner may "grant and convey an exclusive right under his application for patent, or patents, to the whole or any specified part of the United States."[31] Without more, an agreement to enter into an exclusive license generally does not violate antitrust laws or constitute patent misuse.[32] Exclusive dealing agreements that require a licensee not to license other patents or technologies are typically assessed under the rule of reason and do not violate antitrust law unless they harm competition in a relevant market.[33]

Purely vertical license agreements that impose price or output restrictions on the licensee may be viewed as immune from antitrust scrutiny under patent law[34] or they may be assessed under the rule of reason under federal antitrust law.[35] Regardless of how they are treated

---

30. *See* Automatic Radio Mfg. Co. v. Hazeltine Research, 339 U.S. 827, 831 (1950) (finding no evidence of coercion and, therefore, no evidence of tying), *overruled on other grounds by* Lear, Inc. v. Adkins, 395 U.S. 653 (1969). In contrast *see, e.g.*, Paramount Pictures Corp. v. Johnson Broad., 2006 WL 367874, at *2 (S.D. Tex. 2006) (denying summary judgment where there was "a genuine issue of material fact as to whether Plaintiff expressly conditioned its licenses [for two television programs] . . . on Defendant's additionally entering into a license agreement for [another program] . . . .").

31. 35 U.S.C. § 261.

32. *See, e.g.*, D.E. Virtue v. Creamery Package Mfg. Co., 227 U.S. 8, 36-37 (1913). *See* part B of this chapter regarding antitrust merger law considerations for the acquisition of an exclusive license to a patent.

33. *See, e.g.*, United States v. Microsoft Corp., 253 F.3d 34, 61-64 (D.C. Cir. 2001) (en banc) (concluding, in part, that certain license restrictions had anticompetitive effects because they prevented original equipment manufacturers from pre-installing a rival web browser to Microsoft's web browser, thereby protecting Microsoft's monopoly from competition that might otherwise have occurred).

34. United States v. E.I. DuPont de Nemours & Co., 118 F. Supp. 41, 226 (D. Del. 1953), *aff'd*, 351 U.S. 377 (1956) (patent owners may limit the quantities of patented products pursuant to license agreement).

35. *See, e.g.*, State Oil Co. v. Khan, 522 U.S. 3, 19 (1997) (maximum resale price maintenance subject to rule of reason analysis); Leegin Creative Leather Prods. v. PSKS, Inc., 551 U.S. 877, 899-900 (2007) (minimum resale price maintenance analyzed under the rule of reason).

under federal law, such agreements potentially may violate state antitrust laws on resale price maintenance.[36]

Discrimination in royalty rates is not subject to the Robinson-Patman Act insofar as that statute applies only to price discrimination involving the sale of commodities.[37] The Act could apply, however, to a transaction that includes the sale of a commodity as well as a patent license.[38]

### d. Restrictions on Territories, Customers, or Fields of Use

Purely vertical nonprice agreements, such as territorial allocations and customer allocations by a licensor to a licensee, or field-of-use restrictions, are typically assessed under the rule of reason, as are similar agreements that do not involve patents.[39] There are arguments, however, that the patent context provides some additional protection from antitrust liability for such arrangements. Section 261 of the Patent Act provides a patent holder with the statutory right to grant a territorial license.[40] In

---

36.   A number of states have declined to follow *Leegin* and continue to treat minimum resale price maintenance as per se illegal. *See, e.g.*, People v. Bioelements, Inc., File No. 10011659 (Cal. Super. Ct. Riverside County, filed Dec. 30, 2010); consent decree filed Jan. 11, 2011 (enforcement action in which minimum resale price maintenance agreements constituted "vertical price-fixing in per se violation" of the California antitrust statute, the Cartwright Act.); O'Brien v. Leegin Creative Leather Prods., 277 P.3d 1062 (Kan. 2012) (rejecting the rule of reason analysis for minimum resale price maintenance). State law challenges to vertical price restraints have thus far been limited to minimum resale price maintenance arrangements.

37.   15 U.S.C. § 13. *See, e.g.*, La Salle St. Press v. McCormick & Henderson, Inc., 293 F. Supp. 1004, 1005-06 (N.D. Ill. 1968) *aff'd in part and rev'd in part*, 445 F.2d 84 (7th Cir. 1971) (finding the Robinson Patman Act inapplicable because the license at issue did not involve commodities).

38.   *See, e.g.*, Innomed Labs v. ALZA Corp., 368 F.3d 148, 161 (2d Cir. 2004) ("A [tangible] product that is patented, or that contains patented elements, remains a commodity for purposes of the Robinson-Patman Act . . . .").

39.   Continental T.V., Inc. v. GTE Sylvania Inc., 433 U.S. 36, 58 (1977).

40.   35 U.S.C. § 261, *supra* note 20.

addition, the Supreme Court has held that patent owners can grant licensees restricted to a field of use.[41]

e. "Excessive" or Postexpiration Royalties

As a general matter, the Supreme Court has held in *Brulotte v. Thys Co.*[42] that the holder of a bona fide patent can charge whatever price it chooses without triggering antitrust liability.[43]

The Supreme Court also ruled in *Brulotte*, however, that an agreement to charge royalties that continue *after* the patent at issue has expired is unlawful and unenforceable, although the Court's rationale was not clear.[44] This holding has been criticized, the main criticism being that postexpiration royalties could have business justifications that are not anticompetitive. However, *Brulotte* has not been revisited by the Supreme Court.

When a patent is declared invalid, royalties otherwise due on existing licenses are no longer payable.[45] This rule arises because the Supreme Court has held that a licensee may challenge the validity of a licensed patent, as provided for under *Lear, Inc. v. Adkins*,[46] and royalties cease if the licensee prevails in that challenge.[47]

In contrast, at least one court has ruled that the public policy concerns that animate the holding in *Lear*—that a patent (or copyright) licensee contracts only for rights that run with the applicable patent (or copyright) term—do not apply to trade secrets because their scope is not

41.  General Talking Pictures Corp. v. W. Elec. Co., 304 U.S. 175, 181 (1938) ("Patent owners may grant licenses extending to all uses or limited to use in a defined field.").

42.  Brulotte v. Thys Co., 379 U.S. 29 (1964).

43.  *Id.* at 33 ("A patent empowers the owner to exact royalties as high as he can negotiate with the leverage of that monopoly.").

44.  *Compare id.* at 30-31 *with* Scheiber v. Dolby Labs., 293 F.3d 1014, 1016-17 (7th Cir. 2002).

45.  *See, e.g.*, Span-Deck v. Fab-Con, 677 F.2d 1237, 1247 (8th Cir. 1982); Chromalloy Am. Corp. v. Fischmann, 716 F.2d 683, 685-86 (9th Cir. 1983).

46.  Lear, Inc. v. Adkins, 395 U.S. 653, 671-73 (1969).

47.  *Id.; see also* Rates Tech. v. Speakeasy, Inc., 685 F.3d 163, 172-73 (2d Cir. 2012) (following *Lear* and holding that pre-litigation licensing agreements cannot be used to bar licensees from later challenging the validity of a patent), *cert. denied*, 2013 WL 141177 (Jan. 14, 2013).

statutorily limited in time.[48] Specifically, the court rejected an argument that an agreement to pay royalties for rights to the trade secret for the antiseptic liquid compound known as "Listerine" became unenforceable after the trade secret was publicly disclosed.[49]

Subsequently, the Supreme Court upheld a forward-looking license agreement on a product for which a patent application had been filed although the patent was never issued.[50]

### f.   Grantbacks

A licensor sometimes requires the licensee to grant back to it a license to any patented improvements that the licensee makes on the original licensed invention. Such "grantbacks" typically do not raise antitrust concerns insofar as they are nonexclusive, as they are not likely to reduce competition.[51]

In contrast, an exclusive grantback potentially could raise antitrust concerns. For example, if a licensor with monopoly power required exclusive grantbacks from its licensees, such a condition potentially might be viewed as furthering maintenance of that licensor's monopoly power.[52] In addition, if an exclusive license grantback (or even a nonexclusive grantback) had the effect of discouraging the licensee from developing technology that would compete with the licensor's monopoly product, that could potentially raise an antitrust issue.[53]

### 2.   *Horizontal Licenses*

A patent license is "horizontal" if the licensee and licensor are actual or potential competitors and the license restricts competition between them.[54] Horizontal restrictions typically are reviewed under the rule of

---

48.    Warner-Lambert Pharm. Co. v. John J. Reynolds, Inc., 178 F. Supp. 655, 665 (S.D.N.Y. 1959).

49.    *Id.* at 665-67.

50.    Aronson v. Quick Point Pencil Co., 440 U.S. 257, 266 (1979).

51.    *See, e.g.,* IP AND ANTITRUST, *supra* note 17, § 25.2.

52.    *Cf.* Transparent-Wrap Mach. Corp. v. Stokes & Smith Co., 329 U.S. 637, 643 (1947).

53.    *See, e.g.,* INTELLECTUAL PROPERTY GUIDELINES, *supra* note 9, § 5.6 ("Grantbacks may adversely affect competition, however, if they substantially reduce the licensee's incentives to engage in research and development and thereby limit rivalry in innovation markets.").

54.    *See generally* IP AND ANTITRUST, *supra* note 17, § 30.2.

reason if they are "ancillary" to a plausibly procompetitive collaboration or joint venture, but they can be illegal per se under Section 1 of the Sherman Act if they constitute "naked" restrictions on competition.[55]

For example, the Supreme Court has upheld certain cross-licenses between competitors where, but for the cross-license, neither firm could compete against the other because each firm's patent permitted it to "block" the other.[56] Cross-licenses of that nature could be thought of as vertical in nature. In contrast, if two competitors agree to restrict competition and allocate territories between them by means of a licensing arrangement, such an agreement may be found to be illegal, even per se illegal, depending on the circumstances.[57]

The key distinction for horizontal licenses is whether the restrictions are "naked" or, instead, ancillary to some plausibly procompetitive collaboration or venture.[58] A naked restraint is one that is objectively intended to reduce price or output.[59] In contrast, "[a] restraint is ancillary when it may contribute to the success of a cooperative venture that promises greater productivity and output."[60] Ancillary restraints are evaluated generally under the rule of reason.[61] However, courts may also engage in a "quick look" analysis or a more tailored "enquiry meet for

---

55.  The focus of this section is on Section 1 challenges; however, horizontal licenses can also support evidence of exclusionary conduct by a monopolist under Section 2.

56.  Standard Oil Co. v. United States, 283 U.S. 163, 171 n.5 (1931).

57.  *See* Palmer v. BRG of Ga., Inc., 498 U.S. 46, 49-50 (1990) (per curiam) (holding that an agreement between two potential competitors to allocate territory between them to be illegal per se notwithstanding that the agreement involved copyright licenses); Palmer v. BRG of Ga., Inc., 874 F.2d 1417, 1434 (11th Cir. 1989) (explaining defendants' contention that their arrangement was "nothing more than an ordinary copyright royalty arrangement"), *rev'd*, 498 U.S. 46 (1990).

58.  *See* IP AND ANTITRUST, *supra* note 17, § 30.3.

59.  6 PHILLIP E. AREEDA & HERBERT HOVENKAMP, ANTITRUST LAW ¶ 1906 (2012); *see also, e.g.*, White Motor Co. v. United States, 372 U.S. 253, 263 (1963) (discussing examples of naked restraints that have "no purpose except stifling of competition"); *Palmer*, 874 F.2d at 1436 (noting that certain restraints are sufficiently naked if they "directly restrain price or output"); Polk Bros. v. Forest City Enters., 776 F.2d 185, 188 (7th Cir. 1985) (explaining that naked restraints involve a restriction on competition that "is unaccompanied by new production or products . . .").

60.  *Polk Brothers*, 776 F.2d at 189.

61.  *Id.*

the case" depending on how plausible and significant the procompetitive effects appear.[62]

a.   Cross-Licenses Generally

Courts typically refer to the exchange of nonexclusive licenses among patent holders as a "cross-license." Without more, two competitors agreeing to cross-license each other (nonexclusively) regarding their respective noninfringing patents should not present antitrust risks.

As noted above, cross-licenses are often procompetitive where the patent rights in question are either complementary or "blocking."[63] If each of two firms holds a patent that has at least one claim that would exclude the other, then the parties may be considered to hold "blocking patents."[64]

b.   Price Restrictions in Cross-Licenses

If two competitors agreeing to cross-licenses also agree on pricing to be charged to others, such an agreement may be found to be illegal per se, as noted above. For example, in *United States v. Line Material Co.*,[65] the Supreme Court held that a cross-licensing arrangement between two competitors was per se unlawful where the parties also agreed to fix prices charged to other licensees.[66]

---

62.   California Dental Ass'n v. FTC, 526 U.S. 756, 779-81 (1999) The Court in *California Dental* explained that where the anticompetitive effects of a restraint are "intuitively obvious," a truncated or quick look rule of reason approach is appropriate. Such restraints are viewed as facially anticompetitive but are sufficiently novel such that they have not yet been characterized as illegal per se. Under the quick look analysis, a restraint can be condemned without "elaborate industry analysis." *Id.* at 770 (internal citation omitted). In contrast, the "enquiry meet for the case" entails a "less quick look," which requires an analysis of "a restraint's circumstances, details, and logic." *Id.* at 758.

63.   *See* IP AND ANTITRUST, *supra* note 17, § 34.2a.

64.   *See* Standard Oil Co. v. United States, 283 U.S. 163, 171 n.5 (1931).

65.   United States v. Line Material Co., 333 U.S. 287, 311-12 (1948).

66.   *See also* United States v. New Wrinkle, 342 U.S. 379-80 (1952); United States v. Masonite Corp., 316 U.S. 265, 277 (1942).

c.  Output Limitations in Cross-Licenses

Nonexclusive cross-licenses between competitors, without more, are typically viewed as procompetitive and upheld by the courts.[67] However, courts are skeptical of cross-licenses between competing patent holders that restrict output, and such restrictions need to be justified as being procompetitive under the circumstances. For example, in *Hartford-Empire Co. v. United States*,[68] a group of firms limited each others' output through a series of cross-licenses that effectively created a patent "pool" that controlled 94 percent of production in the industry.[69] The Supreme Court affirmed the district court's decision that the patent pool and quantity restrictions were unlawful based on the output restriction.[70]

A license agreement that restricts competition among licensees may be found to be illegal. For example, in *American Equipment Co. v. Tuthill Building Material Co.*,[71] the court condemned as illegal a series of purported licensing arrangements involving the owner of patented brick loading equipment and various brick-maker licensees. The licensing agreements contained restrictions on the amount of bricks each licensee could produce. The patent being licensed, however, did not apply to the manufacture of bricks, but only to the mechanical handling of the formed bricks. As there was no legitimate justification for the patent owner to limit the amount of bricks produced by each brick-maker, the court reasoned that the licensing arrangement "was not a license provision, but was a price fixing, quantity production limitation, the inevitable result of which was the unreasonable restraint of commerce and the creation of a monopoly."[72]

d.  Patent Pools

Patent pools also involve the exchange of licenses between or among two or more patent holders. Where those cross-licenses involve the creation of a joint venture of some kind, courts often refer to the arrangements as patent pools, and restrictions by patent pools are subject

---

67.  *See, e.g., Standard Oil* 283 U.S. at 171 n.5 (upholding cross-licensing agreement regarding "blocking" patents).

68.  Hartford-Empire Co. v. United States, 323 U.S. 386 (1945).

69.  *Id.* at 400.

70.  *See id.* at 422.

71.  American Equip. Co. v. Tuthill Bldg. Material Co., 69 F.2d 406 (7th Cir. 1934).

72.  *Id.* at 409.

to antitrust review. The standard of that review may vary depending on how the participants' patents are viewed.

The Federal Circuit has explained that "a blocking patent is one that at the time of the license an objective manufacturer would believe reasonably might be necessary to practice the technology at issue."[73] Generally, the pooling of bona fide patents that are otherwise blocking or complementary and enable competition typically is viewed under the rule of reason. Thus, if the patent pool lacks market power, it is not likely to violate antitrust law.

In contrast, the pooling of patents is subject to strict antitrust scrutiny where such pooling on its face appears to reduce competition, such as the pooling of *competitive* patents that dominate a market.[74] For example, the FTC challenged as anticompetitive a patent pooling agreement between two manufacturers where the FTC alleged that, but for that agreement, the manufacturers would have competed with their independent technologies, and that their agreement effectively required each of them to charge at least $250 per procedure to sublicensees of the pooled patents.[75]

e.   Territorial Division between Patentee and Licensee

The Patent Act states that a patentee may "grant and convey an exclusive right under his application for patent, or patents, to the whole or any specified part of the United States."[76] In light of this provision, courts typically analyze antitrust claims relating to territorial divisions between a patentee and its licensee, where both parties practice the patent

---

73.   Princo Corp. v. Int'l Trade Comm'n, 563 F.3d 1301, 1310 (Fed. Cir. 2009), *subsequent opinion on reh'g*, 616 F.3d 1318 (Fed. Cir. 2010) (en banc).

74.   *Compare* Standard Oil Co. v. United States, 283 U.S. 163, 174 (1931) ("Where domination exists, a pooling of competing process patents, or an exchange of licenses for the purpose of curtailing the manufacture and supply of an unpatented product, is beyond the privileges conferred by the patents and constitutes a violation of the Sherman Act."), *with Princo Corp.*, 616 F.3d at 1338 (rejecting allegations that patent pool's cross-licensing provisions unlawfully suppressed competing technologies because appellant failed to demonstrate that the foreclosed technologies, "if available for licensing, would have matured into a competitive force" in the relevant market).

75.   Complaint ¶¶ 8-13, Summit Tech. Inc. & VISX, Inc., No. 9286, 1998 WL 34371488 (D. Mass. Mar. 24, 1998).

76.   35 U.S.C. § 261.

to some degree, under the rule of reason. This provision does not, however, permit competing downstream patentees to allocate territories between them or for competing downstream licensees to agree on territorial divisions as between each other.[77]

Territorial restrictions are subject to the first-sale doctrine.[78] Once the licensee sells the patented article, the patent owner loses the right to impose territorial restrictions as to subsequent sales. Post-first-sale territorial restrictions are subject to antitrust review under the standard of review applicable for the type of restriction at issue.[79]

### f. Territorial Division That Benefits Licensees

Courts have not interpreted the Patent Act to permit licensees to agree to licensing schemes that effectively coordinate competition among licensees. For example, in *United States v. Besser Manufacturing Co.,*[80] the court struck down an arrangement in which the owner of patented technology granted exclusive territorial licenses to the two largest competitors in the concrete-block-making industry on condition that the patent owner would not grant licenses to others without first securing the consent of the two competitors.[81] The court found that the requirement of joint consent effectively gave the licensees the power to control the industry and eliminate competition.[82]

### g. Horizontal Field-of-Use and Customer Restrictions between Patentee and Licensee

A "field-of-use" restriction is a provision in a patent license in which the patent holder limits the licensee's rights to particular uses of the patented article or to a particular group of customers. Generally, courts either treat horizontal field-of-use restrictions as expressly allowed under

---

77. *See, e.g.,* United States v. Nat'l Lead Co., 332 U.S. 319 (1947).
78. *See, e.g.,* Adams v. Burke, 84 U.S. 453 (1873); *cf.* United States v. Univis Lens Co., 316 U.S. 241, 250-52 (1942). *See also* 2 ALD, *supra* note 22, at 1097.
79. *See, e.g.,* Mallinckrodt, Inc. v. Medipart, Inc., 976 F.2d 700 (Fed. Cir. 1992).
80. United States v. Besser Mfg. Co., 96 F. Supp. 304 (E.D. Mich. 1951), *aff'd sub nom.* Besser Mfg. Co. v. United States, 343 U.S. 444 (1952).
81. *Id.* at 312; *see also* United States v. Singer Mfg. Co., 205 F. Supp. 394, 430 (S.D.N.Y. 1962), *rev'd*, 374 U.S. 174 (1963).
82. *Besser Mfg. Co.,* 96 F. Supp. at 311.

the Patent Act or evaluate them under a rule of reason standard.[83] Even where the patentee retains a right to some uses while licensing other uses to third parties, such restrictions are likely to be unlawful only if they restrict competition unreasonably.[84] This assumes that the restriction does not violate the first-sale doctrine, in which case the restriction likely would be assessed under the rule of reason.[85] However, competing patent holders generally cannot rely on their patent rights to justify the allocation of territories among themselves.[86]

Horizontal customer restrictions have been treated similar to field-of-use restrictions. For example, in *United States v. Westinghouse Electric Corp.*,[87] the court upheld the customer restrictions at issue and found that Section 1 does not compel patentees to enter into license agreements that "extend to every location and to every possible sale of the licensed product."[88]

### h.   Horizontal Territorial Restrictions That Exceed the Patent's Scope

If a horizontal territorial restriction exceeds the scope of the patent, it may be condemned as illegal per se. In cases where a patent accounts for a small percentage of the value of a product, a territorial restriction relating to the product may not be justified under antitrust law.

For example, in *United States v. Crown Zellerbach Corp.*,[89] a company developed and patented a technology used in paper towel dispensers. The company then licensed the technology to a competitor, specifying that the company and the competitor would each sell the paper towel machines on opposite sides of the Mississippi river. As part of the agreement, the two firms agreed to sell only paper towel machines

---

83.   *See, e.g.*, General Talking Pictures Corp. v. W. Elec. Co., 304 U.S. 175 (1938).

84.   *See, e.g.*, Benger Labs. v. R. K. Laros Co., 209 F. Supp. 639 (E.D. Pa. 1962), *aff'd per curiam*, 317 F.2d 455 (3d Cir. 1963); *see also* INTELLECTUAL PROPERTY GUIDELINES, *supra* note 9, § 2.3 & Example 1.

85.   *See supra* text accompanying note 21; *see also* Mallinckrodt, Inc. v. Medipart, Inc., 976 F.2d 700, 708 (Fed. Cir. 1992).

86.   *See supra* text accompanying notes 68-70 for discussion of Hartford-Empire Co. v. United States, 323 U.S. 386, 406-07 (1945).

87.   United States v. Westinghouse Electric Corp., 471 F. Supp. 532 (N.D. Cal. 1978), *aff'd in part and rev'd in part*, 648 F.2d 642 (9th Cir. 1981).

88.   *Id.* at 541.

89.   United States v. Crown Zellerbach Corp., 141 F. Supp. 118 (N.D. Ill. 1956).

that incorporated the patented technology. The court held that the agreement exceeded the scope of the patent grant because "a patentee who exacts a promise from his licensee not to engage in the manufacture or sale of competing goods not covered by the patent forfeits his patent protections."[90]

## D. Can a Company Be Subject to Antitrust Risk for Refusing to License a Patent?

If one develops intellectual property and obtains a patent, as a general matter the refusal to license that patent to another should not subject the patent holder to antitrust risk. The Supreme Court has observed that a refusal to license a patent "may be said to have been of the very essence of the right conferred by the patent, as it is the privilege of any owner of property to use or not use it, without question of motive."[91] Analogously, Section 271(d)(4) of the Patent Act provides specifically that a patent owner cannot be deemed guilty of misuse of a patent by refusing to use or license the patent.[92]

The Federal Circuit has held that a patentee's refusal to license its intellectual property right can support an antitrust claim under Section 2 only where (1) the patent was obtained through fraud, (2) the lawsuit to enforce the patent was a sham, or (3) the patent holder uses his patent to monopolize a market beyond the scope of the patent.[93] The court emphasized that "[i]n the absence of any indication of illegal tying, fraud on the Patent and Trademark Office, or sham litigation, the patent holder may enforce the statutory right to exclude others from making, using, or selling the claimed invention free from liability under the antitrust laws."[94]

Other courts have taken less deferential positions. For example, in addressing a monopoly claim involving a refusal to license copyrights, the First Circuit ruled that, "while exclusionary conduct can include a monopolist's unilateral refusal to license a copyright, an author's desire

---

90. *Id.* at 127.
91. Continental Paper Bag Co. v. E. Paper Bag Co., 210 U.S. 405, 429 (1908); *cf.* Special Equip. Co. v. Coe, 324 U.S. 370, 378-79 (1945) ("This Court has consistently held that failure of the patentee to make use of a patented invention does not affect the validity of the patent.")
92. 35 U.S.C. § 271(d)(4).
93. *In re* Independent Serv. Orgs. Antitrust Litig., 203 F.3d 1322, 1327 (Fed. Cir. 2000).
94. *Id.*

to exclude others from use of its copyrighted work is a presumptively valid business justification for any immediate harm to consumers."[95]

An even less deferential position has been taken by the Ninth Circuit, in *Image Technical Services v. Eastman Kodak Co.*[96] In *Kodak*, the Ninth Circuit applied a rebuttable presumption test, akin to that used in the First Circuit's *Data General Corp. v. Grumman Systems Support Corp.* decision.[97] The Ninth Circuit then rejected Kodak's justifications based on its ownership of patents that covered a subset of the parts at issue because they were "pretext[ual]" and adopted after the fact.[98] Consequently, Kodak was ordered to sell Kodak parts to competitors at non-discriminatory prices.[99]

### E. We Are Participating in a Standard-Setting Organization That May Relate to Some of Our Patents or Patented Products. What Antitrust Concerns Should We Keep in Mind?

A standard-setting organization (SSO) is an organization in which industry participants may gather to draft, vote on, and adopt technical standards. An SSO may also have policies and rules that govern the standard-setting process. Standards can be beneficial because they allow competing products to interact or interoperate with one another. For example, in the entertainment industry, multiple companies may produce CDs, DVDs, electronic equipment, and other items that implement common technical standards. Some industries may evaluate competing standards, but then gravitate toward one standard over time, such as with the implementation of Blu-ray and the discontinuation of HD-DVD for high-definition video. While standards can have procompetitive benefits, behavior relating to the standard-setting process and the resulting standards can also raise antitrust concerns.

The standard-setting process often can be thought of as a method of competition for *determining* a standard. However, once the standard is adopted, competition among products that *implement* the standard then occurs in the marketplace. The U.S. antitrust enforcement agencies have

---

95.    Data Gen. Corp. v. Grumman Sys. Support Corp., 36 F.3d 1147, 1187 (1st Cir. 1994).

96.    Image Technical Servs. v. Eastman Kodak Co., 125 F.3d 1195 (9th Cir. 1997).

97.    *Data General*, 36 F.3d 1147.

98.    *Kodak*, 125 F.3d at 1219-20.

99.    *Id.* at 1225-26.

recognized the potentially procompetitive benefits of such standard setting and that competition in such context occurs at both levels.[100]

The first potential antitrust concern involving standard setting relates to concerted activity and Section 1 of the Sherman Act, which prohibits agreements that unreasonably restrain trade. SSOs are often comprised of competitors that may work together to draft one or more technical standards. During the standard-setting process, those competitors may agree to approve one particular standard and not to approve other standards. The standard-setting process, depending on the relative "power" of the SSO, may thus potentially displace marketplace competition for the standard. For example, in *Allied Tube & Conduit Corp. v. Indian Head, Inc.*,[101] the National Fire Protection Association (NFPA) had significant influence because most cities and underwriters followed the NFPA's standards for building codes. In rejecting a proposal by the plaintiff to allow polyvinyl conduit in addition to steel conduit to cover electrical wiring in buildings, the NFPA, which included competitors of the plaintiff, effectively foreclosed the plaintiff from the market. It also potentially lessened innovation and reduced competition generally in the market for conduit. As a result, the Supreme Court addressed the potential harm to competition that can occur if one group of participants abuses the standard-setting process.[102]

---

100. In addition, the Standards Development Organization Advancement Act of 2004 provides that the conduct of a standards development organization while engaged in a standards-development activity may not be deemed illegal per se and is not subject to treble damages. *See* 15 U.S.C. §§ 4302, 4303. Those provisions apply to the organization itself, not its participants, and the organization must provide notice to the government to receive the protection from treble damages. *See* 15 U.S.C. §§ 4301, 4305.

101. Allied Tube & Conduit Corp. v. Indian Head, Inc., 486 U.S. 492 (1988).

102. *Id.* at 500-01 ("There is no doubt that the members of [standard-setting] associations often have economic incentives to restrain competition and that the product standards set by such associations have a serious potential for anticompetitive harm. Agreement on a product standard is, after all, implicitly an agreement not to manufacture, distribute, or purchase certain types of products. Accordingly, private standard-setting associations have traditionally been objects of antitrust scrutiny. When, however, private associations promulgate safety standards based on the merits of objective expert judgments and through procedures that prevent the standard-setting process from being biased by members with economic interests in stifling product competition, those private standards can have significant procompetitive advantages.") (citations omitted).

Similarly in *Radiant Burners, Inc. v. Peoples Gas Light & Coke Co.*,[103] the Court addressed the potential harm that can occur to competition when competitors are excluded from practicing an industry standard.[104] In *American Society of Mechanical Engineers v. Hydrolevel Corp.*,[105] the Court noted that an SSO "can be rife with opportunities for anti-competitive activity" and that the SSO itself can be liable for the actions of its agents.[106]

Accordingly, any company that participates in a standard-setting process bears a risk that a competitor whose technology is not adopted will contend that the SSO and its participants foreclosed the competitor by abusing or "hijacking" the process, by excluding the competitor, or by taking some other collective action that restrained competition for the standard or for products implementing the standard. SSOs and their members can design and implement policies and procedures to mitigate such potential risks.

The second potential antitrust concern involving standard setting relates to unilateral activity and Section 2 of the Sherman Act, which prohibits unlawful monopolization and attempted monopolization. If one company uses the standard-setting process or resulting standard to obtain or maintain monopoly power, the company may be subject to a Section 2 claim (or a challenge by the FTC for a violation of Section 5 of the FTC Act). For example, some SSO cases have involved allegations of a "patent ambush" in which a company has patents or patent applications that are essential to implementing a proposed standard but does not disclose them during the standard-setting process. After the standard is adopted, the patent holder may "ambush" the industry by asserting its

---

103. Radiant Burners, Inc. v. Peoples Gas Light & Coke Co., 364 U.S. 656, 660 (1961).
104. *Id.*
105. American Soc'y of Mech. Eng'rs v. Hydrolevel Corp., 456 U.S. 556 (1982).
106. *Id.* at 571, 577–78 ("When ASME's agents act in its name, they are able to affect the lives of large numbers of people and the competitive fortunes of businesses throughout the country. By holding ASME liable under the antitrust laws for the antitrust violations of its agents committed with apparent authority, we recognize the important role of ASME and its agents in the economy, and we help to ensure that standard-setting organizations will act with care when they permit their agents to speak for them. We thus make it less likely that competitive challengers like Hydrolevel will be hindered by agents of organizations like ASME in the future.").

patents, preventing other market participants from implementing the standard, and engaging in a "hold-up" of the industry by refusing to license its patents or by licensing them on unreasonable terms.[107]

Some SSOs have adopted policies and guidelines to reduce the risk of such an ambush and hold-up situation. For example, some SSOs require the disclosure of essential patents at specified points in the process and some require that participants agree that if their patented technology is chosen as part of the standard, they will license their applicable patents on fair, reasonable, and nondiscriminatory (FRAND) terms.

The FTC has been involved in several cases that addressed patent disclosure policies. For example, in *Dell Computer Corp.*,[108] the FTC obtained a consent order after a Dell representative to an SSO stated that Dell did not have any patents related to a standard, but Dell did have patents that it asserted after the standard was adopted.[109] In a more recent case, *Rambus, Inc.*,[110] the FTC brought a complaint against Rambus on a patent ambush theory. The FTC alleged that Rambus unlawfully obtained a monopoly by failing to disclose to an SSO pending patents that were the subject of standards adopted by that SSO. An administrative law judge found that Rambus's failure to its disclose pending patents to the SSO did not amount to exclusionary conduct and dismissed the complaint.[111] The full Commission reversed and in a unanimous decision found that Rambus intentionally misled the SSO by failing to disclose its pending patents and that this deception constituted a violation of Section 2.[112] The D.C. Circuit Court of Appeals later reversed on the grounds

107. *See* Broadcom Corp. v. Qualcomm Inc., 501 F.3d 297, 310-12 (3d Cir. 2007) (providing a summary of cases alleging "patent hold-up").

108. Dell Computer Corp., 121 F.T.C. 616 (1996) (consent order).

109. *See id.* at 617-18.

110. Rambus, Inc., 2004 WL 390647, at *1 (F.T.C. 2004) (initial decision), *vacated by* 2006 WL 2330117 (F.T.C. 2006).

111. *See id.* at *4-5.

112. Rambus Inc., 2006 WL 2330119, at *1 (F.T.C. 2006) (order reversing and vacating initial decision); Press Release, FTC, FTC Finds Rambus Unlawfully Obtained Monopoly Power: Deceptive Conduct Fostered "Hold-Up" of Computer Memory Industry (Aug. 2, 2006), *available at* http://www.ftc.gov/opa/2006/08/rambus.shtm ("Rambus's acts of deception constituted exclusionary conduct under Section 2 of the Sherman Act and contributed significantly to Rambus's acquisition of monopoly power in the four relevant markets.").

that the FTC failed to prove that the SSO would have adopted a different standard but for Rambus's nondisclosure.[113]

Another antitrust area related to unilateral behavior involves licensing commitments that may be made during the standard-setting process. In *Negotiated Data Solutions LLC*,[114] the FTC asserted that a company's refusal to fulfill a licensing commitment made by a predecessor in interest to the patent during a standard-setting process was an unfair method of competition and an unfair act or practice under Section 5 of the FTC Act.[115] In *Broadcom Corp. v. Qualcomm, Inc.*,[116] the Third Circuit Court of Appeals held that a company could face a Section 2 claim if it deceptively made a commitment to license on fair, reasonable, and nondiscriminatory terms to obtain standardization, and then reneged on the commitment after the standard was adopted.[117]

More recently, the FTC has taken the position that a patent holder that discloses its standard-essential patents and commits to license them on FRAND terms may violate Section 5 of the FTC Act by seeking injunctive relief against willing licensees implementing the standard.[118]

## F. We Have a Patent That We Would Like to Enforce against a Competitor. Can We Face any Antitrust Liability if We Bring a Patent Infringement Suit?

Enforcing a patent against a competitor through litigation typically should not expose a patent holder to antitrust liability provided that the patent holder (1) holds a bona fide patent that was not obtained through fraud on the U.S. Patent & Trademark Office (PTO), and (2) litigates in good faith such that it is not engaging in "sham litigation." Enforcement actions that fail either or both of those conditions, however, can raise serious antitrust risks. In addition, the courts and enforcement agencies have struggled to define whether and when the settlement of a bona fide

---

113. Rambus Inc. v. FTC, 522 F.3d 456 (D.C. Cir. 2008).
114. Analysis of Proposed Consent Order to Aid Public Comment, Negotiated Data Solutions LLC, File No. 0510094 (F.T.C. Jan 23, 2008), *available at* http.//www.ftc.gov/os/caselist/0510094/080122analysis.pdf.
115. *Id.*
116. Broadcom Corp. v. Qualcomm, Inc., 501 F.3d 297 (3d Cir. 2007).
117. *See id.* at 314.
118. *See, e.g.*, Statement of the Fed. Trade Comm'n, Robert Bosch GmbH, File No. 121-008, at 2, (F.T.C. Nov. 26, 2012), *available at* http://www.ftc.gov/os/caselist/1210081/121126boschcommissionstateme nt.pdf.

patent dispute can or should give rise to antitrust liability. Recognizing that this topic cannot be covered in depth in this chapter, we provide an overview below.

First, if a patent enforcement action does not reduce competition, then, as a practical matter, it is unlikely that significant antitrust liability would result even if a claim were not barred as a matter of law.

Second, Section 271(d) of the Patent Act states that a patent holder shall not be found liable for patent misuse or illegal extension of the patent right simply for seeking to enforce a patent.[119]

Patent misuse is a defense to infringement, rather than an affirmative antitrust claim. The patent misuse doctrine was discussed extensively in the Federal Circuit's en banc *Princo Corp. v. International Trade Commission*[120] decision. The majority reviewed the history of the doctrine and explained that Supreme Court precedent "established the basic rule of patent misuse: that the patentee may exploit his patent but may not use it to acquire a monopoly not embraced in the patent."[121] Accordingly, "the key inquiry under the patent misuse doctrine is whether, by imposing the condition in question, the patentee has impermissibly broadened the physical or temporal scope of the patent grant and has done so in a manner that has anticompetitive effects."[122]

The baseline for measuring whether a patent holder has broadened the scope of the patent "begins with substantial rights under the patent grant," including the rights (1) "to suppress the invention while continuing to prevent all others from using it"; (2) "to license others, or to refuse to license"; (3) "to charge such royalty as the leverage of the patent monopoly permits"; and (4) "to limit the scope of the license to a particular field of use."[123] Accordingly, patent misuse "has largely been confined to a handful of specific practices" that involve extending the scope of the patent grant.[124]

Section 271(d) of the Patent Act sets forth five types of conduct that may not provide a basis for finding misuse, such as refusing to license the patent or conditioning a license on the purchase of a separate product or patent (i.e., tying), unless the patent owner has market power in the

---

119.  35 U.S.C. § 271(d). Further, all patents are presumed valid under the Patent Act. 35 U.S.C. § 282.
120.  Princo Corp. v. Int'l Trade Comm'n, 616 F.3d 1318 (Fed. Cir. 2010) (en banc).
121.  *Id.* at 1327 (citation and internal quotation marks omitted).
122.  *Id.* at 1328 (citation omitted).
123.  *Id.* at 1328-29 (citation and internal quotation marks omitted).
124.  *Id.* at 1329 (citation omitted).

relevant market for the patent.[125] Patent misuse must involve some type of "patent leverage" to extend the scope of the patent grant.[126] An unrelated antitrust violation—such as a separate agreement between two competitors to suppress a different technology—does not establish a misuse defense. As the court explained, "it does not follow from the possible existence of an antitrust violation" with respect to a nonasserted patent that a patent holder has misused the asserted patent.[127]

However, a company that brings an infringement suit runs the risk that the accused infringer may bring some type of antitrust claim or counterclaim related to the patent holder's enforcement behavior that is separate from patent misuse and is not protected by the Section 271(d) immunity. Behavior may not be immune from attack under Section 2 of the Sherman Act if it involves fraud on the Patent Office, sham litigation or other bad-faith assertions of patent rights, or tying. In addition, the FTC has suggested that conduct that does not violate the Sherman Act may still violate the FTC Act.[128]

The first potential claim that could be raised in response to a patent enforcement action is that the patent holder is asserting a patent that it obtained through fraud on the PTO.[129] For an accused infringer to successfully bring such a claim, referred to as a *Walker Process* claim, it first must prove that the patent was obtained through fraud on the PTO and then it must prove all of the elements of a Section 2 claim (such as that the patent holder has a monopoly position in a properly defined relevant market).

Fraud on the PTO requires a showing that the patent applicant made a misleading statement or omission, that the applicant intended the PTO

---

125.  *Id.* at 1329-30.
126.  *Id.* at 1332.
127.  *Id.*
128.  *See* Analysis of Proposed Consent Order to Aid Public Comment, Negotiated Data Solutions LLC, File No. 0510094 (F.T.C. Jan. 23, 2008) *available at* www.ftc.goc.os/caselist/0150094/080122analysis.pdf; *see also* Jon Leibowitz, Comm'r, FTC, Unfair Methods of Competition in Commerce Are Hereby Declared Unlawful, Remarks Before the FTC Section 5 Workshop (Oct. 17, 2008), *available at* www.ftc.gov/bc/workshops/section5/docs/jleibowitz.pdf ("Reasonable people can disagree over whether N-Data violated the Sherman Act . . . [h]owever, it was clear to the majority of the Commission that reneging on a commitment was not acceptable business behavior and that . . . it would harm American consumers.").
129.  *See* Walker Process Equip. v. Food Mach. & Chem. Corp., 382 U.S. 172 (1965).

to rely on that statement or omission, and that the PTO did rely on it such that the patent would not have issued but for the statement or omission. Effectively, the standard for proving *Walker Process* fraud is similar to the standard for proving inequitable conduct under the Federal Circuit's en banc decision in *Therasense, Inc. v. Becton, Dickinson & Co.*[130] However, inequitable conduct is used as a "shield" that renders a patent unenforceable, while *Walker Process* is used as a "sword" that may render a patent holder liable for treble antitrust damages.[131]

In *Therasense*, the Federal Circuit explained that a patent may be held unenforceable for inequitable conduct only if the accused infringer can prove that the patent applicant (1) misrepresented or omitted material information (2) with the specific intent to deceive the Patent Office.[132] Materiality and intent are separate requirements, each of which must be proven by clear and convincing evidence.[133] In *Therasense*, the Federal Circuit raised the standards for materiality and intent.[134] The level of materiality to establish inequitable conduct is "but-for" materiality, meaning that the party alleging inequitable conduct must prove that the PTO would not have granted the patent but for the misrepresentation or omitting of material information.[135] The plaintiff must also prove that the applicant acted with the "specific intent to deceive" the PTO, i.e., that "the applicant *made a deliberate decision* to withhold a *known* material reference."[136]

The second potential claim that could be raised in response to a patent enforcement action is that the litigation was brought in bad faith or is a sham. A *Handgards*[137] claim alleges that a patent holder brought suit on a patent that it believed to be invalid, unenforceable, or not infringed at the time of enforcement. In that sense a *Handgards* claim differs from a *Walker Process* claim in that a *Handgards* plaintiff alleges that the patent holder "prosecuted infringement actions in bad faith, that is, with

---

130. Therasense, Inc. v. Becton, Dickinson & Co., 649 F.3d 1276 (Fed. Cir. 2011) (en banc).
131. *See* Nobelpharma AB v. Implant Innovations, Inc., 141 F.3d 1059, 1070 (Fed. Cir. 1998).
132. *Therasense*, 649 F.3d at 1287.
133. *Id.*
134. *Id.* at 1290.
135. *Id.* at 1291, 1295. The court recognized an exception to the rule requiring but-for proof in cases of "affirmative egregious misconduct." *Id.* at 1292.
136. *Id.* at 1290 (citation and internal quotation marks omitted).
137. *See* Handgards, Inc. v. Ethicon, Inc., 601 F.2d 986 (9th Cir. 1979) (*Handgards I*).

knowledge that the patents, though lawfully-obtained, were invalid."[138] A *Handgards* claim is a type of "sham" litigation claim.[139]

Since the Ninth Circuit's *Handgards* decisions, the Supreme Court has further addressed sham litigation claims. For an accused infringer to prevail on a sham litigation claim under the Supreme Court's standard in *Professional Real Estate Investors v. Columbia Pictures Industries*, it must prove that the litigation is both objectively and subjectively baseless.[140] This means that no objectively rational patent holder could think it would win the case and that the patent holder just wants to use the process itself, rather than the outcome of the litigation process, to harm the accused infringer.[141] As with *Walker Process* claims, after establishing that the patent litigation is a sham, the accused infringer must establish the additional elements of an antitrust claim.

A third potential claim could arise from the regulatory overlap of patent enforcement where asserting a patent may be alleged to be part of an abuse of governmental process. For example, pharmaceutical patent litigation can arise under The Drug Price Competition and Patent Term Restoration Act of 1984, as amended, commonly known as the Hatch-Waxman Act, which requires patent holders to list certain patents in the "Orange Book."[142] If a patent holder lists a patent in the Orange Book and brings an infringement suit, the accused infringer may allege that the Orange Book listing itself was a sham or was done in bad faith. For example, in *In re Gabapentin Patent Litigation*, a plaintiff raised an antitrust claim that the Orange Book listing was done improperly to restrict generic competition.[143]

---

138.  *Id.* at 994.
139.  Handgards, Inc. v. Ethicon, Inc., 743 F.2d 1282, 1294 (9th Cir. 1984) (*Handgards II*).
140.  *See* Professional Real Estate Investors v. Columbia Pictures Indus., 508 U.S. 49, 60 (1993).
141.  *Id.* at 60-61.
142.  Hatch-Waxman Act, Pub. L. No. 98-417.
143.  *See In re* Gabapentin Patent Litig., 649 F. Supp. 2d 340, 358 (D.N.J. 2009) ("Purepac repeatedly emphasizes that it is targeting Warner-Lambert's overall pattern of alleged abuse of the regulatory process, and that '[t]he anticompetitive effects and legality of the alleged monopolization scheme must be evaluated as a whole.'") (internal citations omitted); *see also In re* Buspirone Patent & Antitrust Litig., 185 F. Supp. 2d 363, 377 (S.D.N.Y. 2002) (finding that patent holder's listing of patent in the FDA Orange Book was done in bad faith, was objectively baseless, and was not protected by *Noerr-Pennington* immunity).

There are also recent examples of antitrust claims that allege an abuse of the Food and Drug Administration (FDA) citizen petition process. The citizen petition process allows individuals to raise with the FDA legitimate concerns about products regulated by the agency. Plaintiffs have alleged that branded pharmaceutical companies have filed sham citizen petitions in an effort to delay entry of a competing generic drug.[144] As mentioned above, plaintiffs alleging sham claims must prove that the petition is both objectively and subjectively baseless. Courts have considered several factors as evidence that a citizen's petition is baseless, including whether: (1) the petition was filed on the eve of generic entry; (2) the petition requests action that the filer knows is contrary to FDA rules and practice; (3) the FDA responds favorably or harshly to the petition; and/or (4) the filing of the petition actually delayed generic entry.[145]

A fourth potential claim that can arise in the enforcement context is a tying claim. See Section C above for a discussion of tying claims in the context of intellectual property and licensing.

Finally, settling a patent infringement suit can also raise antitrust or competition concerns. Section G below discusses "reverse-payment" settlements. However, even a "normal" patent settlement may involve an agreement between competitors. If such an agreement restrains trade in some way, it may not be granted immunity and, therefore, may be subject to antitrust attack simply because it was characterized as a patent settlement rather than a standalone agreement.[146] In addition, Section C above discusses the antitrust issues related to license agreements generally. Those same issues may apply to settlement agreements that contain a license.

---

144. *See, e.g.*, Complaint ¶ 4, A.F.L. - A.G.C. Bldg. Trades Welfare Plan v. Pfizer Inc., No. 12-civ-00931 (S.D.N.Y. Feb. 6, 2012); *In re* Wellbutrin XL Antitrust Litig., 260 F.R.D. 143 (E.D. Pa. 2009).

145. *See* Seth C. Silber, Jonathon Lutinski & Rachel Taylon, *Abuse of the FDA Citizen Petition Process: Ripe for Antitrust Challenge?*, 25 ANTITRUST HEALTHCARE CHRON., no. 2, Jan. 2012 at 26, 36-39.

146. *See* Standard Oil Co. v. United States, 283 U.S. 163, 169-70 (1931) ("The limited monopolies granted to patent owners do not exempt them from the prohibitions of the Sherman Act and supplementary legislation. Hence the necessary effect of patent interchange agreements, and the operations under them, must be carefully examined in order to determine whether violations of the Act result.") (internal citations omitted).

## G. We Are Involved in Patent Infringement Litigation with a Competitor and Would Like to Settle the Case. What Antitrust Issues Should We Consider When Entering a Settlement Agreement?

### 1. Settlements of Patent Litigation Generally

The Supreme Court held in *Standard Oil Co. v. United States* that courts should encourage settlement of "legitimately conflicting claims."[147] For example, in *Boston Scientific Corp. v. Schneider (Europe) AG,*[148] the district court stated that it is "well-established that settlement of patent litigation through a cross-licensing agreement does not in and of itself violate the antitrust laws." Where the settlement covers patents that otherwise would have blocked the settling parties from competing, without more, such a settlement may be upheld on policy grounds.[149] Settlement agreements that contain restrictions on price or otherwise affect competition beyond mere cross-licensing are subject to stricter scrutiny, as noted above, and are not insulated from antitrust scrutiny merely because they are embodied in a settlement agreement (although the settlement context may enhance the business justifications for the arrangement).

### 2. Settlements of Patent Litigation in the Hatch-Waxman Context

In addition to the general settlement considerations discussed above, the settlement of pharmaceutical patent suits brought under the Hatch-Waxman Act has received attention from antitrust enforcement agencies, Congress, and the courts. So-called "reverse-payment" settlements are agreements in which a patent infringement suit brought by a branded drug manufacturer against a proposed generic drug manufacturer is settled by: (1) a payment or some other transfer of value[150] from the

---

147.  *Id.* at 171.
148.  Boston Scientific Corp. v. Schneider (Europe) AG, 983 F. Supp. 245, 269 (D. Mass. 1997), *dismissed sub nom.* Boston Scientific Corp. v. Schneider (USA), Inc., 152 F.3d 947 (Fed. Cir. 1998).
149.  *See, e.g.*, *Standard Oil*, 283 U.S. at 171; Carpet Seaming Tape Licensing Corp. v. Best Seam Inc., 694 F.2d 570, 579-80 (9th Cir. 1982).
150.  The antitrust agencies and the courts have taken varying interpretations of what is considered "compensation" in the form of a transfer of value. For example, the agencies may assert that transfers of value include agreements beyond outright cash payments, such as licensing deals and

patent holder (the branded manufacturer) to the alleged patent infringer (the generic manufacturer); and (2) an agreement by the generic manufacturer not to market the generic drug at issue before a date that is later in time but no later than the date of patent expiration. These payments are termed "reverse" because they are in contrast to more traditional settlements in which an alleged infringer may be expected to make a payment to the patent holder.

Parties that settle a Hatch-Waxman suit, or enter into any other agreement that may affect the launch date of the proposed generic product, may have to report the details of their private settlement to the FTC. The Hatch-Waxman Act, as amended by the Medicare Prescription Drug, Improvement, and Modernization Act of 2003, requires the filing with the FTC and the DOJ of settlements involving Abbreviated New Drug Applications and other agreements between a branded manufacturer and a generic manufacturer.[151]

The FTC and the DOJ have taken the position that reverse-payment settlements are "presumptively unlawful" "payments-for-delay" because they result in two competitors agreeing not to compete in violation of Section 1 of the Sherman Act and Section 5 of the FTC Act.[152]

---

commitments by the brand manufacturer not to launch a competing authorized generic.

151. *See* Medicare Prescription Drug, Improvement, and Modernization Act, Pub. L. No. 108-173 § 1112(a)(2), 117 Stat. 2066 [hereinafter Medicare Modernization Act]. Under the Medicare Modernization Act, the companies must file with the FTC and the DOJ the text or a written description of the agreements within ten business days of execution. The failure to timely file may result in a civil penalty enforcement action brought by the DOJ, or a proceeding brought by the FTC, in which a district court could issue a fine of up to $11,000 for each day the required filing was late. *Id.* § 1115. *See also* Letter from Richard Feinstein, Director, FTC Bureau of Competition, to Helene D. Jaffe, Att'y, Weil, Gotshal & Manges LLP 4 (May 9, 2011) ("The MMA was designed to ensure that the antitrust agencies will be afforded an early opportunity to review agreements that may affect the sale of generic drugs."), *available at* http://www.ftc.gov/os/closings/110510affeletter.pdf.

152. Brief for the United States in Response to the Court's Invitation, *Arkansas Carpenters Health & Welfare Fund v. Bayer, AG*, 2009 WL 8385027, at *10 (2d Cir. July 7, 2009); Fed. Trade Comm'n, How the Federal Trade Commission Works to Promote Competition & Benefit Consumers in a Dynamic Economy, Prepared Statement Before the United States Senate Committee on the Judiciary Subcommittee on Antitrust, Competition Policy and Consumer Rights (June 9, 2010),

Courts have issued varying decisions regarding reverse-payment settlements. In *In re Cardizem CD Antitrust Litigation*,[153] the Sixth Circuit held that a reverse-payment agreement that provided for an interim settlement was per se illegal.[154]

Other circuit courts have found that reverse-payment agreements that settle bona fide patent litigation and that do not exclude competition beyond the scope of the patent at issue are generally immune from antitrust challenge.[155] The Court of Appeals for the Federal Circuit, which handles the appeals of all suits that arise under the patent laws, examines "whether the agreements restrict competition beyond the exclusionary zone of the patent."[156] Absent sham litigation or fraud on the PTO, the Federal Circuit does not consider the validity of the patent in evaluating the settlement.[157]

Recently, the Third Circuit in *In re K-Dur Antitrust Litigation*[158] rejected the scope-of-the-patent analysis.[159] In so doing, the *K-Dur* court held that reverse payments in the pharmaceutical sector are subject to a "quick look" rule-of-reason review. Pursuant to that analysis, reverse payments are "*prima facie* evidence of an unreasonable restraint of trade, which could be rebutted by showing that the payment (1) was for a

---

*available at* http://www.ftc.gov/os/testimony/100609dynamiceconomy .pdf. According to FTC Chairman Jon Leibowitz, "[o]ne of the Commission's top competition priorities is stopping 'pay-for-delay' agreements between brand-name pharmaceutical companies and generic competitors that delay the entry of lower priced generic drugs into the market." *Id.*

153.   *In re* Cardizem CD Antitrust Litig., 332 F.3d 896 (6th Cir. 2003).

154.   *Id.* at 908-09.

155.   *See, e.g.*, FTC v. Watson Pharms., 677 F.3d 1298 (11th Cir. 2012), *cert. granted*, 2012 WL 4758105 (Dec. 7, 2012); *In re* Ciprofloxacin Hydrochloride Antitrust Litig., 544 F.3d 1323 (Fed. Cir. 2008); *In re* Tamoxifen Citrate Antitrust Litig., 466 F.3d 187 (2d Cir. 2006); Schering-Plough Corp. v. FTC, 402 F.3d 1056 (11th Cir. 2005); Andrx Pharms. v. Elan Corp., 421 F.3d 1227 (11th Cir. 2005).

156.   *Ciprofloxacin*, 544 F.3d at 1336.

157.   *Id.*

158.   *In re* K-Dur Antitrust Litig., 686 F.3d 197 (3d Cir. 2012), *petition for cert. filed*, Merck & Co. v. La. Wholesale Drug Co., 81 U.S.L.W. 3090 (Aug. 24, 2012) (No. 12-245) *and petition for cert. filed*, Upsher-Smith Labs. v. La. Wholesale Drug Co, 81 U.S.L.W. 3090. (Aug. 29, 2012) (No. 12-265).

159.   *K-Dur*, 686 F.3d at 217.

purpose other than delayed entry or (2) offers some procompetitive benefit."[160]

Plaintiffs continue to challenge such settlements in court.[161] Commentators have taken various positions regarding the debate.[162] In December 2012, the Supreme Court granted the government's petition for *certiorari* in *FTC v. Watson Pharmaceuticals*,[163] setting potentially setting the stage for a resolution of the split in the circuits regarding reverse-payment settlements.[164] The Supreme Court had not yet issued its ruling as this publication went to press.

---

160.   *Id.* at 218.

161.   Complaint ¶ 16, Chimes Pharm. v. Pfizer Inc., No. 11-5375 (N.D. Cal. Nov. 7, 2011) (alleging agreement between Ranbaxy and Pfizer "constitutes a market allocation agreement between competing providers of Lipitor and its generic equivalent to illegally restrain trade"); *In re* Androgel Antitrust Litig. (No. II), 687 F. Supp. 2d 1371 (N.D. Ga. 2010) (granting in full defendants' motion to dismiss complaint brought by the FTC and denying in part defendants' motion to dismiss complaint brought by private plaintiffs), *aff'd*, FTC v. Watson Pharms., 677 F.3d 1298 (11th Cir. 2012) (affirming dismissal of FTC complaint for failure to state a claim), *cert. granted*, 2012 WL 4758105 (Dec. 7, 2012); King Drug Co. of Florence v. Cephalon, Inc., 702 F. Supp. 2d 514 (E.D. Pa. 2010), *abrogated by K-Dur*, 686 F.3d at 214.

162.   *Compare* IP AND ANTITRUST, *supra* note 17, § 15.3a1(C) (proposing that a payment from a patent holder to an infringement defendant in exchange for the defendant's agreement to delay entry into the market should be found "presumptively unlawful, shifting the burden of proof to the infringement plaintiff" to show that the likelihood of prevailing in the infringement suit is significant and that the payment does not exceed likely litigation costs), *and* C. Scott Hemphill, *Paying for Delay: Pharmaceutical Patent Settlement as a Regulatory Design Problem*, 81 N.Y.U. L. REV. 1553, 1561 (2006) ("[A] settlement should be accorded a presumption of illegality as an unreasonable restraint of trade if the settlement both restricts the generic firm's ability to market a competing drug and includes compensation from the innovator to the generic firm."), *with* Marc G. Schildkraut, *Patent-Splitting Settlements and the Reverse Payment Fallacy*, 71 ANTITRUST L.J. 1033, 1068 (2004) ("[T]here is something to be said for simply declaring settlements arguably within the scope of the patent to be *per se* legal.").

163.   FTC v. Watson Pharm., 677 F.3d 1298 (11th Cir. 2012), *cert. granted*, 2012 WL 4758105 (2012).

164.   The defendants in *K-Dur* also filed petitions for *certiorari* with the Supreme Court. The Court may be holding those petitions pending its ruling in *Watson Pharmaceuticals*. The Court scheduled oral arguments

Both houses of Congress have engaged in legislative efforts to restrict or prohibit reverse-payment settlements. In 2009, legislation aimed at such settlements was considered: the Protecting Consumer Access to Generic Drugs Act in the House of Representatives[165] and the Preserve Access to Affordable Generics Act in the Senate.[166] Although the initial 2009 bills stalled, the legislation was reintroduced in the Senate in January 2011 but was not enacted.[167]

Currently, given the uncertain state of the law, settling pharmaceutical patent litigation in a transaction that results in a payment (or other consideration) flowing from the branded pharmaceutical manufacturer to the generic manufacturer may expose the parties to antitrust scrutiny. Parties contemplating such an agreement should consider the specific facts and circumstances of the case at hand to assess their risks.

## H.  Where Can I Go for More Information?

The foregoing discussion focused on case law. To the extent additional information is needed on any of the topics discussed herein, the best place to start is a treatise, such as the comprehensive *IP and Antitrust*, by Herbert Hovenkamp, Mark D. Janis, Mark A. Lemley, and Christopher R. Leslie. A topical breakdown of the relevant chapters in that treatise is included below, as well as a number of other publications that address the various topics. Another helpful resource is *Antitrust Law Developments*,[168] which includes a detailed chapter covering many of the topics addressed above and below.

### 1.  Patent Acquisition

- 1 Herbert Hovenkamp et al., *IP and Antitrust: An Analysis of Antitrust Principles Applied to Intellectual Property Law* §§ 14.1-14.4 (2d ed. 2010) (*IP and Antitrust*);

---

in *Watson Pharmaceuticals* for March 25, 2013 and the court is expected to render a decision this term.
165.  Protecting Consumer Access to Generic Drugs Act H.R. 1706, 111th Cong. (2009).
166.  Preserve Access to Affordable Generics Act S. 316, 110th Cong. (2007) (reintroduced as S. 369, 111th Cong., Feb. 3, 2009).
167.  Preserve Access to Affordable Generics Act S. 27, 112th Cong. (2011).
168.  1 ALD, *supra* note 22, at 173-78.

- ABA Section of Antitrust Law, *Antitrust Counterattack in Intellectual Property Litigation Handbook* 112-39 (2010) (*Antitrust Counterattack*)).

## 2. Licensing of Intellectual Property

- 1, 2 *IP and Antitrust* §§ 7.4b (vertical agreements), 7.4c (exclusive licenses, exclusive cross-licenses and pools, concerted refusals to deal), 7.4d (settlement terms involving price-, output-, or territory-restricted licenses, field-of-use restrictions), 13.1-13.5 (unilateral refusals to license), 21.1-21.5 (tying), 23.1-23.4 (royalty provisions), 34.1-34.4 (cross-licensing and patent pools);
- DOJ & FTC, *Antitrust Guidelines for the Licensing of Intellectual Property* (1995), *available at* http://www.justice.gov/atr/public/guidelines/0558.pdf. The FTC/DOJ Guidelines are a useful resource, but it is important to note that the Guidelines do not have the power of law and their treatment in the courts may vary;
- *Antitrust Counterattack* at 112-39;
- ABA Section of Antitrust Law, *Federal Antitrust Guidelines for Licensing of Intellectual Property: Origins and Applications* (3d ed. 2010);
- ABA Section of Antitrust Law, *Intellectual Property and Antitrust Handbook* 139-247, 273-318 (2007) (*ABA IP & Antitrust Handbook*);
- ABA Section of Antitrust Law, *Pharmaceutical Industry Antitrust Handbook* 229-82 (2009) (*Pharmaceutical Industry Antitrust Handbook*).

## 3. Joint Ventures Involving Intellectual Property

- 2 *IP and Antitrust* §§ 36.1-36.4;
- *Pharmaceutical Industry Antitrust Handbook* at 229-82.

## 4. Standard-Setting Organizations Relating to Patents or Patented Products

- 2 *IP and Antitrust* §§ 35.1-35.8;
- *Antitrust Counterattack* at 109-12;

- ABA Section of Antitrust Law, *Handbook on Antitrust Aspects of Standard Setting* (2d ed. 2011).

## 5. *Patent Enforcement*

- 1 *IP and Antitrust* §§ 5.4a, 11.1-11.2 (*Walker Process* claims), 5.4b, 11.3a, 11.4b (*Handgards* claims), 11.3b4 (abuse of governmental process generally, *Gabapentin*), 21.1-21.5 (tying);
- *Antitrust Counterattack* at 92-107;
- *ABA IP & Antitrust Handbook* at 318-407.

## 6. *Settlement Agreements Involving Patents*

a.  Settlements of Patent Litigation Generally

- 1 *IP and Antitrust* §§ 7.1-7.4a-d, f (settlements generally, terms involving price-, output-, or territory-restricted licenses, field-of-use restrictions), 7.5 (procedure, disclosure of settlements);
- *ABA IP & Antitrust Handbook* at 247-72.

b.  Settlements of Patent Litigation in the Hatch-Waxman Context

- 1 *IP and Antitrust* § 7.4e;
- *Antitrust Counterattack* at 199-221;
- *ABA IP & Antitrust Handbook* at 247-72;
- *Pharmaceutical Industry Antitrust Handbook* at 283-305.

## CHAPTER VII

# ANTITRUST COMPLIANCE

## A.  I Have Inherited the Responsibility for Managing Our Company's Compliance Program. What Should I Do?

Whether taking over a well-established antitrust compliance program or a rigorous program that is only in its early stages, someone taking on compliance responsibilities should determine what program elements are currently in place and establish priorities for creating or improving them as needed. Ultimately, the goal is to establish a culture of compliance through active oversight and participation by appropriate individuals throughout the organization.

There is no single form of "best practices" for a compliance program, because what will work effectively for any particular company depends on its own specific culture, its people, and the industries in which it operates. Moreover, what was an effective compliance program at one time will no doubt need revisions as the company's business evolves. The following elements tend to be the core components of most effective compliance programs:

- Executives who make it known throughout the company that they are committed to compliance;
- Training programs and written standards that guide executives and employees in appropriate business conduct for their industry and circumstances;
- A method for anonymous employee reporting of potential violations and confidential evaluation of those reports;
- Periodic evaluations to detect possible breaches;
- Business units that work cooperatively with company counsel responsible for compliance; and
- Counsel experienced in providing antitrust advice.

Most companies decide to design their compliance program to meet the standards set out by the U.S. Sentencing Commission (USSC) in its

United States Sentencing Guidelines for the sentencing of organizations,[1] as well as the competition compliance guidance brochure that was released by the European Commission in late 2011.[2] Both of these are discussed in more detail below. Because a compliance program cannot be instituted overnight throughout a company, the specific individuals assigned overall responsibility for the compliance and ethics program should set a list of priorities for elements of the compliance program that need to be adjusted or introduced and obtain approvals for implementation of these elements from executives at the top of the organization.

### B.  Are There Sample Compliance Programs That I Can Implement in My Company?

Compliance programs should be company-specific, and each company's program should be tailored to meet the specific needs of that organization based upon an assessment of the risks arising from the activities of that company. Differences between companies, even within the same industry, may require substantial differences in their respective compliance programs.

The program's overall design needs to fit the company culture. Its manuals and written products will be effective reference tools only if they are tailored specifically to the company with particular business units and issues in mind. Similarly, its training programs need to address the company's products, services, and business units, with modules that focus on issues relevant to particular employees' responsibilities and competitive relationships. That said, sample materials that may be helpful in developing a tailored compliance program are available in American Bar Association publications related to compliance, which are detailed in answer to Question N below.

Although development of a compliance program can *begin* with a sample or with another company's program, someone who knows the company's business will need to tailor it carefully. The company's

---

1.  U.S. SENTENCING COMM'N, U.S. SENTENCING GUIDELINES MANUAL § 8B2.1 (effective Nov. 1, 2012) [hereinafter SENTENCING GUIDELINES] *available                    at*                    http://www.ussc.gov/Guidelines/ 2012_Guidelines/Manual_HTML/Chapter_8.htm.

2.  In November 2011, the European Commission published a brochure, "Compliance Matters," which describes key competition rules and sets out generally recognized basic methods to help companies ensure compliance with EU competition rules.

competitive circumstances should be addressed with specificity. For example, a research scientist or engineer developing a new widget will need instructions about permissible responses to a competitor who asks her about the current projects on which she is currently working, and a member of the sales force will need to know how to react to a salesman from a competitor who suggests dividing territories. All employees need a common baseline knowledge of antitrust issues, but each employee also needs details relevant to their own possible challenges.

## C. What Are the Components of an Effective Compliance Program?

### 1. Standards in the Sentencing Guidelines a Good Starting Point

The Sentencing Guidelines, which contain the factors taken into account in the calculation of fines for organizations found guilty of criminal conduct, also provide significant guidance to companies in the structuring of their corporate antitrust compliance program. The USSC recognized that, "despite its best efforts to prevent wrongdoing in its ranks," even the most careful of organizations may nonetheless be found criminally liable for a single employee's illegal conduct. "[T]o alleviate the harshest aspects of this institutional vulnerability," the USSC provides more lenient corporate sentences for offenders who, at the time of the offense, had implemented an "effective compliance and ethics program"[3] that meets certain eligibility criteria.

Overall, an effective program is one in which the company acts to "exercise due diligence" and "promote an organizational culture that encourages ethical conduct and a commitment to compliance."[4] The Guidelines specify minimum requirements for such a program, which are generally as follows:

- Establish standards and procedures to prevent and detect criminal conduct;
- Exercise reasonable oversight of a compliance and ethics program, with active involvement and direct reporting authority

---

3.  Paula Desio, Deputy Gen. Counsel, U.S. Sentencing Comm'n, An Overview of the Organizational Guidelines, *available at* http://www.ussc.gov/Guidelines/Organizational_Guidelines/ORGOVER VIEW.pdf. *See also generally* Chapter Eight of the SENTENCING GUIDELINES, *supra* note 1, § 8B2.1.

4.  *Id.* § 8B2.1.

from the individual(s) responsible for the corporation's compliance program to the corporation's Board of Directors;

- Ensure that no individual involved in overseeing compliance has engaged in illegal activities or other conduct inconsistent with an effective compliance program;
- Communicate periodically the company's compliance standards and procedures and conduct effective training of such;
- Monitor, audit, and periodically evaluate compliance with the program, including providing anonymous or confidential means for reporting potential breaches;
- Promote compliance consistently throughout the company, establishing appropriate incentives and disciplinary procedures for compliance; and
- Take reasonable steps to respond appropriately if criminal conduct is detected to prevent further such conduct, including making modifications required.[5]

Practitioners generally agree that an effective compliance program is critical for a company, both to avoid antitrust violations and to identify potentially dangerous conduct before a violation takes place.[6]

The company's compliance program and compliance monitoring may also afford the company the ability to discover its own antitrust malfeasance and to consider whether it should seek leniency by self-reporting. The Department of Justice's (DOJ) Leniency Program, which it describes as "its most important investigative tool for detecting cartel activity," provides amnesty or leniency to corporations and individuals who report their cartel activity and then follow that reporting with full cooperation in the ensuing DOJ investigation. For the first reporter of cartel activity, leniency can mean avoiding criminal conviction, fines,

---

5.    *Id.* § 8B2.1(b).

6.    Unlike other areas of criminal law enforcement, the DOJ has not given companies credit in antitrust sentencing for having an effective compliance program, often as the result of "substantial suthority personnel" having participated in, condoned, or being willfully ignorant of the offense. *See id.* § 8B2.5(f) (in effect prior to November 30, 2010). At least one former DOJ antitrust official has urged changing this policy, arguing that leniency credit would encourage companies to develop internal programs that may prevent criminal antitrust behavior. Joseph Murphy & William Kolasky, *The Role of Anti-Cartel Compliance Programs In Preventing Cartel Behavior*, 26 ANTITRUST 61, 63 (Spring 2012).

and prison sentences altogether, if the requirements of the Leniency Program are met.[7]

The renewal of the Antitrust Criminal Penalty Enhancement and Reform Act (ACPERA) provides even further incentive for an effective compliance program. ACPERA places a limitation on what could be recovered from a leniency applicant in any federal or state civil litigation, except actions brought by the state, to the actual damages sustained that are attributable to the commerce done by the leniency applicant, as opposed to treble damages.[8]

## 2. *Ensure the Company Has an Appropriate Antitrust Compliance Manual*

A company's Antitrust Compliance Manual serves as the backbone of its effective antitrust compliance program. Built on the company's Code of Conduct and Ethics (or similar overall compliance principles), the Antitrust Compliance Manual is the foundational document for the program.

If the company already has an antitrust manual, counsel should evaluate its current applicability or ask outside antitrust counsel to do so. The manual should be drafted in language that will be meaningful to employees and should be readily available (e.g., on a company intranet site) as a reference resource. At least annually, compliance counsel should obtain a signature from those employees whose job responsibilities put them in a position to need compliance training stating that the manual is available to them, that they have read the manual, that they understand its principles, and that they agree to abide by its standards. In addition to the company's executives, this annual compliance reminder should include at least those employees who interact with competitors or participate in trade associations, as well as their respective managers and supervisors.

Generally, the antitrust manual will briefly describe the basic antitrust laws using language that will be clear and can be understood by all employees. It should describe the types of business conduct that may be illegal under the antitrust laws, such as (1) agreements between competitors that reduce competition on price, quality, service, or innovation and conduct; (2) exchanges of competitively sensitive

---

7.  Details of the DOJ Leniency Program are found on the agency's website at http://www.justice.gov/atr/public/criminal/leniency.html.

8.  Antitrust Criminal Penalty Enhancement & Reform Act of 2004, Public Law 108-237; 15 U.S.C. § 1, as amended (2010).

information between competitors; (3) conduct by a company with a large market share that prevents competitors from competing effectively; and (4) certain agreements between manufacturers and distributors or retailers that unnecessarily restrict the competitive marketplace. Memorable examples that relate specifically to the company's business can help ensure that employees understand the practical application of this guidance to their own work.

In addition, the antitrust manual should emphasize that both criminal and civil penalties may be imposed, that individuals as well as companies may be charged, and that private plaintiffs may be awarded treble damages in certain circumstances for violations of the antitrust laws. Companies often choose to establish relatively conservative standards for compliance so as to avoid not only actual criminal or civil violations of the antitrust laws but also to lower the risk that a third party could successfully mount a legal challenge to the company's conduct under the antitrust laws in the first place.

The overriding principle of the manual, and all relevant training, should be that employees need to understand the basic principles of antitrust and that they need to recognize when to seek legal advice about whether a situation raises antitrust issues. Overall, employees need to understand enough about the laws to give them the ability to spot a potential issue that should be discussed with the company's counsel. Those assigned responsibility for the compliance and ethics program should emphasize that in-house (and where appropriate outside) counsel are accessible for all types of questions.

Samples of antitrust manuals and training materials are available in American Bar Association publications related to antitrust compliance listed in response to question N below.

### 3. *Evaluate the Company's Antitrust Training Program to Ensure That It Is Tailored to the Company and Includes Training for Each Category of Employee*

As discussed more fully below (see part 2 of Question G), employees and executives require effective training that has been tailored to the company's specific circumstances. In addition, employees with different areas of responsibility need training that provides them with information relevant to their positions. For example, executives who are interacting with other executives in trade association meetings need to know the antitrust limits for their conversations with industry colleagues and how to end participation in an inappropriate meeting or conversation; sales personnel for the largest company in an industry who are negotiating terms with a distributor need to know what types of conduct may give rise to claims that they were inappropriately attempting to exercise market power or dominance. Most importantly, each and every member of the organization needs to know to call for legal advice whenever they have questions or concerns.

### 4. *Even an Effective Compliance Program Requires Periodic Updating and Should Be Regularly Evaluated*

Companies change over time, as do industries, and those changes bring new competitive conditions. Employees and executives move between firms, and mergers and acquisitions may change a company's make-up and corporate structure. In addition, legal standards evolve over time. These and other types of changes can significantly affect the types of compliance program materials that will best serve an organization. Thus, even if new compliance counsel has inherited a vibrant antitrust compliance program, the elements already in place should receive a fresh evaluation every few years.

An effective program will fit the company culture, its industry, and its specific competitive conditions and will no doubt evolve over time. Corporate counsel should re-evaluate the program frequently and revise written materials, training, and approaches, as appropriate.

### D. I Understand That It Is Sometimes Difficult to Maintain Attorney-Client Privilege When Working in Antitrust Compliance. What Are the Important Issues?

Although attorney-client privilege differs by jurisdiction—and significantly so between the United States and certain foreign jurisdictions—its general precept is that confidential communications between an attorney and client for the purpose of obtaining legal advice will qualify for protection under the privilege. Compliance raises some difficult considerations in this context because a company's training sessions and compliance documents are not necessarily considered confidential communications for the purpose of obtaining legal advice.

Training that involves only general advice about antitrust law and company standards of conduct or written materials of general applicability *may* not be considered legal advice that would be covered by attorney-client privilege depending on the jurisdiction or specific factual circumstances. On the other hand, questions asked by employees during compliance training about how best to handle a particular situation would probably be considered privileged, because such an exchange is a request for legal advice. The cases that differentiate one from the other, however, are fact-specific, and attorneys engaged in compliance should remain cognizant of the privilege issues that may be raised by efforts involved in managing their company's compliance program.

The court in *In re Sulfuric Acid Antitrust Litigation*,[9] for example, held that an outside counsel's hypothetical situations found in the defendant's antitrust compliance manuals were "not the product of any requests for advice in specific circumstances" and therefore were not privileged.[10] The outside counsel had an ongoing client relationship with the defendant and had written hypothetical descriptions of circumstances based on his general knowledge of his client's business and the client's past requests for legal advice. This decision left open the possibility that had the attorney's sections of the compliance manual been based upon real examples of the client's questions, they might have been entitled to privilege.

Importantly, communications with in-house counsel are treated differently in the United States than in some foreign countries, and those assigned responsibility for compliance should be particularly wary of this factor. In April 2010, the EU Court of Justice (ECJ) upheld a decision involving Akzo Nobel Chemicals Ltd. in which the EU common law of privilege between in-house attorneys and management of their companies was put into question.[11] The ECJ decided that, in connection with EU competition law investigations undertaken by the European Commission, communications between company management and their in-house counsel are not protected by attorney-client privilege.[12] The rationale for the decision is that, as an employee of the company, in-

---

9.  *In re* Sulfuric Acid Antitrust Litig., 235 F.R.D. 407, *supplemented by* 432 F. Supp. 2d 794 (N.D. Ill. 2006).
10. *In re Sulfuric Acid*, 432 F. Supp. 2d at 797.
11. Case C-550/07, Akzo Nobel Chemicals Ltd. v. Comm'n, 2010 E.C.R. I-8309 (Eur. Ct. Justice).
12. *Id.* ¶¶ 166-70. The decision was limited to EU proceedings, such as European Commission antitrust investigations, and would not apply to EU Member States that have national legislation conferring privilege when certain conditions are met.

house counsel is not independent of the company and therefore the privilege cannot attach.[13]

To enhance privilege protection in conducting compliance activities, in-house counsel should consider:

- Including outside counsel when feasible in matters outside the United States;
- Communicating with individuals about the purpose of requested compliance materials and documenting the purpose of the project;
- Stating at the outset of the compliance materials that their purpose is to provide advice to executives and employees in connection with their job responsibilities for the company;
- Not including business advice in the context of a compliance manual or training session;
- Stating explicitly that the compliance manual and training sessions are for the purpose of providing legal advice and that the company considers it a privileged communication; and
- Avoiding using a blanket claim of privilege on every document broadly related to compliance because that could dilute the argument that a particular document was written to provide advice for a specific circumstance.
- Instructing employees seeking legal advice either to discuss their questions with in-house counsel in person or by phone, or, if in written form, to do so copying outside counsel.

Even with adherence to these principles, compliance counsel should assume that the basic Code of Conduct and Ethics and the Antitrust Compliance Manual may well be discoverable. These materials, as well as all related training materials, should be drafted with this possibility in mind.

---

13. *Id.* ¶¶ 147-53. See also, Case 155/79, AM & S Europe Ltd. v. Comm'n, 1982 E.C.R. 1575 (Eur. Ct. Justice).

### E. My Company Assigned Me Responsibility to Implement and Manage Our Compliance Program, but the Top Executives at My Company Do Not Take Compliance Seriously at All. What Should I Do?

Without management support, implementing an effective compliance program will be next to impossible, and this question thus raises one of the toughest issue the individual with responsibility for the compliance program will encounter.

A company's executives lead the firm in developing excellent products, service, and innovation, and the executives are no less critically important for an effective antitrust compliance program. As in all other spheres of a company's operations and productivity, the tone with respect to compliance with laws and ethics should be set at the top of the organization and reinforced by top management. Executive management should reinforce that the company wants to achieve its profitability goals legally and ethically and that employee disregard of the principles laid out in the code of conduct and antitrust manual will not be tolerated.

The CEO, the Board of Directors, and other company executives need to lead by example, to participate actively in compliance matters, and to provide support for compliance efforts. The entire company will benefit from the culture of compliance this top level management involvement entails, and without this leadership, the company is more likely to suffer an erosion of its ethics principles and possibly even a heightened risk of violations.

An experienced compliance officer for a major U.S. corporation, who will remain unnamed, recently provided succinct advice for a compliance counsel whose executives are not interested in furthering compliance: "Run." Although somewhat glib, this exemplifies the importance of obtaining executive buy-in of the compliance program. Executives need to understand that, while compliance may be seen as generating costs instead of profits, a compliance failure comes at far greater costs:

### 1.  The Costs of Improper Conduct Are Severe

Executives without interest in maintaining an effective compliance program need to hear the terrible consequences the company may suffer for violating the laws.

Criminal prosecutions of companies and individuals continue to rise, with the U.S. Department of Justice exacting ever more significant fines and restitution payments—an average of approximately $850 million annually from 2008 through 2012 and more than $1.35 billion in fiscal 2012 alone.[14] Individuals are serving even longer prison terms, with sentences greater than two years in some instances.[15]

In addition, civil suits expose companies to further liability. Monetary costs to corporations for any antitrust malfeasance may mean criminal fines, treble damages, significant legal expenses, and quantifiable harm to the company's public image. Moreover, defending against these types of suits will divert key executives and employees who would be better focused on the company's business.

Fines for violations of the competition laws in Europe have also increased dramatically over the last decade as the European Commission (EC) has focused greater attention on prosecuting price fixing. The EC recently imposed fines of EUR 1.47 billion for seven international groups of companies for participating in cartels involving cathode ray tubes.[16] Between 2007 and 2011, cartels were fined more than EUR 10

---

14. *See generally* U.S. Dep't of Justice, Division Update Spring 2011, *available at* http://www.justice.gov/atr/public/division-update/2012/criminal-program.html; Press Release, Gibson Dunn, 2012 Year-End Criminal Antitrust and Competition Law Update (Jan. 7, 2013) *available at* http://www.gibsondunn.com/publications/pages/2012YearEnd-Criminal-Antitrust-Competition-Update.aspx

15. *See, e.g.*, Press Release, U.S. Dep't of Justice, Taiwan-Based AU Optronics Corporation Sentenced To Pay $500 Million Criminal Fine For Role in LCD Price-Fixing Conspiracy, (Sept. 20, 2012), *available at* http://www.justice.gov/atr/public/press_releases/2012/287189.htm (two executives each sentenced to three years for role in cartel); Press Release, U.S. Dep't of Justice, Former Owner of Illinois Technology Company Sentenced to Serve 30 Months in Prison for Role in Multi-State Scheme to Defraud Federal E-Rate Program, (Feb. 9, 2012), *available at* http://www.justice.gov/atr/public/press_releases/2012/280071.htm.

16. Press Release, European Commission, Antitrust: Commission fines producers of TV and computer monitor tubes € 1.47 billion for two decade-long cartels (Brussels, Dec. 5, 2012), *available at* http://europa.eu/rapid/press-release_IP-12-1317_en.htm.

billion.[17] European fines may be set as high as 10 percent of the company's annual "turnover" (or, sales).[18]

## 2. There Are Significant Incentives for an Effective Compliance Program by Top Management.

Recent revisions to the Sentencing Guidelines include elements that draw company leadership even more directly into an "effective" compliance program.[19] In 2010, the USSC unanimously voted to modify the Sentencing Guidelines' standards for an effective corporate compliance and ethics program making even more clear the notion that compliance goes to the very top—the Board of Directors. As modified, a reporting role from the individual or individuals responsible for the compliance program to the Board is given greater importance. When a high-level company official has "participated in, condoned, or was willfully ignorant of the offense" the Sentencing Guidelines still view a compliance program as effective notwithstanding this complicity if, among other requirements, "the individual or individuals with operational responsibility for the compliance and ethics program have direct reporting obligations to the governing authority or an appropriate subgroup thereof (e.g., an audit committee of the board of directors)."[20] A company without this direct reporting obligation, will not have an "effective" compliance program under the Sentencing Guidelines in the event that a high-level individual in the company has committed wrongdoing.

---

17.  More statistics for EU fines can be found in the European Union Cartel Statistics as of June 27, 2012, *available at* http://ec.europa.eu/competition/cartels/statistics/statistics.pdf.

18.  Factsheet, European Comm'n, Fines For Breaking Competition Law (2011) *available at* http://ec.europa.eu/competition/antitrust/compliance/factsheet_fines_nov_2011_en.pdf.

19.  SENTENCING GUIDELINES, *supra* note 1, § 8C2.5(f).

20.  SENTENCING GUIDELINES, *supra* note 1, § 8C2.5(f)(3)(C) (citations omitted). Other requirements include:

> (ii) the compliance and ethics program detected the offense before discovery outside the organization or before such discovery was reasonably likely; (iii) the organization promptly reported the offense to appropriate governmental authorities; and (iv) no individual with operation responsibility for the compliance and ethics program participated in, condoned, or was willfully ignorant of the offense.

*Id.*

### F. How Can My Company Get Employees to Take Compliance Seriously?

Companies can foster a culture of compliance into the fabric of the organization that employees will adopt. When management and the Board of Directors take compliance seriously, employees will follow— although it will likely take significant time and effort. Companies with a top-down message to employees that "compliance matters" can instill that thinking in their employees. Merely saying the words, however, will not be sufficient. Company leaders must empower an appropriate individual or individuals with responsibilities for the compliance program and provide direct access to the top to instill this compliance culture in a company. The company also will need to invest in the appropriate tools to build an effective antitrust compliance program, including meaningful training materials as well as means for identifying possible transgressions.

In addition, employees often take pride in working for an ethical company. A positive attitude about compliance from the top down can provide a model that the company's leaders believe in operating ethically and will reward performance based on compliance with the law.

### G. What Specific Techniques Best Encourage Proper Employee Attention to Compliance?

#### 1. *Employees Need to Hear about Personal Liability in Addition to Corporate Penalties*

As with key executives, the fear of serious adverse consequences is a significant motivating tool for employees. Emphasizing to employees the possibility of personal liability is often more effective than focusing on corporate exposure. If employees hear stories of just a few recent prison terms imposed on corporate middle managers, they undoubtedly will remember the lessons.

#### 2. *Effective Training on a Regular Basis Is Critical to Maintaining Employee Focus on Compliance*

The goal of antitrust training is not to impart detailed legal knowledge to employees, but rather to provide basic sensitivity to antitrust issues or circumstances related to each employee's areas of responsibility. Employees and executives need to recognize situations in which they should contact counsel for advice.

Most compliance counsel advise that training needs to be done in person. Although written materials can reinforce points and provide back-up information and on-line training may be an effective and efficient supplement, antitrust principles should be discussed in live training sessions at regular intervals. Most counselors suggest an hour or two of tailored training annually. These sessions provide an opportunity for employees to ask questions and hear fellow employees' concerns. Perhaps more important, the trainer is able to adjust the topics even more specifically for the audience, provide real-life examples that are relevant to the specific employees, and identify issues for later follow-up.

At the very least, the following categories of individuals should be considered for in-person training sessions:

- senior managers;
- employees involved in mergers, acquisitions, and licensing;
- employees with customer, competitor, or supplier contact;
- employees who analyze competitors or perform competitive benchmarking;
- employees who attend trade association committees or regularly participate in trade association meetings;
- employees who work with a joint venture that includes a competitor, supplier, or customer;
- employees with pricing authority; and
- employees who develop marketing strategy.

Moreover, it is advisable to provide specialized training to any employees who are engaged in a merger or acquisition with a company that is a competitor or potential competitor. This situation may raise special issues and should be given particular attention at the time of the pending transaction.

### 3. Training Programs Should Cover Basic Points As Well As Items Specific to the Company

Typical antitrust training programs begin by describing the myriad of ways an antitrust violation (or the mere appearance of one) can be dangerous: criminal and civil fines, company and individual liability, prison terms for individuals, private antitrust actions and class action litigation that can drag on for many years, and treble damages. This laundry list, when delivered appropriately, tends to foster careful attention.

The substantive discussion typically includes the following topics in varying detail depending upon the group of employees present:

- per se offenses;
- distribution issues and how to interact with customers;
- monopolization and dominance;
- dangers of sharing confidential information;
- communications with competitors; and
- trade association conduct.

Finally, the most important part of a training is the name and phone number of counsel. Those attending need to fully understand that antitrust law is fact-specific and that there is no substitute for discussing a particular situation with their in-house (or where appropriate outside) attorney. Employees need to feel encouraged to call, even with questions they fear may be silly.

Most antitrust compliance advisors emphasize that training should include the specific suggestion that questions be posed not in writing or by e-mail but rather by phone call or in person. A live conversation provides the opportunity for exchange of more factual information than is often communicated in cryptic e-mails, and because antitrust issues are very fact-driven, follow-up questions and discussion are most often important. A conversation also avoids the possibility of a poorly worded e-mail that could be misinterpreted by others outside the company if it were later discovered.

Compliance training should be provided regularly, for example once per year, although all topics need not be covered repeatedly with the entire group. Companies often train new employees soon after they arrive with a full overview of general antitrust principles. It may then be most effective to follow-up with more specific job-related training for these employees as they mature into their positions.

All training should be accompanied by attendance sheets. Moreover, employees should sign statements that they have received, read and understand the company's compliance materials and will abide by the company's policies.

Many companies supplement live training sessions with computerized training modules. While these and Internet-based training materials may be helpful as add-ons, they may not be considered sufficient standing alone under the Sentencing Guidelines.

## H. What Should We Do to Encourage Employees to Report Noncompliance?

### 1. *Ensure Top Management Has Delivered the Message That Noncompliance and Toleration of Noncompliance by Others Is Unacceptable*

The company's leadership should be unequivocal that every employee is responsible not only for obeying the laws and company's policies but also for providing information about others who may not be doing so. The CEO often provides a written statement to this effect to introduce the Antitrust Compliance Manual, and a senior manager should deliver this message at each training session.

### 2. *Middle Managers Are Essential to Encouraging Reporting of Noncompliance*

Managers should deliver a consistent message that adherence to the company's compliance standards is of critical importance. They must demonstrate both in their actions and their words that noncompliance comes with significant adverse consequences and that every employee is personally responsible for staying within the prescribed standards of conduct. Moreover, it should be clearly stated that each employee is responsible for reporting malfeasance and that tolerating another's noncompliance may bring adverse consequences as well.

### 3. *Encourage Employees Directly to Report Possible Anticompetitive Activity*

For most companies, their own employees are in the best position to provide information about compliance issues. Employees often will know of a potential problem long before a periodic audit could catch the issue.

During training sessions, employees should be instructed that reporting a possible anticompetitive action will often be their best protection from personal liability. If, for example, an employee is approached by a competitor to engage in an illegal boycott or a price-fixing agreement, that employee should not only turn down the suggestion firmly but also report the instance to counsel in a timely manner. Counsel will document the incident and, if appropriate, take further steps with counsel for the other party.

The often more difficult reporting situation is one that involves two employees of the same company. Companies should provide a convenient means for employees to report suspicious activity anonymously. Toll-free hotlines and online submissions may be used to accept anonymous tips regarding potentially illegal conduct.

Companies can increase the likelihood that illegal conduct will be reported by setting up positive incentives for doing so. Employees who report suspicious conduct should be assured that the reporting individual's identity will remain confidential and that no retaliation may be undertaken against the whistleblower. The information itself needs to be held in confidence except to the extent that the company finds it necessary to investigate and remedy wrongdoing.

Throughout the organization, a company must make certain that it appropriately disciplines those who either fail to adhere to the company's policies or who tolerate others' overstepping of defined antitrust boundaries. By instituting this policy firmly and uniformly, employees will be more diligent in reporting potentially troublesome behavior and will seek out advice before treading into difficult behavior.

## I.   We Just Received an Anonymous Tip That Some of Our Sales Executives May Be Involved in Fixing Prices (or Other Anticompetitive Behavior). How Should We React?

### 1.   *Every Company Needs to Have a Rapid Response Plan in Place*

The Antitrust Compliance Manual and all training materials need to provide information for employees about what to do first in response to serious allegations of anticompetitive conduct. First, the person who receives this type of information should immediately call an in-house attorney. Supervisors and managers need to understand that they should not try to handle allegations or tips about a potential violation of the antitrust laws themselves. Efforts to do so could create a dangerous paper trail that could later be used in follow-on litigation. Attorneys for the company can best handle the tip in a privileged setting. The company should provide twenty-four-hour contact information for the purpose of these types of reports.

## 2. When the Company Receives a Report, Quick and Decisive Action Is Paramount

The company's rapid response may keep it from suffering adverse consequences at all—such as when an employee seeks advice before taking any wrongful steps—but even if a potential violation has already been committed, speedy action may serve to significantly lessen sanctions.

If potentially inappropriate activity has occurred, the company needs to take steps immediately to prevent further potential violations and evaluate possible remedial actions. The exact procedures will vary depending upon the conduct at issue, but generally, a company will:

- hire experienced outside counsel or deputize trusted in-house counsel to evaluate the conduct, advise as to its legality or illegality, and recommend whether to report the conduct to antitrust authorities;
- establish document preservation guidelines to ensure no documents are destroyed that may relate to an investigation of the conduct and to further ensure that the company is not later accused of destroying evidence relevant to a government's inquiry into the matter; and
- conduct a preliminary factual investigation as soon as possible, using both documents and interviews to identify relevant individuals and information.

It is important to note that interviewees may need to be or ask to be represented by their own counsel, particularly when the situation may involve potentially criminal conduct by the individual being interviewed. The company's counsel represents the company's interests rather than those of any particular individual. This should also be clearly stated in the Antitrust Compliance Manual and in compliance training. Any interview of an individual whose interest may diverge from the company's at some point must be given specific information that the attorneys conducting the interview represent the company and not the employee, along with an explanation that the attorney-client privilege with respect to the interview belongs to the company.[21] The company

---

21. The statements to employees (1) that the interviewing attorney represents the company and not the individual, and (2) that the interview is covered by the company's attorney-client and work product protection as opposed

may suggest appropriate counsel for the employees in such a situation, and often will agree to pay for such counsel; however, the actual choice of counsel should be left to the employee and such individual counsel will always report only to their client and not to the company that may be paying the counsel's fees. Typically, counsel for the individuals in such a situation will work collaboratively with counsel for the company, to the extent the interests of the company and the individual align.

### 3. The Company Needs to Develop a Factual Basis for Deciding Whether to Apply for Amnesty or Leniency

Amnesty is available only to the first company reporting wrongful behavior, so the speed with which a company decides whether to self-report can be vitally important. However, the decision to seek amnesty is often not an easy decision. Although the amnesty applicant is exempt from criminal exposure and may qualify for single damages, instead of joint and several liability for treble damages, private suits will remain, and the amnesty applicant will have admitted wrongdoing (which can be used against it in follow-on civil litigation). If the company has arguments that it may not have violated the law, self-reporting and admitting liability may not be the best course. Because the company needs to understand the full factual situation to make this decision, a prompt investigation is critical.[22]

When a company discovers a potential antitrust criminal violation and has begun an internal investigation to gather information, it may seek and obtain a "marker" from the DOJ's Antitrust Division to preserve its place as first in line (meriting amnesty consideration) to provide counsel for the company time to gather information for a full leniency application. The marker, which will be part of a conditional leniency agreement, holds the company's position in line for leniency for a finite period of time agreed to between counsel for the company and the DOJ.[23]

---

to the employee's privilege, are referred to as *Upjohn warnings*. *See* Upjohn Co. v. United States, 449 U.S. 383, 394-96 (1981).

22. Note also that potential corporate wrongdoing may trigger an affirmative legal duty on behalf of a public corporation to correct misrepresentations that have been made (such as in a public filing with the U.S. Securities & Exchange Commission).

23. *See generally*, U.S. DEP'T OF JUSTICE, U.S. DEP'T OF JUSTICE LENIENCY PROGRAM, *available at* http://www.justice.gov/atr/public/criminal/leniency.html. *See also*, Scott D. Hammond, Deputy Asst. Atty. Gen. for

Leniency applicants must not have been the leader or originator of the anticompetitive activity being reported, and applicants must agree to cooperate fully with the DOJ's investigation to qualify for amnesty. When provided to DOJ, the company's leniency application will need to include an admission of participation in a criminal antitrust violation and will include a proffer (or multiple proffers—typically presented in oral form) of detailed evidence of the company's own malfeasance and that of its coconspirators.[24]

In the meantime, the company must undertake corrective steps and also ensure that its employees have ceased the improper conduct that is the subject of the marker. Any continuation of the conspiracy by a rogue employee may negate the company's first place marker, as will any holding back of relevant information by the company.[25]

### J.  Are There Things a Company Should Do to Be Prepared in Case the FBI Arrives to Conduct a Dawn Raid?

Dawn raids by antitrust enforcers are becoming more common and more thorough, and they occur both domestically and internationally. No company should leave its managers and employees without a set of procedures to employ in the unlikely event that law enforcement agents arrive to execute a warrant or ask questions.

Specifically, employees should be counseled to take the following steps:

- Remain courteous at all times. Harsh words will not help anyone.
- Review the search warrant and the agents' credentials.
- Immediately call counsel and keep calling different attorneys for the company until you speak with one of them.
- Ask the law enforcers to wait until counsel arrives before beginning their search. Typically, they will not wait as asked. You should not do anything to impede them if they decide to begin their search without counsel.

---

Criminal Enforcement, Antitrust Division, U.S. Dep't of Justice, Recent Developments Relating to the Antitrust Division's Corporate Leniency Program (Mar. 5, 2009) *available at* http://www.justice.gov/atr/public/speeches/244840.htm.

24.   *See generally,* U.S. DEP'T OF JUSTICE LENIENCY PROGRAM, available at http://www.justice.gov/atr/public/criminal/leniency.html

25.   *Id.*

- Send home the nonessential employees who are working in the area to be searched.[26]
- Ensure that no one on the premises takes any steps to destroy information.
- Inform employees that they are free to speak to law enforcement officials but that they are under no obligation to do so, that no adverse inference may be made by a choice not to be interviewed at this time, and that their interests may be best served by consulting with counsel.
- When asked to do so, provide agents information about how to find documents identified in the warrant.
- You are not required to provide substantive answers to questions about the business until counsel has arrived and instructed you to answer.
- Carefully watch where the law enforcement officials search, making notes, and request a copy of everything they take. They should also give you a receipt.

In recent raids, the FBI has simultaneously appeared both at company locations and at employees' homes. By doing so, they preserve the element of surprise and, catching people off guard in their driveways,

---

26. Those employees who are *essential* to identify the location of documents subject to the subpoena should remain on the company's premises; without them present, the enforcers would need to search more broadly to locate the materials responsive to the subpoena, and such a search would be more disruptive to the company's overall business. If the company were to keep *non-essential* employees present, however, there is a greater possibility that the company could be subject to claims that some documents have been altered or destroyed—if, for example, an enforcer observes an employee apparently entering keystrokes at a computer work station. Also, if all employees are available to enforcers, some of them may feel they need to submit to on-the-spot interviews. For these reasons, companies generally release from work at the facility during the search those employees not needed to identify the location of materials responsive to the subpoena.

   In the unlikely event that the enforcers request all employees to remain in place, the company's counsel will need to make a judgment call. Unless the employees are under arrest, the enforcers have no right to keep them present at the facility during the search. The company will need to weigh, however, whether it wishes to cooperate fully with the enforcers' request that employees remain or whether it wishes to ask some or all non-essential employees to leave the premises.

may obtain interviews from individuals fearful of seeming uncooperative. Employees need to receive specific training that they are free but not required to answer any substantive questions in such situations and that it may be in their best interest to consult with a lawyer before consenting to an interview. The FBI's warrant may require employees to hand over documents, but their first actions should be to call counsel and receive advice before taking any further steps.

In the European Union, dawn raids are common. While not all of the national competition authorities are empowered to conduct dawn raids, the European Commission officials and several of the member states can and do routinely conduct them.[27] The European Commission is allowed to carry out an inspection of the business premises of target companies (as well as homes and cars of individuals) to inspect and copy documents and to ask questions of employees. The raid must be based on specified reasonable grounds for suspecting anticompetitive activity, but the Commission need not obtain a search warrant beforehand if they are raiding only the company's business premises. All of the information collected may be used as evidence in any regulatory action against the companies involved.

## K. How Can I Monitor Whether Our Compliance Program Is Working?

Several tools are available to monitor the effectiveness of the company's program. Typically, those delegated day-to-day operational responsibility for the compliance and ethics program should do the following:

- Listen carefully for potential compliance issues or problems when answering questions—whether in one-on-one counseling, in training, or in casual conversations with company officials and employees;
- Periodically monitor or examine a business unit or an entire company, even when no wrongdoing is suspected, to identify possible problem areas for further compliance attention;
- Carefully follow-up each employee tip. This is most often the very most effective tool for compliance monitoring;

---

27.     Dawn raids are provided for under Article 20 of Regulation 1/2003.

- Periodically review corporate documents related to strategic planning, pricing policies, and other areas that have the greatest antitrust exposure.

A global company has special compliance challenges, which require additional steps. For example, each office should have a person specifically designated for compliance matters. Because cultural differences exist across borders, those assigned overall responsibility for the compliance and ethics program at headquarters should not assume knowledge of nuances and specific practices sufficient to spot potential compliance difficulties. Involving personnel in each office provides more effective coverage and an easier method for questions to be asked. In this context, however particular attention needs to be given to the issue of privilege in jurisdictions where in-house counsel communications are not protected.

Make it easy for employees to report possible violations. Companies often set up a phone line and an Internet e-mail box for anonymous tips. Employees should feel free to ask questions or report situations that appear suspicious to them. They should be promised that there will be no retaliation for reporting what they believe to be misbehavior, which should give an added measure of comfort along with the anonymity of the call line or e-mail box.

## L.  We Are a Global Company. How Can We Make Sure Our Compliance Program Is Effective in Other Jurisdictions?

Counsel are wise to consider compliance on a global basis, and multinational companies require an antitrust compliance program that is effectively implemented throughout their operations. Although the task of complying with antitrust or competition laws in multiple jurisdictions may seem daunting, it can be managed.

Because the basic principles are consistent, personnel around the world can be instructed—at a minimum—to follow the rules that there shall be:

- No price fixing;
- No customer allocations
- No territorial or market allocations; and
- No bid rigging.

Locally based company personnel and attorneys qualified in the jurisdiction should evaluate more specific legal differences and business practices particular to their area that could require attention in the company's compliance program.

When all of the jurisdictions have been covered individually, most companies find it prudent to implement a uniform policy across all offices. The most stringent requirements will govern, unless the company cannot operate pursuant to those limitations and needs to identify a particular exception for one location. Having the policy as uniform as possible allows for training across offices and consistency in communication to all employees. A uniform policy provides a greater likelihood that the company will develop the kind of culture of compliance that can keep it operating within legal parameters globally. It also facilitates training in companies where employees frequently transfer among offices.

A company's Code of Ethics and its Antitrust Compliance Manual should be translated into the language of each office. Antitrust principles may not be intuitive, especially to employees in countries where competition enforcement is a relatively recent phenomenon, and language barriers will only create additional, unnecessary risks.

As with training generally, often a simple list of "do's" and "don'ts" will be an effective communication tool. This can be followed up with a set of likely scenarios for employees, so that the statements are put into an applied format. Including a role-playing session in live training sessions may be helpful as well, as both a teaching tool and also to check comprehension. In addition, it is typically a good practice to include local managers in the training so that respected superiors are helping to deliver the compliance message.

Particular care needs to be given to employees in countries where cooperation among industry members is commonplace. Pointing out the prison sentences served by fellow countrymen can create the right impact for some. Foreign-based employees also need to understand that their company is at risk—and they personally are also at risk—of violating U.S. antitrust laws, even if all of their illegal conduct is outside the United States, with intermediate assemblies outside the United States, and only final products sold into the United States. The recent guilty pleas in the automotive parts cases may provide an apt object lesson on this point.[28]

## M. We Operate Our Business Units on an Integrated North American Basis. Are There Significant Differences in Canadian Antitrust Laws That We Should Be Aware of?

Canada's competition laws have been revised significantly in recent years, and corporate compliance programs need to take into account both these changes as well as the differences between U.S. and Canadian standards.

### 1. Canada's Competition Act Includes Both Civil and Criminal Offenses

Pursuant to revisions that became effective in 2010, the Competition Act's criminal provisions were amended to make horizontal price fixing a per se offense—a change from when criminal liability would attach only where the conduct "unduly" prevented or lessened competition.[29] The amendments also impose greater financial penalties and jail terms for antitrust violations.[30] Companies may avoid liability if they can demonstrate that their agreements are "ancillary" to and reasonably necessary to implement another, legitimate agreement.[31]

Criminal charges may also be brought for bid rigging and false or misleading advertising. In addition, private parties who have been

---

28.    *See, e.g.*, Press Release, U.S. Dep't of Justice, Yazaki Corp., Denso Corp. and Four Yazaki Executives Agree to Plead Guilty to Automobile Parts Price-Fixing and Bid-Rigging Conspiracies, (Jan. 30, 2012) *available at* http://www.justice.gov/atr/public/press_releases/2012/279734.htm; and Press Release, U.S. Dep't of Justice, Japanese Automobile Parts Manufacturer Agrees to Plead Guilty to Price Fixing and Obstruction of Justice, (Oct. 30, 2012) *available at* http://www.justice.gov/atr/public/press_releases/2012/288353.htm.

29.    R.S.C. 1985, c. C-34.

30.    Maximum sanctions for violations under the new cartel provisions are fourteen years imprisonment and a C$25 million fine per count. R.S.C. 1985, c. C-34 § 45(2). Previously, maximum penalties were five years imprisonment and C$10 million per count. R.S.C. 1985, c. C-34 § 45(1) (2002), *available at* http://laws-lois.justice.gc.ca/eng/acts/C-34/section-45-20021231.html.

31.    R.S.C. 1985, c. C-34 § 45(4).

harmed by the cartel provisions of the Competition Act may seek damages in a civil action.[32]

Noncriminal conduct is termed "reviewable" and is actionable before the Canadian Competition Tribunal and, for some offenses, in suits by private parties. Conduct that is reviewed under the civil provisions of the Competition Act include misleading advertising, refusals to deal, resale price maintenance, exclusive dealing, tying, and abuse of dominance. The Competition Bureau has issued guidance regarding its enforcement intentions in its *Competitor Collaboration Guidelines*.[33]

## 2.  *An Effective Antitrust Compliance Program Can Reduce Penalties under Canadian Law*

As is the case in other jurisdictions, companies may receive quantifiable benefits, including mitigation of sentencing in the event that wrongdoing occurs, by having in place an effective compliance program. Canadian authorities have provided factors that would be found in an effective compliance program;[34] these are similar to those named by authorities elsewhere:

- Senior management involvement and support, including reporting to the Board of Directors, annual risk assessments, and designation of an individual or individuals with responsibility for the compliance program among the senior management;
- Documented corporate compliance policies and procedures that are widely available throughout the organization;
- Ongoing training and educational programs for management and staff;
- Monitoring, auditing, and reporting mechanisms; and
- Consistent disciplinary procedures and incentives.[35]

---

32.  *Id.* § 36.
33.  COMPETITION BUREAU OF CANADA, COMPETITOR COLLABORATION GUIDELINES (2009), *available at* http://www.competitionbureau.gc.ca /eic/site/cb-bc.nsf/eng/03177.html. Although these predate the new legislation's effective date, they were issued after the statute's passage and incorporate the new provisions that became effective in 2010.
34.  *See* Bulletin, Competition Bureau of Canada, Corporate Compliance Programs (Sept. 10, 2008), *available at* http://www.competitionbureau .gc.ca/eic/site/cb-bc.nsf/eng/02732.html.
35.  *Id.* at Part IV.

In addition, conspirators may avoid prosecution altogether, or receive lenient treatment, by entering Competition Bureau programs for immunity or leniency. Immunity from criminal prosecution may be granted when a company is the first to report a cartel and it cooperates with the Bureau's investigation, including reporting on violations discovered in its own internal investigation and malfeasance by its coconspirators.[36] Leniency may be available for cooperating companies as well, even if they are not the first to report.[37]

## N. Where Can I Go for More Information?

### 1. Counseling

- ABA Section of Antitrust Law, *Antitrust Compliance: Perspectives and Resources for Corporate Counselor*s (2d ed. 2010);
- Theodore L. Banks & Frederick Z. Banks, *Corporate Legal Compliance Handbook* (2d ed. 2012);
- Olesya Dmitracova, *Firms Do Better if Obey Governance Rules—UK Study,* Reuters (February 26, 2008);
- Karen A. Gibbs & Thy B. Bui, *Antitrust Counseling on Bundling in High-Technology Industries*, 3.7 *The Corporate Counselor* 1 (Sept. 2008);
- William M. Hannay, *Designing an Effective Antitrust Compliance Program*, 11 *Corporate Compliance Series* (Thompson/West 1996 & updates);
- David Higbee & Djordje Petkoski, *Compliance: When Procedure becomes Substance* (2008);
- Susie L. Hoeller, *The Intersection of Antitrust With Product Safety—The Need For Greater Collaboration By Antitrust And Regulatory Lawyers When Counseling Corporate Clients, The Antitrust Source* (February 2008), *available at*

---

36. *See* Bulletin, Competition Bureau of Canada, Immunity Program under the Competition Act (June 7, 2010) *available at* http://www.competitionbureau.gc.ca/eic/site/cb-bc.nsf/eng/03248.html.

37. *See* Bulletin, Competition Bureau of Canada, Leniency Program (Sept. 29, 2010), *available at* http://www.competitionbureau.gc.ca/eic/site/cb-bc.nsf/vwapj/LeniencyProgram-sept-2010-e.pdf/$FILE/LeniencyProgram-sept-2010-e.pdf.

http://www.abanet.org/antitrust/at-source/08/02/Feb08-Hoeller.pdf;

- Jaclyn Jaeger, *Economic Crime: How to Reduce the Risks, Compliance Week* (Jan. 2008);
- U.S. Department of Justice, *Compliance Assistance Resources for Businesses*, *available at* http://www.justice.gov /atr/public/business-resources.html;
- U.S. Department of Justice, *Criminal Enforcement*, *available at* http://www.justice.gov/atr/public/criminal/index.html;
- Federal Trade Commission, *FTC Guide to the Antitrust Laws*, *available at* http://ftc.gov/bc/antitrust/factsheets/ antitrustlawsguide.pdf;
- Federal Trade Commission, *Inside BC*, Bureau of Competition 2012 User's Guide, *available at* http://www.ftc.gov/bc/ BCUsersGuide.pdf.

## 2. *Criminal Enforcement, Amnesty and Leniency*

- Thomas O. Barnett, U.S. Department of Justice, Global Antitrust Enforcement, Presented at the Georgetown Law Global Antitrust Enforcement Symposium (Sept. 26, 2007), *available at* http://www.usdeoj.gov/atr/public/speeches/226334.pdf;
- Thomas O. Barnett, U.S. Department of Justice, Seven Steps To Better Cartel Enforcement, Presentation to the 11th Annual Competition Law & Policy Workshop (June 2, 2006), *available at* http://www.usdoj.gov/atr/public/speeches/216453.pdf;
- Scott D. Hammond, Deputy Assistant Attorney General for Criminal Enforcement, Antitrust Division, U.S. Department of Justice, The Evolution of Criminal Antitrust Enforcement Over the Last Two Decades, Remarks at the 24th Annual National Institute on White Collar Crime (February 25, 2010) *available at* http://www.justice.gov/atr/public/speeches/255515.htm;
- Scott D. Hammond, Deputy Assistant Attorney General for Criminal Enforcement, Antitrust Division, U.S. Department of Justice, Recent Developments Relating to the Antitrust Division's Corporate Leniency Program (March 5, 2009) *available at* http://www.justice.gov/atr/public/speeches/ 244840.htm;
- Scott Hammond on *Stoldt-Nielsen, Global Competition Review* 13-14 (May 2008), *available at* http://www.usdoj.gov/atr/public/ speeches/234840.pdf;

- Scott D. Hammond, U.S. Department of Justice, Recent Developments, Trends, and Milestones in the Antitrust Division's Criminal Enforcement Program, Remarks at the ABA Section of Antitrust Law 56th Annual Spring Meeting (Mar. 26, 2008), *available at* http://www.usdoj.gov/atr/public/speeches/ 232716.pdf;
- Scott D. Hammond, U.S. Department of Justice, Charting New Waters in International Cartel Prosecutions, Remarks Before the 20th Annual National Institute on White Collar Crime (Mar. 2, 2006), *available at* http://www.usdoj.gov/atr/public/speeches/ 214861.pdf;
- Scott D. Hammond & Belinda A. Barnett, U.S. Department of Justice, Frequently Asked Questions Regarding The Antitrust Division's Leniency Program and Model Leniency Letters (Nov. 19, 2008), *available at* http://www.usdoj.gov/atr/public/criminal/ 239583.htm;
- U.S. Department of Justice, Corporate Leniency Policy (Aug. 10, 1993), *available at* http://www.usdoj.gov/atr/public/guidelines/ 0091.pdf;
- U.S. Department of Justice, Individual Leniency Policy (Aug. 10, 1994), *available at* http://www.usdoj.gov/atr/public/ guidelines/0092.htm;
- Jeffrey M. Kaplan, Joseph E. Murphy & Winthrop M. Swenson, *Compliance Programs and the Corporate Sentencing Guidelines* (Thompson/West 2005);
- Gregory J. Werden, Scott D. Hammond & Belinda A. Barnett, Antitrust Division, U.S. Department of Justice, Recidivism Eliminated: Cartel Enforcement in the United States since 1999, Remarks before the Global Antitrust Enforcement Symposium (September 22, 2011) *available at* http://www.justice.gov/atr/ public/speeches/275388.pdf;
- Gregory J. Werden, Scott D. Hammond & Belinda A. Barnett, Antitrust Division, U.S. Department of Justice, Deterrence and Detection of Cartels: Using All The Tools and Sanctions, Remarks before the 26th Annual National Institute on White Collar Crime (March 1, 2012) *available at* http://www.justice.gov/atr/public/speeches/283738.pdf.

## 3. Global Compliance

- Australian Competition & Consumer Commission, Compliance and Enforcement Policy (February 20, 2013), *available at* http://www.accc.gov.au/content/item.phtml?itemId=867964&nodeId=78b0956fa087fe1ea3b08b9817ffa964&fn=ACCC%20Compliance%20and%20Enforcement%20Policy.pdf;
- Australian Competition & Consumer Commission, ACCC Immunity Policy for Cartel Conduct (February 7, 2011), *available at* http://www.accc.gov.au/content/index.phtml/itemId/879795;
- Canadian Competition Bureau, Immunity Program under the Competition Act (June 7, 2010), *available at* http://www.competitionbureau.gc.ca/eic/site/cb-bc.nsf/eng/03248.html;
- Canadian Competition Bureau, Corporate Compliance Programs Final Version (Sept. 27, 2010), *available at* http://www.competitionbureau.gc.ca/eic/site/cb-bc.nsf/vwapj/CorporateCompliancePrograms-sept-2010-e.pdf/$FILE/CorporateCompliancePrograms-sept-2010-e.pdf;
- Canadian Competition Bureau, Leniency Program (Sept. 29, 2010), *available at* http://www.competitionbureau.gc.ca/eic/site/cb-bc.nsf/eng/03288.html;
- Kiran S. Desai, *Antitrust Compliance Programs, European Antitrust Review* (2005);
- European Commission, Compliance Matters: What Companies Can Do Better To Respect EU Competition Rules (November 2011), *available at* http://ec.europa.eu/competition/antitrust/compliance/compliance_matters_en.pdf;
- European Commission, Notice of Immunity From Fines and Reduction of Fines in Cartel Cases, OJ C298/11 (2006), *available at* http://eur-lex.europa.eu/LexUriServ/LexUriServ.do?uri=CELEX:52006XC1208(04):EN:NOT;
- International Competition Network, *Anti-Cartel Enforcement Manual*, Chapter on Cartel Awareness, Outreach and Compliance (March 2012), *available at* http://internationalcompetitionnetwork.org/uploads/library/doc835.pdf;
- Japan Fair Trade Commission, Rules on Reporting and Submission of Materials Regarding Immunity From or

Reduction of Surcharges (2005), *available at* http://www.jftc.go.jp/e-page/legislation/ama/immunity.pdf;

- Fair Trade Commission, Republic of Korea, Commission on Compliance for Fair Trade, Code of Conduct for Corporate Compliance Programs (July 2001), *available at* http://www.ftc.go.kr/eng/laws/code.php;
- Fair Trade Commission, Republic of Korea, Notification on Implementation of Leniency Program for Corrective Measures against Confessors (July 2006), *available at* http://ftc.go.kr/data/hwp/20070323_102028.pdf;
- Michele Lee, *Building an Effective Antitrust Compliance Program: International and Cultural Challenges*, ABA Section of Antitrust Law Antitrust Compliance Bulletin (Mar. 2006);
- R. Hewitt Pate, U.S. Department of Justice, Current Issues In International Antitrust Enforcement, Remarks Before the Fordham Corporate Law Institute 31st Annual Conference on International Antitrust Law & Policy (Oct. 7, 2004), *available at* http://www.usdoj.gov/atr/public/ speeches/206479.pdf;
- R. Hewitt Pate, U.S. Department of Justice, Securing The Benefits Of Global Competition, Remarks Presented at the Tokyo American Center (Sept. 10, 2004), *available at* http://www.usdoj.gov/atr/public/ speeches/205389.pdf;
- Turkey Competition Authority, Regulation on Active Cooperation for Detecting Cartels (Feb. 2009), *available at* http://www.rekabet.gov.tr/dosyalar/images/file/iktisadiarastirmalar/1(1).pdf;
- U.K. Office of Fair Trading, OFT's Guidance as to the Appropriate Amount of Penalty (Dec. 2004), *available at* http://www.oft.gov.uk/shared_oft/business_leaflets/ca98_guidelines/oft423.pdf;
- U.K. Office of Fair Trading, The Cartel Offence: Guidance on the Issue of No-Action Letters for Individuals (Apr. 2003), *available at* http://www.oft.gov.uk/shared_oft/business_leaflets/ enterprise_act/ oft513.pdf;
- U.K. Office of Fair Trading, How Your Business Can Achieve Compliance: A Guide to Achieving Compliance With Competition Law (March 2005), *available at* http://www.oft.gov.uk/NRrdonlyres/78AD1280-4EB8-46D4-A52B-207F9AFEAAE1/0/oft424.pdf;
- U.K. Office of Fair Trading, Leniency and No-Action, OFT's Guidance Note on the Handling of Applications (Dec. 2008),

*available      at*      http://www.oft.gov.uk/shared_oft/reports/
comp_policy/oft803.pdf.

## 4.  Trade Associations

- ABA Section of Antitrust Law, *An Antitrust Guide for Trade Association Professionals and Members* (2004);
- ABA Section of Antitrust Law, *Antitrust and Associations Handbook* (March 2009);
- Jon Leibowitz, Federal Trade Commission, The Good, the Bad and the Ugly: Trade Associations and Antitrust, Remarks Before the ABA Section of Antitrust Law Annual Meeting (Mar. 30, 2005), *available at* http://www.ftc.gov/speeches/leibowitz/050510goodbadugly.pdf.

## 5.  Training

- *On-Line Antitrust Compliance Training: The ABCs and ZYZs, Antitrust Source* (July 10, 2003);
- Clark Aldrich, *Learning by Doing: The Essential Guide to Simulations, Computer Games, and Pedagogy in E-Learning and other Educational Experiences* (2005);
- Michael Allen, *Designing Successful e-Learning* (2007);
- Roger Buckley & Jim Caple, *The Theory and Practice of Training* (4th ed. 2000);
- Lisa A. Burke, *High-Impact Training Solutions* (2001);
- Saul Carliner & Patti Shank, *E-Learning Handbook* (2008);
- Robert M. Gagne, Leslie J. Briggs & Walter W. Wagner, *Principles of Instructional Design* (4th ed. 1992);
- Steven H. Gluckman & Peter Glowacki, *E-Learning for Law Firms* (2006);
- William M. Hannay, *Designing an Effective Antitrust Compliance Program* (2003);
- William Horton, *E-Learning by Design* (2006);
- Mehdi Khosrow-Pour, *Web-Based Instructional Design* (2002);
- Kurt Kraiger, *Creating, Implementing and Managing Effective Training and Development* (2002);
- Kar-Tin Lee & Jennifer Duncan-Howell, *How Do We Know E-Learning Works? Or Does It?* 4 *E-Learning* 482 (2007);
- Elliott Masie, *Learning Rants, Raves and Reflections* (2005);

- Luvai F. Motiawalia, *Mobile Learning: A Framework and Evaluation*, 49 *Computers & Education* 581 (2007);
- George M. Piskurich, *The ASTD Handbook of Training Design and Delivery* (2000);
- Allison Rosett & Kendra Sheldon, *Beyond the Podium: Delivering Training and Performance in a Digital World* (2001);
- Alastair Rylatt, *Learning Unlimited* (2d ed. 2000);
- Roger C. Schank, *Designing World-Class E-Learning* (2002);
- Mel Silberman, *The ASTD 2006 Training & Performance Sourcebook* (2006);
- David E. Stone & Constance L. Koskinen, *Planning and Design for Web-Based Training* (2002).

## CHAPTER VIII

# DEALING WITH THE ANTITRUST AUTHORITIES

## A. Somebody from the Department of Justice (or Other Government Agency) Just Called. What Should I Do?

The proper response to any government inquiry depends on the nature of the inquiry itself. There are any number of situations in which an individual or company might be contacted by someone from the government. The contact could, for example, involve the surprise execution of a search warrant in a criminal investigation, a demand for information related to a civil investigation, an attempt to gather information about the company as part of an agency study of an industry, or an informal contact to gather information about a transaction between other companies with which your client may do business or compete. Depending on the situation, your client's response could be completely voluntary, or it could be compelled by law (with significant civil and/or criminal sanctions resulting from a failure to respond or a failure to respond truthfully).

The government may commence an investigation based on information obtained from a variety of sources, including competitors, news reports, premerger notification filings, state agencies, and private litigation.[1] Care is required in responding to any contact from a government investigator (no matter how informal or friendly the contact might seem) because the possible consequences of an inappropriate or careless response are serious. Until the full context of a government inquiry is understood, an accurate evaluation of the matter or decision on the appropriate nature of your response may not be possible.

*Criminal Investigations.* Antitrust violations may be prosecuted both criminally and civilly under the Sherman Act. The Department of Justice

---

1.    U.S. Dep't of Justice, Antitrust Division Manual III-6 [hereinafter AT Manual]. The AT Manual is available from the Government Printing Office and, by chapter, in .pdf format at http://www.justice.gov/ atr/public/divisionmanual/index.html.

(DOJ), as part of the executive branch, is the only federal agency with the constitutional authority to pursue criminal prosecutions under the Sherman Act. Criminal penalties under the Sherman Act are substantial. The current maximum Sherman Act corporate fine is $100 million per violation, and the maximum individual fine per violation is $1 million.[2] In addition, the maximum prison term is 10 years per Sherman Act violation.

A surprise search warrant served in connection with an antitrust investigation is extremely serious and means that the government has a strong suspicion, and probably some evidence as well, of criminal conduct. The DOJ and state attorneys general use search warrants to obtain documents, electronic files, and physical items from corporations and individuals either for use in a grand jury investigation or in support of an indictment when there is probable cause to believe that the seized items are evidence of the commission of a crime. Federal Rule of Criminal Procedure 41 governs the procedures for search warrants. The publicly available DOJ Antitrust Division Manual describes the circumstances in which the DOJ will use search warrants to gather evidence and procedures relating to their use.[3] Receipt of a search warrant or grand jury subpoena may indicate that your company, another company, or certain individuals are under investigation for antitrust violations.

Counsel must immediately take charge of the company's response to the government in such criminal investigations. When the DOJ serves a search warrant, an in-house lawyer or outside counsel should go to the site of a search as soon as possible to ensure that the search is properly conducted. He or she should confirm the validity of the search warrant,[4] obtain identification of all of the individuals conducting the search, object if the scope of the search is beyond that authorized by the search

---

2.    U.S. Dep't of Justice, Price Fixing, Bid Rigging, and Market Allocation Schemes: What They Are and What to Look For - An Antitrust Primer, *available at* http://www.justice.gov/atr/public/guidelines/211578.htm.

3.    *See* AT Manual, *supra* note 1, at III-96-III-97.

4.    Fed. R. Crim. P. 41. In general, the search warrant must be validly issued by competent judicial authority, must describe with particularity the property to be seized, state that the property is evidence of a specified criminal offense, provide an exact description of the location to be searched, and note the period of time within which the search is to be executed.

warrant,[5] attempt to list the items being seized,[6] and ensure that company employees are aware of their rights not to answer certain types of questions.[7] The search should not in any way be impeded, as such conduct may constitute obstruction of justice.[8] The government is entitled to seize the originals of documents.[9] As a consequence, the subject of the search must either reach an agreement with the government regarding the handling of the documents and access to them for the purpose of making copies, or must file a motion for return of the documents with the federal district court in the district in which the property was seized. In general, the subject of a search warrant is entitled to reasonable access for the purpose of making copies, provided that there are adequate provisions made for the security of the originals.[10]

The following issues must be assessed promptly when a company or individual served with either a search warrant or grand jury subpoena: (1) the nature and possible targets of the probe; (2) possible conflicts of interest arising out of representing the company and individuals; (3) possible assertion of a privilege by subpoenaed individuals; (4) whether leniency should be sought for the company or individuals; and (5) communicating with government lawyers regarding the nature of testimony sought and possible immunity.[11] Senior management should

---

5.  Items found in plain view that pertain to the criminal investigation may be seized, even if they are not specified on the search warrant. *See* Horton v. California, 496 U.S. 128 (1990) (items found in plain view during a lawful search for other evidence authorized by a valid warrant were lawfully seized).

6.  If the scope of the search warrant is broad enough, its execution by the agents may make it difficult or impossible to continue business operations unless immediate access to the items taken is obtained through court order or by agreement with the government. The ability of the subject's counsel to get access to the documents may depend on the thoroughness of the record made during the search of the records seized.

7.  A search warrant cannot compel individuals to make statements to the agents. Instead, a grand jury subpoena must be issued and the proper procedures followed by the government before individuals can be compelled to tell what they know about the matters being investigated. FED. R. CRIM. P. 6, 17.

8.  *See* 18 U.S.C. § 1503(a) (it is a felony to "corruptly . . . endeavor[] to influence, obstruct, or impede, the due administration of justice").

9.  *See* FED. R. CRIM. P. 41.

10. FED. R. CRIM. P. 41(e).

11. *See* AT MANUAL, *supra* note 1, providing extensive guidance regarding grand jury procedures and issues.

be informed of the seriousness of the inquiry, and it is critical to retain counsel with substantial experience representing clients in criminal antitrust investigations.

*Civil Investigations.* On the federal level, both the DOJ and the Federal Trade Commission (FTC) have authority to conduct civil antitrust investigations, and may gather information by a number of means.

A Civil Investigative Demand (CID) is a precomplaint discovery subpoena issued by the DOJ or FTC to obtain information relevant to a civil investigation[12] that can be used in court, before administrative agency proceedings, or before a grand jury. A CID recipient may challenge the CID on a variety of grounds, seek to narrow its scope by agreement with the government, or comply without challenge.[13] There are four types of precomplaint compulsory process that can be issued by the FTC: annual or special reports, access orders, subpoenas, and CIDs.[14]

A request from the DOJ or the FTC for voluntary cooperation in an investigation, including voluntary production of documents and voluntary interviews, also requires careful evaluation by counsel before a decision is made as to what extent one should cooperate or whether to cooperate at all. The government may not agree to restrict its contact with individuals, even if they are known to be represented by counsel; therefore, it is essential in early stages to obtain advice regarding the rights of the individuals not to make any statements to the government without careful consideration of the implications and possible risks.[15]

Whether the request is an informal request for cooperation, a CID, or some other formal request, counsel should take certain immediate steps regarding potentially responsive documents. First, counsel should ensure that a statement is issued to relevant company personnel instructing them to preserve all documents (including electronic messages and files)

---

12.   The Antitrust Civil Process Act (ACPA), 15 U.S.C. §§ 1311-14 authorizes the issuance of CIDs. *See* 15 U.S.C. § 1312(a).

13.   *See, e.g.,* 15 U.S.C. § 1314(b). To compel compliance, the DOJ must obtain an order from a district court where the recipient resides, is found, or transacts business; CIDs are not self-enforcing. *See* 15 U.S.C. § 1314(a).

14.   15 U.S.C. §§ 46(b), 49, 57b-1(c).

15.   *See* 64 Fed. Reg. 19273 (1999), 28 C.F.R. Part 77. "[A]ttorneys for the government shall conform their conduct and activities to" all rules that prescribe ethical conduct for attorneys enacted by the federal local court and by the state where the attorney engages in the attorney's duties. 28 C.F.R. § 77.3.

relating to the issues under investigation. Even the unintentional destruction of records can have severe consequences. Counsel also should consider whether any documents turned over or copied by the government will divulge trade secrets or other confidential company information if divulged to others. If so, steps should be taken to gain the maximum protection for the documents from inquiries made by competitors under the Freedom of Information Act or by litigants in private lawsuits against your company.[16] Counsel also should evaluate the document request with an eye toward negotiating a narrowing of its scope. Counsel for larger organizations should give special attention to the problem of assuring that responsive documents have been gathered and reviewed and develop a plan for communicating the request to all business units reasonably likely to have such documents and for gathering those documents. Documentation of the steps taken will be key in these situations.

Counsel should also begin gathering information about the subject of the government inquiry. Counsel should interview all company individuals contacted by the government to learn as much as possible about the subject of the inquiry before further steps are taken to respond. This is particularly so when the inquiry appears to be focusing on the conduct of your company or its employees. Counsel should attempt to determine (1) the identity and agency affiliation of the person making the contact, (2) the general nature of the information sought, (3) the target of the investigation, (4) the authority for the contact, and (5) the timing involved in the investigation.

Until the full scope of the investigation is understood, counsel generally should seek to defer an immediate decision on whether to recommend that company employees cooperate with an informal interview request. This will give counsel time to evaluate whether the company is a target, whether the information possessed by the individuals may be problematic for the company, and whether to recommend that the individuals involved retain separate counsel. Counsel also should locate and review any documents that may appear to

---

16. 15 U.S.C. § 1314(g) exempts documents produced pursuant to a CID from disclosure under the Freedom of Information Act. In responding to other types of government requests for information, counsel may be able to successfully negotiate with lawyers for the government that documents produced will remain confidential. However, it sometimes may be advisable to structure the response to an information request as a formal response (rather than a voluntary submission) in order to get the broadest possible confidentiality protection.

have a bearing on the matters under investigation and ensure that any individuals providing information to the government are correctly recalling historical events and their context. Counsel should consider informing the government agency that all current employees are represented by common counsel (inside or outside) and requesting that the government agency make all future contacts through such counsel.[17] Business personnel should be instructed to refer all future inquiries relating to the company and the investigation to designated inside or outside counsel and to advise counsel of any future contact immediately.

Counsel should remain actively involved even if the antitrust authorities profess to need information from the company only as part of an investigation of another company. A government inquiry that targets another company may have a variety of business and legal implications. Merely because your company is not a target of the government's investigation does not necessarily mean that the information your company provides will not harm your company in the pending investigation, or with respect to unrelated conduct. The information provided may implicate your company, or your company's business may have a significant interest in the outcome of the investigation. Counsel also should consider the value to the company of maintaining good relations with the government, especially because the government is usually able to compel a company to provide the information it seeks in any event. Moreover, government investigations may have consequences for a company's future plans. For example, what a company says to the government in response to a proposed merger of two other companies in the same industry as the company may affect the analysis of that company's future merger plans and the legal or factual positions the company may want to take in future transactions of its own. In many (if not most) cases, it will be possible to meet multiple good-faith objectives of the government and the company by negotiating appropriate limits to the scope of document production and by preparing individuals carefully for informal interviews or grand jury appearances.

---

17. Counsel for the company should be careful in assuming that his or her representation should extend to all of the individuals affected by the inquiry. The attorney-client privilege will extend to many of the current employees of the company, but likely not to all. Upjohn Co. v. United States, 449 U.S. 383 (1981). In addition, the interests of the individuals and of the company may not be coextensive, in that the company's interests may dictate a different approach to investigation than if the individuals' interests are exclusively considered.

## B. Our International Division Just Called with Some Legal Questions. Do They Need to Worry about Antitrust Laws Too?

The international division will be subject to the antitrust laws in the countries in which it operates and possibly to the antitrust laws of other countries that are affected by the business activities.

Most nations—including nearly all developed nations and many developing ones—have antitrust or competition laws. For instance, many nations in Asia-Pacific have enacted antitrust laws, including Australia, China, Japan, New Zealand, India, Korea and Taiwan. A number of developing Latin American, Middle Eastern, and African countries have antitrust laws on the books as well. These laws are generally similar to the antitrust laws in the United States. For example, most countries have prohibitions similar to those found in Section 1 of the Sherman Act against agreements in restraint of trade, and over 85 countries have enacted premerger notification regimes. Counsel for any multinational corporation is well advised to become familiar with the competition laws of the countries in which his or her company does business.[18] Early involvement of skilled counsel conversant with the relevant antitrust laws is critical to assuring compliance with the unique characteristics of local law.

Enforcement of antitrust laws has taken on an increasingly international character. While enforcement of antitrust laws has traditionally been a domestic matter, more and more governments are beginning to work cooperatively to enforce antitrust laws. There are a variety of mechanisms that facilitate such cooperation. For example, the International Competition Network (ICN) now includes over 100 jurisdictions as members. The objectives of the ICN are to provide support for new competition agencies and to promote greater international antitrust enforcement cooperation and convergence,

---

18. There are a variety of Internet resources available that can assist counsel in becoming generally familiar with the antitrust laws of specific nations and regions. For example, The Asia-Pacific Economic Cooperation Website, www.apec.org, contains a wealth of information about the competition laws of member countries, which include the United States, Canada, Australia, Japan, the People's Republic of China, Russia, Mexico, and other countries. Information about European Union competition laws can be found at www.europa.eu.int. The Website of the Organization for Economic Co-operation and Development (OECD), www.oecd.org, contains information about the competition laws of its members.

including the creation of international "best practices" in the merger review process. The Organization for Economic Co-operation and Development (OECD) also has adopted a recommendation that its member countries cooperate to enforce their competition laws. In addition, a number of countries, both within and outside of the European Union, have entered into bilateral agreements that provide, among other things, for information exchanges regarding restrictive practices that may affect the interests of one of the countries. Examples are the cooperation agreements between the United States and the European Commission of 1991 and 1998, which, among other things, permit a party to ask the competition authorities of the other nation to investigate and, if warranted, to remedy anticompetitive activity.[19]

Criminal antitrust violations involving multiple jurisdictions can result in serious penalties. Recently, competition authorities in the United States and in Europe have levied record fines against companies and individuals and obtained unprecedented prison sentences in connection with international price-fixing schemes. In fiscal year 2011, the DOJ filed 90 criminal cases and levied more than $576 million in criminal fines.[20] Prior to 1994, the largest single corporate criminal fine levied by the DOJ was $6 million. As of the end of 2011, however, Sherman Act violations have resulted in 91 criminal fines of $10 million or more, including 19 fines of $100 million or more. During the same year, the average prison sentence for defendants sentenced in Division matters was nearly 17 months, with a total of 18,295 prison days imposed on criminal antitrust defendants during 2010-2011.[21]

Activities outside the United States that affect commerce in the United States may be subject to U.S. antitrust laws. The DOJ has made extraterritorial enforcement of U.S. antitrust laws a high priority. The test

---

19.   *See* Agreement Between the United States of America and the Commission of the European Communities Regarding the Application of Their Competition Laws, U.S.-Eur., (Sept. 23, 1991), *available at* http://www.justice.gov/atr/public/international/docs/0525.htm; *see also* Agreement Between the Government of the United States of America and the European Communities on the Application of Positive Comity Principles in the Enforcement of Their Competition Laws, U.S.-Eur., (June 4, 1998), *available at* http://www.justice.gov/atr/public/international/docs/1781.htm.

20.   *See* U.S. DEP'T OF JUSTICE, ANTITRUST DIVISION, DIVISION UPDATE, Spring 2012, *available at* http://www.justice.gov/atr/public/division-update/2012/index.html.

21.   *Id.*

for whether foreign conduct provides authorities in the United States with subject matter jurisdiction is whether it has a "direct, substantial and reasonably foreseeable effect" on domestic markets or on an opportunity to export from the United States.[22]

As with U.S. antitrust enforcement agencies, the European Commission has not been hesitant to impose severe penalties on antitrust offenders. The European Commission has broad investigative and regulatory powers to enforce its competition laws and has imposed significant fines when it has found such violations to have occurred.

Many countries have enacted merger notification regimes similar to the Hart-Scott-Rodino Act. The applicability of these requirements often depends upon the size of the parties, the market share of the parties, or both. The Merger Control Regulation of the European Union, for example, applies only to mergers with a "community dimension," which are mergers that meet fairly high turnover thresholds (both worldwide and within the community).[23] There also are variations from jurisdiction to jurisdiction regarding domicile requirements, the definition of relevant markets, and the types of contact that constitute presence in a jurisdiction. Likewise, the types of information that must be provided also vary greatly among jurisdictions, as do the applicable review periods.[24]

## C. Some of Our Competitors (or Suppliers or Customers) Are Being Investigated by the Department of Justice (or Other Government Agency). My Company Is Not under Investigation, but Is There Anything I Should Do?

If a company learns that an antitrust enforcement agency is investigating one or more other industry participants—such as competitors, suppliers, or customers—the actions the company should take in response depend largely upon the specifics of the investigation. If the government is investigating potential illegal agreements among the

---

22. Foreign Trade Antitrust Improvements Act of 1982, Pub. L. No. 97-290, title iv, § 402, 96 Stat. 1246 (1999), codified at 15 U.S.C. § 6a.

23. Individual member states may, however, have lower notification thresholds.

24. It is important to carefully review the laws of the specific jurisdictions that may be affected by a merger. The Web site of the International Competition Network includes links to information about foreign merger control laws. *See* http://www.internationalcompetitionnetwork.org/working-groups/current/merger/templates.aspx.

company's competitors, the company may consider conducting an internal review of its activities to assess whether any of its employees have been involved in any agreements with the targets of the investigation. Any subsequent actions likely depend on the outcome of that internal review.

Alternatively, if the government is investigating potential anticompetitive conduct involving the company's suppliers or customers, the company should consider whether it is a potential victim of any such conduct and has grounds for seeking legal recourse. Additionally, the company might consider whether the business has an interest in the outcome of the investigation—for example, if a merger is being investigated that could subject the company to higher prices in the future.

In any event, depending upon the facts of the investigation, the company should be prepared for the possibility of the government asking the company to provide documents and information. While the government frequently utilizes voluntary requests for information from third parties, at least initially, the government does have the authority to issue compulsory process to third parties that it believes may have information relevant to its investigations. Responding to a third-party subpoena or CID can be time consuming and costly. However, government agencies typically are more flexible in negotiating the response to a subpoena or CID issued to a third party. For example, a third party that cooperates with the investigating agency may be able to obtain limitations to the CID or subpoena that may avoid full compliance with certain burdensome obligations, such as the production of a full privilege log. The agency also has the authority to grant extensions of the time period in which to respond to a request for information or to defer the production of some of the categories of information initially requested.

In some cases, the government may request a deposition or an "investigational hearing," as referred to by the FTC. While obviously an imposition on the company, in some cases providing oral testimony may be less burdensome than providing documents or written responses to interrogatories. Alternatively, the government may accept a sworn written statement or declaration in lieu of deposition or hearing testimony. There are various advantages and disadvantages to these approaches. Submitting a written declaration—as opposed to sitting for a deposition—gives parties greater control over the content of any evidence submitted into the record. However, working with the investigating agency to prepare and review a written declaration may be no less time-consuming than preparing for and attending a one-day deposition.

If a company receives a third-party request for information from an enforcement agency, it may disclose the fact of the investigation to the target(s). Whether a party should disclose this may depend upon the facts and circumstances of the investigation, as well as the relationship between the company and the target(s). If, for example, the company believes it may be the victim of alleged anticompetitive behavior engaged in by a supplier with whom it currently does business, disclosure that the company is cooperating with the government investigation could compromise both the strategy for pursuing legal remedies against the supplier as well as the ongoing commercial relationship between the parties. However, if the investigation focuses on conduct or a merger that does not affect the company and in which the company has no interest, disclosing that the government has requested information (and, potentially, seeking coordination on discovery requests) could minimize the extent to which the targets themselves seek duplicative or additional information from the company.

A typical question that arises among third-party respondents is whether the target(s) of the investigation will have access to any material provided to the government. Information provided to the government by a third party is subject to statutory confidentiality protections that largely limit the target's access to the information.[25] Moreover, the investigating agencies ordinarily are averse to revealing their investigative process and have a natural inclination to avoid disclosing too much to the target. The agencies cannot promise absolute protection for information provided voluntarily as opposed to pursuant to compulsory process. However, both the FTC and DOJ typically will not disclose voluntarily produced information unless required by law or to further a legitimate law enforcement purpose, and both have policies in place designed to maximize the protection afforded to information produced on a voluntary

---

25. 15 U.S.C. § 18a(h) prohibits disclosure of any information provided to the DOJ pursuant to the Hart-Scott-Rodino Act, except "as may be relevant to any administrative or judicial action or proceeding" to which the FTC or DOJ is a party, or to Congress. Information obtained from CIDs is governed by the Antitrust Civil Process Act, 15 U.S.C. § 1313(c)-(d), which provides that materials received in response to a CID may not be made public unless the party submitting the information has waived confidentiality. However, CID material may be used in courts, administrative bodies, or grand juries. HSR and CID materials also are exempted from disclosure under the Freedom of Information Act (FOIA), 5 U.S.C. § 552.

basis.[26] If and when the FTC or DOJ files a lawsuit challenging the conduct under investigation, the defendant will have access to third-party evidence. To the extent this evidence consists of competitively or commercially sensitive information, the court typically will enter a protective order limiting access to the defendant's lawyers.

Alternatively, the target(s) of the investigation might enter into a consent decree settlement resolving the government's concerns. If the company believes it has been harmed by the actions of the settling defendants, it may ask whether the settlement may be used as prima facie evidence of an antitrust violation in any subsequent private litigation. According to statute, neither FTC findings in an action brought under the antitrust laws or Section 5 of the FTC Act, nor consent decree settlements entered into prior to the taking of any testimony, can be given collateral estoppel effect or used as prima facie evidence in other actions.[27]

### D. My Company Is under Investigation for Price Fixing (or Other Anticompetitive Conduct). Another Participant in the Same Conduct Has Already Pleaded Guilty and Received Amnesty, so There Is No Point in Cooperating Now, Is There?

One way for a company to avoid indictment for a criminal antitrust violation is to make a successful application for amnesty under the DOJ's Corporate Leniency Policy.[28] A successful amnesty applicant can avoid prosecution for itself and usually its employees. However, the DOJ only will grant amnesty to the first qualified applicant involved in an antitrust conspiracy. Subsequent applicants will not enjoy a complete pass from prosecution; however, their level of cooperation with the DOJ could have a bearing on the ultimate disposition of their criminal liability.

Time is of the essence in making a leniency application. As the DOJ

---

26. For example, FTC Rule 4.10(d) provides that the agency will not release materials obtained voluntarily in lieu of process in a law enforcement investigation, except in certain circumstances, so long as those materials are designated "confidential." The DOJ has similar policies in place. Moreover, voluntarily produced information may be exempt from disclosure to the extent it qualifies for protection under FOIA (e.g., the information is "confidential business information").

27. *See* 15 U.S.C. § 16(a).

28. Dep't of Justice, Antitrust Division, Corporate Leniency Policy, *available at* http://www.justice.gov/atr/public/guidelines/0091.htm.

has noted on several occasions, the second company to apply for leniency has been beaten by a prior applicant by only a few hours. If a company decides that it may want to pursue an amnesty application but is still conducting an internal investigation to determine the extent of any potential criminal liability, it can obtain a "marker" from the DOJ.[29] The marker puts the DOJ on notice of a potential criminal violation, prevents any other applicant from "leapfrogging" over the company, and allows the company to complete its investigation.

The requirements for a grant of amnesty under the DOJ's Corporate Leniency Policy depend on whether an application is made before or after an investigation has been opened. A corporation may be granted amnesty after an investigation has begun if the following seven conditions are met:[30]

- the corporation is the first to come forward and qualify for leniency with respect to the illegal activity being reported;
- the Antitrust Division, at the time the application is made, does not yet have sufficient evidence that is likely to result in a sustainable conviction at the time of the corporation's reporting;
- the corporation, upon discovery of the illegal activity, acted promptly to terminate its involvement;
- the corporation provides complete disclosure and on-going cooperation that advances the Antitrust Division's investigation;
- the confession of wrongdoing is truly a corporate act, not an isolated confession by an individual executive or official;
- the corporation makes restitution to injured parties where possible; and
- the Antitrust Division determines that granting leniency would not be unfair to others, considering the nature of the illegal activity, the confessing corporation's role in that activity, and the timing of the corporation's decision to come forward.

---

29. *See* Scott D. Hammond, Deputy Ass't Att'y Gen., & Belinda A. Barnett, Sr. Counsel to the Deputy Ass't Att'y Gen., Antitrust Div., Frequently Asked Questions Regarding the Antitrust Division's Leniency Program and Model Leniency Letters (Nov. 19, 2008), *available at* http://www.justice.gov/atr/public/criminal/239583.pdf.

30. DEP'T OF JUSTICE, ANTITRUST DIVISION, CORPORATE LENIENCY POLICY, *available at* http://www.justice.gov/atr/public/guidelines/0091.htm.

In order to receive amnesty before the DOJ has commenced an investigation, instead of conditions (1) and (2) applying, the DOJ must not yet have received information about the illegal activity from another source. And instead of condition (7), the applicant must not have coerced others to participate in the illegal activity or have been a leader or originator of the illegal activity.

The Antitrust Criminal Penalty and Enforcement Act of 2004 provides additional potential benefits to a party granted amnesty by the DOJ. If the party receiving amnesty has provided timely and adequate cooperation during the investigation, as determined by a trial court, its liability in any subsequent civil antitrust damages actions is limited to the actual damages "attributable to the commerce done by the [corporation] in the goods or services affected by the violation."[31] Thus, not only are damages "detrebled," but the successful amnesty applicant is not subject to joint and several liability in any action involving multiple defendants or plaintiff's attorneys' fees. The opportunity to avoid treble damages and joint and several liability has served as an additional meaningful inducement for cartel members to seek amnesty and cooperate with the government.

Even if complete amnesty is not an option, a company might still choose to cooperate with DOJ in order to obtain more favorable treatment or a more favorable resolution through a plea agreement. If the company cooperates with the investigation and provides useful information, it may be able to secure reduced penalties and prosecutions of fewer individual company employees. In addition, the DOJ has adopted an "Amnesty Plus" policy under which a company that did not make a timely amnesty application who nonetheless continues to cooperate and uncovers evidence of a separate conspiracy is eligible for amnesty for the second conspiracy. The DOJ may also recommend a substantial reduction in the company's criminal liability for the first conspiracy.[32]

It is also important to bear in mind that over 50 other jurisdictions also have leniency programs, many of which do not have a "winner take all" structure. The European Union, for example, offers cooperating companies that are not "first in the door" in the amnesty race the

31.   Pub. L. No. 108-237, § 213, 118 Stat. 661, 666-67 (2004).
32.   *See* Scott D. Hammond, Deputy Ass't Att'y Gen., Antitrust Div., Recent Developments, Trends, and Milestones in the Antitrust Division's Criminal Enforcement Program, Presented at the ABA Section of Antitrust Law Annual Spring Meeting 15 (Mar. 26, 2008), *available at* http://www.justice.gov/atr/public/speeches/232716.pdf.

possibility of a fine reduction, depending on the amount of added value the company provides through cooperation.[33] Thus, even if a company is not the first successful amnesty applicant, there are many compelling reasons why it should consider cooperating with the antitrust authorities.

## E. It Is Just an E-mail to My Boss and a Few Other Engineers. Nobody outside the Company Will Ever See It, Right?

Almost any written communication, whether it be a short memo, e-mail, or notes in a personal calendar, may be subject to production in a government investigation or private litigation. As a result, care must be taken in the creation and retention of documents in order to avoid misleading impressions or creating problems when none exist. Discovery in antitrust matters is as broad as in any other legal matter and there are many situations when a client's e-mail or other documents are likely to be seen by people outside the company (whether antitrust authorities or private plaintiffs).

Resolution of antitrust issues often is fact-intensive, requiring a great deal of discovery. It is not unusual in an antitrust matter for hundreds of boxes of many types of documents—correspondence, e-mail, reports, presentations—to be exchanged by the parties or inspected by governmental enforcers. Moreover, the obligation to produce documents in an investigation or litigation applies no matter what form the document takes: formal memo, draft memo, e-mail, documents stored only on computer or backup tape (even if in non-readable form), audiotape, videotape, notation in a calendar, credit card receipt, cocktail napkin scribble, etc. Simply marking a document "privileged," "confidential," or "internal eyes only," will not necessarily protect it from production.

Counsel should advise clients on the responsible creation and retention of documents, including e-mail documents. Document writers should assume all documents will be discovered and reviewed by individuals who are unfamiliar with the industry or, worse, suspicious of the writer's motives. Writers should stick to facts and information they know and avoid speculation or words that can be misconstrued. Writers should be able to explain a document, including why it was created and sent to the recipients, to individuals unfamiliar with (and perhaps hostile to) the company or industry. Writers should be especially careful with e-

---

33. *See* European Commission Competition Authority, "Leniency", *available at* http://ec.europa.eu/competition/cartels/leniency/leniency.html

mail, where the informality might lead some to be less careful in the words they choose. Finally, all company policies for document retention and destruction should be followed.

Once discovery requests are made, counsel should advise clients on the proper retention and collection of relevant documents. Counsel must advise those who reasonably can be expected to possess potentially relevant documents, whether corporate officers or administrative assistants, not to destroy documents until further notice from counsel. Indeed, it is generally advisable to send an e-mail or memorandum to a wider group, advising them of the company's document retention policy and the need to comply with it. Counsel must search for and produce relevant documents in ways that comply with the discovery request while causing the least interference with the ongoing business. Counsel should document the search and production process to head off any future accusations of noncompliance.

Other discovery issues for counsel in antitrust matters are unlikely to pose issues substantially different from other investigations or lawsuits. Counsel can attempt to negotiate limitations on the scope of discovery with the requesting party, whether a governmental investigator or private litigant. Absent agreement, however, courts generally have agreed to a broad scope of discovery in antitrust matters by explaining that the burden of production is outweighed by the need for all relevant information in fact-intensive matters. Courts have allowed broad discovery in terms of relevant time period,[34] geographic area,[35] relevant products,[36] and corporate affiliates.[37] As in other matters, documents that meet the appropriate definition of privilege can be withheld. Finally, courts have been willing to entertain motions for protective orders for confidential information and trade secrets, especially those that strike a balance between the need for secrecy of one party with the need of the other party to prosecute a case properly.[38]

---

34. *See, e.g.*, Wilder Enters. v. Allied Artists Pictures, 632 F. 2d 1135 (4th Cir. 1980).
35. *See, e.g.*, Park Ave. Radiology Assocs. v. Methodist Health Sys., 1995-1 Trade Cas. (CCH) ¶ 70,895 (6th Cir. 1995).
36. *See, e.g.*, General Motors v. Johnson Matthey, Inc., 887 F. Supp. 1240 (E.D. Wis. 1995).
37. *See, e.g.*, American Angus Ass'n v. Sysco Corp., 158 F.R.D. 372 (W.D. N.C. 1994).
38. *See, e.g.*, *In re* Indep. Serv. Orgs. Antitrust Litig., 1995-2 Trade Cas. (CCH) ¶ 71,099 (D. Kan. 1995).

## F. Where Can I Go for More Information?

### 1. Approach by the Government

- ABA Section of Antitrust Law, *The Handbook of U.S. Antitrust Sources* (2012);
- ABA Section of Antitrust Law, *Department of Justice Civil Antitrust Practice & Procedure Manual* (2012);
- ABA Section of Antitrust Law, *FTC Practice & Procedure Manual* (2007);
- *State Antitrust Practice & Statutes* (4th ed. 2009);
- U.S. Department of Justice, *An Antitrust Primer for Federal Law Enforcement Personnel* (April 2005), *available at* http://www.justice.gov/atr/public/guidelines/209114.htm.

### 2. Application of Antitrust Laws outside the United States

- ABA Section of Antitrust Law, *Antitrust Law Developments* (7th ed. 2012);
- ABA Section of Antitrust Law, *Competition Laws Outside the United States* (2d ed. 2011).

### 3. Government Investigations of Competitors

- U.S. Department of Justice, *Department of Justice Civil Antitrust Practice & Procedure Manual* (2012);
- ABA Section of Antitrust Law, *The Handbook of U.S. Antitrust Sources* (2012);
- ABA Section of Antitrust Law, *FTC Practice & Procedure Manual* (2007).

### 4. Dealing with Government Investigations When a Coconspirator Has Already Pleaded Guilty

- U.S. Department of Justice, *Department of Justice Civil Antitrust Practice and Procedure Manual* (2012);
- ABA Section of Antitrust Law, *Criminal Antitrust Litigation Handbook* (2d ed. 2006);
- U.S. Department of Justice, Antitrust Division, Leniency Program, *available at* http://www.justice.gov/atr/public/criminal/leniency.html.

## 5. Government Access to Company Documents

- ABA Section of Antitrust Law, *Antitrust Law Developments* (7th ed. 2012);
- ABA Section of Antitrust Law, *Antitrust Discovery Handbook* (2d ed. 2003);
- ABA Section of Antitrust Law, *Antitrust Compliance: Perspectives and Resources for Corporate Counselors* (2d ed. 2010).